THE SCANDAL OF THE GOSPELS

THE SCANDAL
OF THE GOSPELS

JESUS, STORY, AND OFFENSE

DAVID McCRACKEN

New York   Oxford
OXFORD UNIVERSITY PRESS
1994

Oxford University Press

Oxford   New York   Toronto
Delhi   Bombay   Calcutta   Madras   Karachi
Kuala Lumpur   Singapore   Hong Kong   Tokyo
Nairobi   Dar es Salaam   Cape Town
Melbourne   Auckland   Madrid

and associated companies in
Berlin   Ibadan

Copyright © 1994 by David McCracken

Published by Oxford University Press, Inc.
200 Madison Avenue, New York, New York 10016

Oxford is a registered trademark of Oxford University Press, Inc.

Library of Congress Cataloging-in-Publication Data
McCracken, David.
The scandal of the Gospels : Jesus, story, and offense /
David McCracken.
p. cm.   Includes bibliographical references and index.
ISBN 0-19-508428-4
1. Jesus Christ—Person and offices—Biblical teaching.   2. Bible.
N.T. Gospels—Criticism, Narrative.   3. Narration in the Bible.
I. Title.   II. Title: Jesus, story, and offense.
BT205.M43   1994
232—dc20   93-13093

2 4 6 8 9 7 5 3 1

Printed in the United States of America
on acid-free paper

For
Rusty Palmer

Preface

Scandal fascinates. Yet, someone may reasonably protest, this hardly justifies attaching scandal—a low form of human activity that we associate with the tabloid press, corrupt politicians, or rampant sexual license—to the Bible. It seems (the objection might proceed) singularly inappropriate to the Bible, and if it should exist—the story of David and Bathsheba pops into mind—it is preferable not to impose our low form of "scandal" on it, or even our higher, more intellectually respectable form—the scandal of logical contradiction, which is also inappropriate, since the Bible is not an argument or a treatise.

So might a skeptical or respectable reader approach a book on scandal in the Bible, and I would agree that the Bible is radically different from a tabloid or a treatise. And yet the parts of the Bible that are my particular concern in this book are narratives, stories, a form that is also the stuff of tabloids and even of some philosophical treatises. Tabloids, treatises, and the Bible all deal with some semblance of the world we live in, with things we find desirable or repulsive, and with actions that are almost beyond imagining. And though the conjunction of scandal and Bible may seem inappropriate, I am going to claim here that scandal is demonstrably and importantly present in the Bible, both in ways that overlap our low and high forms of scandal and, more importantly, in ways that do not.

I do not claim that scandal is *undeniably* present in the Bible; the history of reading the Bible is to a large extent a history of finding ways to deny its scandal. But even though we understandably may not *want* scandal in the Bible, it is present nonetheless, most obviously in the Greek word *skandalon*, which I call "scandal" or "offense" but which takes its meaning from an accumulation of specific, vivid, powerful images: traps, snares, stumbling blocks, things that obstruct, and things that cause a fall. The action of these images appears frequently throughout the Bible, and while it is commonly recognized in some forms, such as the stumbling blocks encountered by the Israelites or the stumbling blocks that followers of Jesus are enjoined not to place before "little ones," it is almost entirely ignored in its most profound form: the essential offense.

The essential offense builds on and transcends our mundane scandals of desire and our intellectual scandals of contradiction. In the Hebrew Bible, Yahweh not only lays stumbling blocks before the Israelites but *becomes* the stumbling block. In the New Testament, this image of Yahweh is transposed to Jesus, who warns his followers not to scandalize others but who is himself, dramatically and repeatedly, a scandal to those who encounter him. Jesus is the essential offense. Jesus must be an offense, a scandal, to the respectable, ordinary world, because the respectable, ordinary world is naturally offended by what is not respectable, not ordinary. In the Gospels, Jesus associates with the low and the corrupt; identifies with the poor, the sick, and the outcast; and dies a supposed criminal, which is offensive to many. But also, in the same stories, he is said to be the Son of God, which is an offense to the world of common sense. By his very nature, his presence, his words, and his actions, Jesus in the Gospels poses the possibility of offense to those who encounter him. And yet, as he says, "Blessed is anyone who takes no offense at me." Offense is not the desired end, but it is an essential part of a Gospel character's encounter with Jesus.

In the crisis of encounter, response is all. There are only two fundamental Gospel responses—offense or faith—and either response is of ultimate importance to life, but, since characters live in narrative as humans live in time, the response is not the end of the story. Offense repeatedly confronts and provokes even the faithful, who find it difficult to be faithful in the face of scandal and difficult not to be scandalous themselves. Offense is the recurring moment of crisis as characters in the Gospels move toward idolatry or truth.

Jesus must be the possibility of offense to all who encounter

him, and this applies not just to characters but to readers as well.
The possibility of offense ought to be an essential part of a reader's
encounter with the Gospel. But now the possibility has diminished;
we have translated and interpreted the Gospels to minimize and
domesticate the offense, making it barely recognizable. This is itself
a scandal that needs to be exposed, not so we can feel superior to
the perpetrators of scandal but so we can encounter the Gospel
scandals that exist in the text.

The scandal–offense–stumbling block becomes vivid and powerful when we return to reading the Gospels as stories. Their two
forms of offense—first, the worldly offenses of desires, idolatry, and
human obstacles to faith and, second, the essential offense of Jesus—flourish in narrative contexts. Gospels are stories to be heard,
and the power of these stories comes not from doctrines or messages
contained in them but from the stories themselves, as stories. Jesus
is a dramatized hero of the four Gospels; he is the *skandalon* who
blesses those who are not, dramatically, offended by him; and he
himself characteristically tells stories, full of worldly scandals, that
he calls parables. These parables, I will argue, are not modes of
instruction but rather forms of offense. Furthermore, the stories
about Jesus—the Gospels—place the scandalous Jesus before the
reader and become, themselves, occasions for offense.

As occasions for offense, Gospels constitute not only a source
of fascination but also a danger to readers. We have become expert
at dealing with this danger through mitigating it by interpretation—
sometimes by allegorical interpretation that substitutes one thing
for another, sometimes by historical interpretation that explains
away offensive passages as interpolations *because* they are offensive, and sometimes by critical interpretation that renders the text
acceptable and even comfortable. But my argument is that Gospel
stories are inherently scandalous for characters in them and for readers of them. Like parables, Gospels call on us to "hear," not to interpret. "Hearing," in the gospel sense, is different from interpreting or
from rational understanding, and this odd "hearing" requires the
stumbling block, which obstructs. It also reveals. But the revelation
cannot exist without the obstruction.

By making use of Søren Kierkegaard's writings and paying attention to Gospel stories, I am trying to reanimate the biblical *skandalon* that is central to the Gospels.

During the process of writing this book, I have incurred debts that
are a pleasure to acknowledge: to David Van Liew and friends who

(without knowing it) led me to start this project; to the late Esther Branch and friends who responded to the ideas here; to members of my 1990 graduate seminar on biblical narratives; to Doug Collins, whose perfectly timed gifts were invaluable; and to Steve Eberhart, Paul Flucke, Eugene Lemcio, Helene Solheim, Mark Lloyd Taylor, and Dale Turner. I would also like to thank the University of Washington Graduate School for its award of the Humanities Research Professorship, which provided time for research and writing.

I owe special thanks to all the members of my family, especially my wife, Marcia, who have made extraordinary support something almost ordinary, and to colleagues who have generously read and commented on parts of the manuscript: Don Bialostosky, Doug Collins, Alan Fisher, Mona Modiano, and Eugene Webb. To the friend who responded to ideas and prose with what Mikhail Bakhtin called the "questioning, provoking, answering, agreeing, objecting activity," this book is gratefully dedicated.

Seattle   D. McC.
May 1993

Contents

I

THE OFFENSE

Act just once in such a manner that your action expresses that you fear God alone and man not at all—you will immediately in some measure cause a scandal.

SØREN KIERKEGAARD, *Journals and Papers*

And blessed is anyone who takes no offense at me.

JESUS IN MATTHEW 11:6, LUKE 7:23

1

Introduction:
The Offense and Us

In 1848, Søren Kierkegaard wrote, "Offense is never mentioned these days—alas." Now, however, it is not quite true that offense is never mentioned; it—or its near relation, scandal—is mentioned, for example, by Lévi-Strauss, Derrida, and Bakhtin, but it is also not quite true that in 1848 offense was "never mentioned." It had in fact been discussed at some length by Johannes Climacus in *Philosophical Fragments* and *Concluding Unscientific Postscript* and by Vigilius Haufniensus in *The Concept of Anxiety*, and it was about to be discussed at still greater length by Anti-Climacus in *The Sickness unto Death* and later in *Practice in Christianity*. All of these books, of course, were written by Kierkegaard himself; the putative authors, representing different points of view, were part of his ventriloquistic strategy to awaken his readers to things unknown to the Hegelians and the established church. Offense, for Kierkegaard, is something of profound human and religious importance, as is apparent from the full lament, of which I have quoted only a part: "Offense," he wrote in his journal, "is never mentioned these days—alas, and even to the disciples, the believing disciples, Christ said: You will be offended in me" (*Journals* 3: 3028; cf. Matt. 26:31 and Mark 14:27). But the truth is that in this sense the offense is still seldom mentioned, in spite of Kierkegaard's best efforts to awaken the world to what he called the essential offense. Kierkegaard would find his "alas" no less applicable today than in 1848.

3

In spite of the fact that the offense is not much mentioned, it is hard to avoid it altogether, either in or outside the Bible. Before looking at biblical narratives, I want to consider, very briefly, some implications of offenses that we are accustomed to living with, to acknowledge my indebtedness to Kierkegaard in this enterprise, to raise the problem of modern Bible translations (a serious problem for me, since they tend to translate my subject out of existence), and to mention a few recent critics and philosophers who have been fascinated by offense or scandal.

Encountering and Suppressing Offense

We are all to some degree familiar with offense; whether we give it, take it, or avoid it, we know that it is the nature of offense to threaten us or our kind—our group, profession, race, or nationality. Our sense of self, our beliefs, or our ways of seeing things are challenged whenever we encounter an offense. When we feel an offense deeply, it is most likely because it challenges something of fundamental importance to us. And even though many of us prefer not to be challenged or threatened at all, we know that especially in a diverse, democratic society there must be some spirit of toleration, creating a tension between the individual's or group's comfortable security and the right to be offensive.

How to manage this tension is no easy matter. For example, in 1989, when the United States Supreme Court found unconstitutional a Texas statute prohibiting flag burning, Justice William Brennan argued in the majority opinion, "If there is a bedrock principle underlying the First Amendment, it is that the Government may not prohibit the expression of an idea simply because society finds the idea itself offensive or disagreeable." On the other hand, Chief Justice William Rehnquist, in his minority opinion, argued that the Texas statute should be upheld because the flag burning in question was "a form of protest that was profoundly offensive to many" (*New York Times*, June 22, 1989, A12).

Rehnquist's opinion seems to rest on a desire for harmony, for uniformity that to some extent represses diversity, and for protection of the beliefs of the majority in a community. Brennan's position, on the other hand, willingly accepts the existence of disharmony, of diversity that supersedes uniformity, and of threats to whatever constitutes our "I," our sense of self within a community. In spite of the undeniable attractions of institutional and personal comfort and security, Brennan argues on the basis of freedom of

expression that even profound offense must be tolerated and pro-
tected. Mikhail Bakhtin raises the stakes even higher: truth, in his
view, lives only on the threshold where the dialogic encounter
among words, persons, and ideas takes place, and that encounter is
often a scandalous or offensive one. For Bakhtin, a world without
the possibility of offense is a world without the possibility of truth.
Even so, in the sufficiently tricky business of managing our lives
and forming responses to those we encounter, many of us find ourselves harboring a divided practical, if not theoretical, attitude toward offense. Many of those who on principle defend offense would
prefer not to encounter it, and those who relish offense usually find
it more blessed to give than to receive.

The tension that is built into any response to offense, I believe,
has much to do with our recurring fascination with the Bible, which
is less a collection of doctrines than a collection of narratives, or
to many readers *the* narrative. The Bible is full of offense—actual,
dramatic offense to characters in the narrative, as well as offense to
readers. I find the term *fascination* useful in this context, since
what repels us is often as fascinating as what attracts us. Theodor
Adorno says of Kierkegaard, "Fascination is the most dangerous
power in his work" (11). By this he means that the reader or critic is
drawn, willingly or not, into the landscape of Kierkegaard's pseudonymous authors, his cunning choice of words, his dialectical seduction, and his paradoxical claim that subjectivity is truth, in such a
way that the reader succumbs to its "magical provenance," becoming
a prisoner in that landscape and a blind pursuer of (to Adorno) Kierkegaardian error. Adorno himself assumes the role of a fox hunter,
self-consciously pursuing the fox in its landscape of "infinitely re-
flected interiority" with the intention of catching the fox—Kierkegaard—in traps the fox himself has set (11–12).

The Bible, too, has its fascinating and dangerous landscape—
including traps, snares, foxes, wolves, and, if not a magical, at least
an illogical provenance. My role in this enterprise is not to smoke
out the fox but to encounter the fascination and at the same time to
observe the laying of traps, snares, and offenses, without trying to
account for them as historical artifacts or trying to extricate myself
from them by deconstructing them. I write from within a Kierkegaardian landscape, observing the laying of traps without trying to
chart a route whereby they may be avoided and without suggesting
that they can or should be avoided. In fact, I want to argue that the
complex of traps–snares–stumbling blocks–offenses–scandals, which
abide in the Greek word *skandalon*, is an essential part of the Jewish

and Christian Bibles, and that it is essentially, dangerously, and fascinatingly embodied in Gospel narratives. A corollary to my argument is that the *skandalon* is sufficiently offensive that readers and institutions naturally want to domesticate it to nullify its dangerous power.

The very notion of biblical truth presupposes and thrives on offense, but, though there is no hiding all of the offense, we as readers are oblivious to much of it. It is regularly translated out, and interpreted out, of the Bible. And that is a scandal worthy of study, because without the offense a reader has a severe handicap when encountering ideas and characters of the Gospels, especially the hero, Jesus. The offense I want to consider here is a distinctively biblical idea; it was developed in the Bible for the sake of its story, its theology, and its readers, none of which can be altogether disentangled from the others. Without it, we miss the biblical representation of the hero and his actions, and we miss the fundamental power of much of the hero's dialogue, including the speech genre always associated with Jesus: parables.

In defense of our blindness, we may say that the offense is understandably translated out of the New Testament: there is no good, single word to be found to serve as an equivalent for the idea and the word—*skandalon*—that contained a certain power two thousand years ago. It is true that the Bible still demonstrably has the power to offend, as well as to move in other ways. But the loss of a word for the idea and the dissipation of parts of the idea into many words pose serious difficulties. The Greek *skandalon* became the Latin *scandalum*, which became the English *scandal*, but in spite of the similarity no one would argue that they mean the same thing. In the verb form, the Latin *offendere* is close to the Greek *skandalizein*; both mean "to cause to stumble," and both have found their way into English. But, as Owen Barfield has pointed out, "for us there is a subtle difference between *scandalize* and *offend*; for [while] *scandalize* and *scandal* merely hint at the liveliness of an emotion, *offend* and *offence* convey a sober warning of its probable results" (*History in English Words*, 96). In fact, I suspect that the meanings of these words have changed since Barfield observed this distinction sixty-five years ago. *Offense* still conveys a warning of results to the offender, but it also increasingly conveys the challenge that must be endured by the person who has been offended (such as the patriotic citizen), regardless of the consequences to the offender (the flag burner).

This increasing emphasis on the offended is particularly relevant to my argument about the Gospels, where characters and readers are repeatedly challenged by an offensive Jesus. Jesus poses the possibility of offense to those who may themselves be an offense to God, and he offers them an escape from their offensiveness only through offense. The offenders (Jesus's audience within the text) are sometimes offended by Jesus and sometimes not, but Jesus himself repeatedly takes the form of an offense, a stumbling block. And his offensiveness is reciprocated: in the end, those who are offended crucify him. After the death, the cross itself becomes the scandal: Paul refers to "the offense of the cross," an offense that he does not want to be "removed" (Gal. 5:11). But whether it comes from Jesus or the cross or elsewhere, the challenge to the individual's most fundamental and cherished beliefs is at the heart of the New Testament *skandalon*.[1]

Our word *scandal* is charged with passion, the unexpected, and the violation of norms—all of which are relevant to my topic—and I continue to make use of the word here, but it is too late in the history of *scandal* to think that it can be extricated from its now usually sexual or political confines to allow it alone to carry the biblical weight the text requires, which indeed is sometimes sexual or political but far less exclusively so. René Girard has pointed out that modern scandal excites indignation, "a feverish desire to differentiate between the guilty and the innocent. . . . The person who is scandalized wants to bring the affair out into the open; he has a burning desire to see the scandal in the clear light of day and pillory the guilty party" (*Things Hidden*, 426). Our scandal is a form of violence, as indeed it is in the Bible—the cross being an instrument of violence—but it is also a way of suppressing the biblical offense. A scandal may titillate or outrage us; either way, the titillation or moral indignation effectively prevents any challenge of the sort that offense brings to the assumptions and truths we hold most dear and the idols we cherish most deeply. Offense violates our assumptions about what our world is or what we think it ought to be. Whatever is unofficial, unestablished, non-normal, deviant, or nonstandard, in our view, carries with it the possibility of offense.

The difficulties of translation are inevitably formidable, and it is not remarkable that there is no uniform translation for the numerous appearances of *ton skandalon*, "the stumbling block" or "the offense," and its verb form *skandalizō*, "I cause to stumble" or "I offend."[2] It *is* remarkable, however, that the Revised Standard Version (RSV) *never* translates the noun with any form of "offense" or "scandal," thereby giving special poignancy to Kierkegaard's lament that "the offense is never mentioned these days"—these days now being nearly a hundred and fifty years later. Whenever *skandalon* appears in the Greek text, it is translated in the RSV as "cause for stumbling," "cause of sin," "difficulty," "hindrance," "hindrance in the way," "make fall," "pitfall," "stumbling block," "temptation," or "temptation to sin." With these varied translations, is it any wonder that we fail to recognize a common idea repeatedly surfacing in the New Testament? The verb *skandalizō* has fewer, but still varied, translations in the RSV: "cause of falling," "cause to fall," "cause to sin," "fall away," "give offense," "make fall," "offend," and "take offense." There is no form of "stumble" or of "scandal" here, but, in fewer than one-quarter of the appearances, there is some form of "offense." The diffusion of an important idea contained in this word is not limited to the RSV. It occurs in all modern translations, although, happily, the *New* Revised Standard Version (NRSV) is a distinct improvement. It uses some form of "offense" or "stumbling" for most of the noun forms of *skand-* and for slightly more than half of the verb forms.[3]

I do not want to suggest, however, that the idea of the offense resides only in appearances of the Greek word *skandalon*. On the contrary, it is essentially a dramatic action, at work in the narratives of the Gospels. To recognize it at work, however, and to recognize its power as an action, we must recognize that it has a name, *skandalon*—a name repeatedly used in crucial contexts by Jesus, by all of the Gospel writers, by Paul, and by Peter. Furthermore, in addition to appearing dramatically, with no name at all, it is sometimes referred to in other ways—sometimes in other words for "stumbling" or "offense" (*proskomma*), "an occasion for taking offense" (*proskopē*), or even "fall" (*ptōsis*).

Some Contemporary Varieties of Offense

With the exception of a very few scholars, mainly German, only three modern writers have, to my knowledge, paid serious attention to the significance of the biblical offense: Girard, Bakhtin, and, most important, Kierkegaard.[4] René Girard uses the idea in conjunction with his theory of "mimetic desire"—essentially the idea that we humans desire not some object as such but whatever is already desired by a rival or model. We desire only what is given value by another. Girard has applied his theory not only to literature (especially Dostoyevski, Stendhal, Proust, and Shakespeare) but also to

anthropology, psychology, and theology—challenging the anthropologists with a new theory of the origin of violence (in *Violence
and the Sacred*), psychologists with non-Freudian notions of desire
(in *Things Hidden since the Foundation of the World*), and biblical
scholars with desacralizing interpretations (in *The Scapegoat* and
Job: The Victim of His People). The idea of the *skandalon* is crucial
to Girard's larger argument about violence. The *skandalon* is the
obstacle that one is obsessed by, or, as he says, the "obstacle-model
of mimetic rivalry" (*Things Hidden*, 416), which in fact is not usually real at all but a metaphysical illusion created by the mechanism
of desire, imitation, and rivalry. In the Hebrew Bible, the quintessential scandal is idolatry (421); in the New Testament, it is the
"other as an object of metaphysical fascination" (425). In both cases,
and throughout history, the underlying principle of this obsession
is violence, the principle of dominating and being dominated. This
mechanism of violence, in Girard's view, is exposed by the New
Testament, which teaches that rivalry and violence can be suppressed only through childlike imitation (as opposed to mimetic
rivalry) in the biblical logic of love.

Unlike Girard, Mikhail Bakhtin (to whom I will return in chapter 8) has little to say about biblical narratives, but he does argue
that the "scandal scenes" in Dostoyevski and other writers lead back
to "the basic narrative genres of ancient Christian literature—'Gospels,' 'Acts of the Apostles,' 'Apocalypse,' and 'Lives of the Saints
and Martyrs'" (*Problems*, 135). Both Girard and Bakhtin may have
encountered the *skandalon* in their reading of Kierkegaard, although it is not until late in the development of Girard's theory
(*Things Hidden* [1978] and *The Scapegoat* [1982]) that he equates
the *skandalon* with his earlier idea of mimetic desire, and he never
explicitly connects it to Kierkegaard.[5] Similarly, Bakhtin says little
about Kierkegaard in his writings, but he read Kierkegaard in German translations and began to learn Danish to read his works in the
original language (Clark and Holquist, 27).

Whatever the origin of their interest in scandal, it is certain that
Kierkegaard is the preeminent modern philosopher of the *skandalon*
or (in the Princeton translations of Kierkegaard's works) the "offense." In *The Sickness unto Death* (1849), Anti-Climacus calls the
offense "Christianity's crucial criterion" and "an eternal, essential
component of Christianity." In both his signed and his pseudonymous writings, Kierkegaard emphasizes its importance in order to
show the folly of Christians' ignoring "Christ's own instructions,

which frequently and so concernedly caution against offense; that is, he [Christ] personally points out that the possibility of offense is there and must be there" (83–84).

Kierkegaard has attempted with extraordinary explicitness and indirection to make his readers see the essential offense and to grasp its importance. He cannot be said to have succeeded on a grand scale. Offense was not much mentioned in his day or ours. Most people do not want to encounter an offense, much less *the* offense, any more than they want to live in fear and trembling.

But it should be noted that the idea of scandal or offense has a certain attraction. It has appealed recently to structuralists and post-structuralists, as well as to Bakhtin and Girard. Claude Lévi-Strauss begins his discussion of the prohibition of incest (in *The Elementary Structures of Kinship*) by establishing a double criterion for analysis: whatever is universal is natural, and whatever is governed by rules or norms is cultural, the two orders of nature and culture being mutually exculsive. "We are then confronted," he says, "with a fact, or rather, a group of facts, which . . . are not far removed from a scandal," namely, the prohibition of incest. This near scandal is not incest itself (as it might be in a supermarket tabloid) but rather the prohibition of incest, because the prohibition appears to be both natural *and* cultural, contradicting what is self-evident — that nature and culture are "two mutually exclusive orders" (8).

Jacques Derrida has found this contradiction to be a revealing one. In his lecture "Structure, Sign and Play in the Discourse of the Human Sciences," he argues that Lévi-Strauss's scandal — it is no longer a near scandal — occurs at the point where the "difference [between nature and culture], which has always been assumed to be self-evident, finds itself erased or questioned." This, then, opens the way for Derridean deconstruction: the disappearing difference allows one either to "deconstitute" "the founding concepts of the entire history of philosophy" or to abandon the "truth value" of traditional philosophy while making use of its methods (*Writing and Difference*, 283–84). In a similar manner, the semiotician and novelist Umberto Eco makes use of the word in his essay "The Scandal of Metaphor," because of the erasure of what seem to be self-evident differences.

In all of these cases (as in a tabloid, though in a different way), scandal is fundamentally a violation of rules or of norms. The "mutually exclusive orders" that the incest prohibition combines in Lévi-Strauss are, of course, culturally determined orders; the near scandal is that the rule of mutual exclusivity does not hold in the prohibition of incest. For Derrida, the full-blown scandal is somewhat different: it is the violation of a rule of explainability. He refers to a "scandalous fact" as "a nucleus of opacity within a network of transparent significations," but when the network is deconstructed, the non-transparent "nucleus of opacity" is no longer a scandal. Derrida calls into question the difference between nature and culture and, indeed, "the whole of philosophical conceptualization" that produced the nature/culture distinction in the first place. Thus, the scandal (which is not really a scandal at all once one sees the distinctions collapse) is a useful stumbling block, making possible the deconstruction of traditional norms, concepts, and philosophy. It reveals that there is "no longer any truth value" in the old concepts (*Writing and Difference*, 283–84).[6]

There is clearly a relation between the Derridean scandal and the biblical *skandalon*: both violate norms, and both are stumbling blocks. But Derrida's scandal is finally nonexistent; once the erroneous distinctions are abolished, the scandal "can no longer be said to be a scandalous fact." (And, likewise, though for entirely different reasons, the *skandalon* for Girard is ultimately an "illusion.") Scandal is, in Derrida's view, a useful deconstructive tool that deconstructs the accepted truths of old concepts and then deconstructs itself. The biblical *skandalon*, on the other hand, is not a tool but an action. It does not deconstruct old concepts; it hardens them. Or, alternatively, it reveals truth, although not truth as a philosophical concept or doctrine. In its biblical form, the *skandalon* is encountered by individuals on the way to idolatry or to truth.

Whatever else one may think of them, Harold Bloom's J and Yahweh are properly scandalous. J, the most ancient author of the Torah, is, in Bloom's account, a comic, ironic, paradoxical, cunning woman, perhaps a granddaughter of David, living in the degenerate court of Reheboam. She is, as Bloom sees her, the greatest Jewish writer, who prefigures, in a curious mixture, the genius of William Shakespeare, Jane Austen, and Franz Kafka. In *The Book of J*, Bloom presents us with "the scandal of how J has been weakly misread by normative conventions" (282), and his J, in the tenth century B.C.E., presented us with "the scandal of an all-too-human God who finally resists either moralizing or a removal to the high heavens." Further: "To complement her scandalous God, she also gave the normative a fairly scandalous group of matriarchs and patriarchs, passionate men and women not always ruled by scruples, reverence, or the spirit of fairness, let alone the spirit of self-abnegation" (199). Bloom is, as always, the strong reader, providing us with something like the Kierkegaardian essential offense in the "all-too-human God" who resists human desires. Bloom also follows Kierkegaard in his scandalous demolition of what Bloom calls "the guardians of normative Judaism, Christianity, and Islam," who "muted and evaded J's outrageous Yahweh." And, for good measure, Bloom offers us a highbrow version of the *National Enquirer*, peopled by an unscrupulous, passionate bunch of matriarchs and patriarchs.

These are some particular appearances of offense and scandal today, but in some more general senses offense and scandal are inescapable. Works such as Picasso's *Guernica* and Diaghilev and Stravinsky's *Rite of Spring* scandalized the artistic establishments of their day, and, even now, in their familiarity, they still convey a power that resides in or near offense. But new art continues to scandalize people and institutions, and we expect it to, even to the point of taking scandal and controversy as signs of vitality. Many novelists—from Flannery O'Connor and Philip Roth to one's favorite provocateur of the moment—manage to offend a substantial number of their own readers. And it is a sign of the times that literary critics and historians privilege what was scandalous in the past, especially if it also can be shown to be a scandal in the present.[7] Later, in chapter 9, I will make use of the idea that stories are by nature scandalous, which is even plausible, once one understands scandal in a certain way. One critic has recently claimed that *all* literature is scandal, not because it is radical or new but because it is by nature conservative or even reactionary and, as such, is a challenge to the progressive evolution of history.[8] Ernst Behler has convincingly argued that the ironic manner of expression, so central to modern discourse, "automatically constitutes an offense to common reason and understanding—an offense not necessarily intended by the ironist but somehow involuntarily connected with his claim and almost regularly taken as such by the public" (111).

These claims for the prevalence of scandal and offense come to be extraordinarily comprehensive, but my enterprise is more specific. When I speak of offense, scandal, and *skandalon*, I refer (with some exceptions, which I note) to the specifically biblical and Kierkegaardian senses described in the following chapters and to the closely related sense of Bakhtin (chapter 8). But these limited senses are not without their own challenges and complexities.

A brief guide to what lies ahead will indicate where I find the challenges and how I proceed with them. In chapter 2, after describing a particular narrative instance of offense in Matthew 15 involving the Pharisees and a Canaanite woman, I look back at how the idea of offense appears and is developed in the Hebrew Bible, and I then go on to examine Paul's and Peter's New Testament transformations of Hebrew images into images of Jesus as an offense. Although I will be showing that the offense is an idea necessarily and positively associated with the divine, I must then move in an apparently contrary direction in chapter 3 by observing Jesus and Paul speaking *against* offense. (As Blake observed, there is no progression without contraries.) To examine the depth and richness of the idea, I turn in chapter 4 to the philosopher of offense, Søren Kierkegaard, who explores the idea in various dramatic permutations throughout his career as author, and who finally enacts it through his attack on "Christendom."

Through these approaches, I hope in part I to convey a sense of the biblical offense as a significant idea with both ancient and modern ramifications. This provides the framework for attending, in part II, to the problems of reading biblical narratives, including parables. I begin in chapter 5 with Mark's and Matthew's much-discussed statements about parables, which I use to explain the proposition that parables speak about, and are, offenses—an idea I place in the context of the current debate over parables. I turn in chapter 6 to Matthew's great "parable chapter" (Matt. 13), offering a narrative reading of the entire chapter, and in chapter 7 to another passage (in Matt. 17 and 18) in order to develop further the Gospel idea of *skandalon* and the necessity of its working within a narrative context. Because Bakhtin's ideas usefully extend the Kierkegaardian ideas of encounter, collision, and offense, I develop, in chapter 8, a more specifically dialogic view of Gospel narratives through a reading of Luke's parable of the Good Samaritan in its narrative context. Finally, in chapter 9, I apply the notions of dialogic interaction and scandalous encounters to John's Gospel. Using Lotman's and Kermode's broad views of scandal as news and story, I try to suggest why narrative is essential to the biblical offense in John.

Mindful both of Bloom's and Kierkegaard's scandal of normative misreading and their lament over the suppressed offense, I am attempting here to reintroduce Bible readers to the biblical *skandalon*, to illuminate the workings of Gospel narratives as actions grounded in offense, and, more specifically, to explore parables as actions presented by their offensive interlocutor, Jesus. My interest is not simply in how the offense operates in the narrative but also in how we as readers and interpreters conveniently eliminate its dangerous and fascinating qualities. Avoiding offense is a deep need, even (perhaps especially) when it appears in sacred texts.

2

Biblical Offense at Work: Defilement and Blindness

The Pharisees and the Canaanite Woman

The first half of Matthew 15 is a good place to begin looking at the workings of the biblical offense since it contains a plethora of offenses. Jesus's fame as teacher, preacher, and healer has spread sufficiently by this point in Matthew's narrative that Pharisees and scribes have come to Galilee from Jerusalem, many miles away, to encounter the man. The first action that is reported of the Pharisees and scribes, however, is that they are offended not at Jesus but at his disciples, who have transgressed the tradition of the elders by not washing their hands when they eat. They approach Jesus with their complaint in the form of a question. Instead of answering the question, Jesus questions them: "And why do you break the commandment of God for the sake of your tradition?" (Matt. 15:3). God's commandment, he charges, contradicts what they say. He explains their offense against God, and he goes on to insult them directly and unmistakably, quoting Scripture against them personally. In no uncertain terms, Jesus confronts the Pharisees with the possibility of offense: "You hypocrites! Isaiah prophesied rightly about you when he said: 'This people honors me with their lips, but their hearts are far from me; in vain do they worship me, teaching human precepts as doctrines'" (Matt. 15:7–9).

Jesus then turns away from the Pharisees and to the people,

calling on them to "listen and understand" and explaining to them the true nature of defilement: "it is not what goes into the mouth that defiles a person, but it is what comes out of the mouth that defiles" (Matt. 15:11). The crowd, which had not asked about defilement, gets the straightforward answer, while the Pharisees, who had asked, get a question and a rebuke that seems more likely to make them angry than to mollify and enlighten them.

In the narrative, Jesus does not stay for an answer to the question he puts to the Pharisees or for a response to his accusations. Instead, he speaks to the crowd, and the Pharisees, as actors, drop out of the narrative. But they do not disappear entirely, for Jesus's disciples report on the Pharisees' response to his harsh words: "Then the disciples approached and said to him, 'Do you know that the Pharisees took offense [*eskandalisthēsan*, the root being *skandal*] when they heard what you said?'" (Matt. 15:12).

It is no wonder "the Pharisees took offense," since Jesus has called them hypocrites and turned their Scripture against them, personally. Jesus professes neither surprise nor indifference to the disciples' report but answers them with two parabolic sayings, one about plants ("Every plant that my heavenly Father has not planted will be uprooted," Matt. 15:13) and another, which is applied directly to the Pharisees, about blind men ("Let them alone; they are blind guides of the blind. And if one blind person guides another, both will fall into a pit," Matt. 15:14). The Pharisees are offended, and, like the blind, they will fall. The two actions of being offended and falling are the effects—really the single effect—of the *skandalon*.

Jesus's response may seem harsh and surprising to the disciples or, for that matter, to readers. Many readers might expect Jesus to suggest that we *help* blind men who are about to fall into a pit. The Scripture says, "You shall not . . . put a stumbling block [translated *skandalon* in the Septuagint, LXX] before the blind" (Lev. 19:14). But in this case the blind have chosen their particular form of blindness, and they are to be left alone. Specifically, they have chosen to be offended by the disciples and by Jesus, and they have chosen not to hear Jesus and Isaiah (as interpreted by Jesus). And when the Pharisees will not grasp the message about themselves, the crowd is given the opportunity to "listen and understand."

The Pharisees, however, are not alone in failing to listen and understand. The crowd also may fail, though we are not told. In a brilliant essay on the Gerasene demoniac, Jean Starobinski argues that in the course of the Gospel narrative, "evil is always on the side of plurality," echoing Kierkegaard's dictum that "the crowd is untruth" (341), but the crowd in this particular passage drops out as a narrative actor as quickly as the Pharisees do. The disciples, however, remain: "But Peter said to him, 'Explain this parable to us.' Then he [Jesus] said, 'Are you also still without understanding? Do you not see . . . ?'" (Matt. 15:15–17). Once again, Jesus is not gentle, even with his own disciple. He does not, to be sure, offensively call Peter a hypocrite or a numskull, but he clearly implies that Peter *should* understand by this point. Furthermore, he does not do what Peter requests; he does not explain "this parable" by saying that the plant or the blind man refers to the Pharisees, or whatever else he might have said to make the meaning of the metaphor plain to Peter. Instead, he returns to his explanation of defilement, repeating to Peter what he has already told the crowd ("These are what defile a person," Matt. 15:20, cf. 15:11) and amplifying it. His answer suggests that Jesus knows the nature of Peter's misunderstanding better than Peter does. Peter does not need help with a parable about the offended Pharisees; he has not heard or understood the teaching about defilement, even though he and the other disciples—the eaters with unwashed hands—were the source of the original offense to the Pharisees, which led to their complaint and to Jesus's teaching.

Jesus's phrase "*still* without understanding" indicates that there already had been misunderstanding in the disciples' earlier question—"Do you know that the Pharisees took offense when they heard what you said?"—and that the parabolic sayings have not cleared up the misunderstanding. The disciples seem to think that what Jesus said might not have been appropriate behavior, or that it might possibly have been unintentional, or that perhaps an apology, or a few kind words to the offended Pharisees, might be in order. But Jesus's answer makes it quite clear that the offense was intentional and that the offended Pharisees' guidance ("they are blind guides") will lead to a fall.

This episode is not resolved as narrative in any conclusive way: the Pharisees, who have come a long way to encounter Jesus, have dropped out of the narrative in the state of offense; the crowd has been given an opportunity to hear and understand, but whether they do or not is left unreported; and the disciples have witnessed everything that has happened but have "still" not understood, and they are given another explanation. Whether they understand *this* time, however, is also left unreported; the narrative stops immediately after the explanation. The inconclusive conclusion of this part of the narrative is that the Pharisees are offended and that the crowd and the disciples may or may not understand what is involved in the offense. But even though the episode is over, the narrative is not. The geographical location shifts; the Pharisees are gone (replaced by their opposite, one non-Jewish woman), and the crowd is gone (in fact, Jesus "withdrew," from Galilee, Pharisees, and crowds); but Jesus and the disciples—the constants from the previous episode— remain. The narrative goes on, developing the themes of defilement, not hearing, and offense:

> Jesus left that place and went away to the district of Tyre and Sidon. Just then a Canaanite woman from that region came out and started shouting, "Have mercy on me, Lord, Son of David; my daughter is tormented by a demon." But he did not answer her at all. And his disciples came and urged him, saying, "Send her away, for she keeps shouting after us." He answered, "I was sent only to the lost sheep of the house of Israel." But she came and knelt before him, saying, "Lord, help me." He answered, "It is not fair to take the children's food and throw it to the dogs." She said, "Yes, Lord, yet even the dogs eat the crumbs that fall from their masters' table." Then Jesus answered her, "Woman, great is your faith! Let it be done for you as you wish." And her daughter was healed instantly. (Matt. 15:21-28)

Much in this passage is in striking contrast to the previous episode, but the contrast serves only to continue the development of issues raised earlier. Although the Pharisees in addressing Jesus used no title, the non-Jewish woman addresses Jesus with a Jewish, messianic title, "Lord, Son of David." Jesus, who rebuked the Pharisees for their Jewish traditions that transgress God's commandments, apparently refuses to help the woman because she is not a Jew, not one of "the lost sheep of the house of Israel," not one of "the children." She is a dog, not worthy to eat at the table. The Pharisees had felt that the disciples were not worthy to eat at the traditional Jewish table because of their unwashed hands, but being a dog is a far lower order of uncleanness. This episode is a dramatic enactment of issues raised in the earlier episode. In it, Jesus had reformulated the distinction between defilement and cleanness not on the basis of tradition (Matt. 15:2, 6) or doctrine (15:9) but on the basis of what "proceeds from the heart" (15:18-19, 8). The issue of *hearing* in the preceding passage, where it was a problem for the Pharisees, the crowd, and the disciples, now seems to be Jesus's "problem." He acts as if he does not hear her ("But he did not answer her a word"), although, of course, physical hearing is no more the issue here than it was in the preceding passage. Acoustically, the disciples are hearing all too well: "Send her away, for she keeps shouting after us."

But they still do not understand Jesus's curious treatment of the people who come to encounter him.

In the episode of the Canaanite woman, Jesus is at the center of a series of three confrontations. First, the woman states her request ("Have mercy on me"), surprisingly addressing Jesus as "Lord, Son of David" and succinctly explaining the problem. Jesus's response to this encounter is silence. In the second confrontation, the woman disappears temporarily from the represented scene, as the disciples beg Jesus to send her away. The narrative dramatizes only the confrontations, but there is other action, not even offstage but simply unreported as it occurs. We infer from the disciples' request not that Jesus's silence has caused the woman to give up trying to have her daughter cured by this Jew but that she has continued to plead her case to the disciples. And although they want her to go away, they cannot, on their authority alone, succeed in getting rid of her, and she is proving to be a nuisance. They therefore appeal to the higher authority, Jesus. However, Jesus's response to them is not directly a response to *their* request but a response to the woman's first request: he does not say that he will or will not send her away, but instead he says, indirectly, that he cannot have mercy on her because she is not of "the house of Israel."

Although this explanation is spoken to the disciples, the woman, as it turns out, hears it as well. When she reenters the narrative, she is not "shouting after" Jesus, as the disciples reported she did to them; instead, in the third dramatized encounter of this episode, she kneels, "saying" a simple plea: "Lord, help me." Jesus's response to her this time is emphatic and direct, and it poses a much stronger possibility of offense than silence, or ignoring her: "It is not fair to take the children's food and throw it to the dogs" (15:26). The metaphor has changed, from lost sheep to children, but the meaning is clear: she is not a Jew, she is a dog. There is no mistaking the astonishing insult—you are a Canaanite dog—and it is clear that the woman does not mistake it: "Yes, Lord, yet even the dogs eat the crumbs that fall from their masters' table" (15:27).

More astonishing than the insult is the woman's response; she, unlike the Pharisees, affirms the insult ("Yes, Lord"), choosing not to be offended. She has acknowledged his lordship and his Jewishness from the outset ("Lord, Son of David"). Even in the face of an insult that would normally send one away from the giver of the insult, enraged or in despair, she continues to acknowledge his lordship and therefore is willing to accept the role of dog. She, like the dogs, will willingly take the crumbs, for these crumbs, she believes, are life-giving bread from the Lord, and they will heal her daughter. Jesus's response—"Woman, great is your faith!"—is in direct contrast to his response to Peter in the preceding chapter, when Peter began to sink in the water ("You of little faith, why did you doubt?" Matt. 14:31) and to all the disciples in the following chapter when they forget Jesus's use of bread and teaching about bread ("You of little faith. . . . Do you still not perceive?" Matt. 16:8–9).

The Pharisees are offended; the Canaanite woman is not offended. The stark contrast is revelatory, for the opposite of offense is faith, but the only way to faith is through the possibility of offense.

The central issue of this passage is usually defined as the primacy of Jesus's mission to the Jews and his struggle between that mission and a possible mission to the Gentiles. But this issue is an offensive vehicle for raising a larger question about cleanness and defilement, and Jesus has been at pains, in spite of repeated misunderstanding, to redefine the distinction between cleanness and defilement on the basis of what "proceeds from the heart." Jesus says of the Pharisees that "their hearts are far from [God]," but the Canaanite woman's heart is with her daughter and with the Son of David, who can heal her daughter. The central issue of this passage is *not* Jesus's mission to Jews versus Gentiles; it is not even cleanness versus defilement. The central issue is offense versus faith. And it is posed in a highly offensive way: pious and law-abiding Pharisees lack faith, and a Gentile dog has great faith. What Jesus said to John the Baptist's disciples in Matthew 11:6 broods over this narrative as a kind of suspended challenge to characters in the text and to readers of the text: "Blessed is anyone who takes no offense at me."

In spite of this explicit statement about the blessedness of not taking offense, and in spite of repeated offenses and potential offenses issuing from the mouth of Jesus, many readers of the Gospels do not want to recognize the possibility of offense that Jesus embodies. Indeed, this passage, which appears also in Mark with some variations, is itself so offensive that some commentators have decided that it is a textual corruption *because* it is offensive. "'The dogs' is *impossibly* [my emphasis] harsh and unfeeling on the lips of Jesus," we are told in the exegesis of *The Interpreter's Bible*. The explanation for this impossibility is that the "language of the tradition has been affected by . . . the prejudices of Jewish Christians" during the course of the oral tradition. Thus, "one of the most difficult sections in the Gospel" is neatly disposed of (Buttrick, 7: 754–

55). Other commentators try to deny that the reply to the woman is harsh or offensive. One argument is that the word *dog* is in the diminutive form; the woman might be offended by being called a dog but not by being called a little dog, or a puppy. C. S. Mann, in the *Anchor Bible*, rejects this argument (presumably on the grounds that, as others have pointed out, the Hellenistic use of this form does not consistently weaken or diminish the noun), but he argues that the "near harshness" of Jesus's reply is mitigated because the dogs are domestic animals.[1] In his view, no offense is intended. Jesus is uncertain whether his ministry extends to this Gentile woman or not, and his reply reflects his hesitation: "There was evidently hesitation in Jesus's mind as to the limits of his ministry, and the reaction voiced in this verse expresses this. The woman's reply suggests that she recognized the hesitation and took advantage of it" (Mann, 321). Another interpreter argues similarly that the meaning of Jesus's saying depends on the speaker's "tone and facial expression" (Filson, 178), but the narrative itself offers little evidence of Jesus's geniality, hesitation, or "inward bafflement" (Buttrick, 7: 442). The diminutive form of *dogs* (in spite of the varying Hellenistic uses of the form) has to bear virtually all the weight, and the dogs have even led some to portray this scene as an exceptionally cozy one—a pleasant setting, in a humble peasant's home, with a few people around, and puppies under the table (Bundy, 280–81).

Other interpreters see the passage as a play of wit, with the woman's witty riposte about dogs and crumbs winning the day for her. The scholar who has perhaps done more than anyone to illuminate the meanings of the passage, T. A. Burkill, dismisses many of these interpretations as belonging "to the realm of pure speculation" (112). He does not accept the argument that Jesus's saying is anything but insulting, following Joseph Klausner, who observed that Jesus's answer is "so brusque and chauvinistic that if any other Jewish teacher of the time had said such a thing Christians would never have forgiven Judaism for it" (294). Burkill points out that "as in English, so in other languages, to call a woman 'a little bitch' is no less abusive than to call her 'a bitch' without qualification. In the parable the dogs may not be street scavengers, but the fact remains that they are not truly members of the household, as the children are; they are *under* the table, not *at* the table, and their consumption of the crumbs is an unintended consequence of the act of feeding the children" (114).[2] Burkill explains the passage by trying to reconstruct its transmission in light of the early church. At the outset, in

his view, was the insulting saying, which might have been a proverb, indicating something like our proverb "Charity begins at home,"
with the clear intention of excluding non-Jews. After Jesus's death,
certain elements in the Jewish-Christian groups wanted to widen
church membership and added the woman's reply and the subse-
quent healing of the daughter to the original story, thereby reversing
the force of it in order to bring it into line with their own theological
views. Mark took this version and added the topographical framework, and Matthew took Mark's version and inserted a few more
revisions.

In Burkill's interpretation, as with other interpretations, the narrative has nothing whatsoever to do with the biblical offense ("Blessed
is anyone who takes no offense at me"). But although the offense
has no place in his interpretation, Burkill makes a revealing comment when he wonders why Luke did not include the story in *his*
Gospel: "Luke may have been offended by the reference to Gentiles
as dogs . . . , and for this reason decided to omit the story" (75). This
comment reveals an unexplored assumption that I concur with—
namely, that the story contains at its center the double possibility
of offense, first, to a character in the story and, second, to a reader
of the story. Of course, Burkill's speculation about Luke rests on
the assumption that Luke was, like the Canaanite woman, a Gentile
and therefore likely to be offended. But one might wonder why, if
the woman in the story chooses not to be offended, Luke should
choose otherwise. Or whether Luke, as a Gentile writer, found the
offense to the Pharisees acceptable while he found the offense to the
Canaanite woman unacceptable. (In fact, Luke omits the episode
about the Pharisees as well as the story about the Canaanite woman.)
Or whether the Jewish writers of the New Testament found Jesus's
attack on the Pharisees offensive and were tempted to leave them
out but had no problem including an offense to a Gentile. We are
back at trying to account for the text on the basis of the "prejudices"
of the authors, and, with due respect to the power of ethnic and
national considerations over us, the insignificance of such considerations is central to this narrative. Defilement is not an ethnic issue;
it comes from the "heart," transcending ethnic considerations. This
Jesus teaches through his dramatic actions, and the offense in the
narrative challenges the reader to encounter the teaching.

The possibility of offense to Luke or any other reader posed by
this story of the Canaanite woman is hard to escape if we will read
the story *as story*, read it in its narrative context (most immediately,

the context of the offense against the Pharisees), and read it without extratextual assumptions about what is possible or impossible for Jesus to do or to say. That is, if we assume that Jesus is a kind, gentle, and loving hero and that such traits are antithetical to offensiveness, we as readers will do whatever we can to ameliorate any apparent offensiveness in the text. Or if we assume that ethnic explanations of character explain much about actions, we as readers will have a tendency to adopt ethnic explanations of actions no matter what the text may imply about such explanations. Jesus's saying that links a woman to dogs, and hence the entire story, *is* offensive, but that does not guarantee that the reader will encounter the offense. Lionel Trilling once said of Jane Austen's *Mansfield Park* that its greatness is commensurate with its power to offend (211). Likewise, in this biblical episode, the power of the narrative lies precisely in a series of offenses to characters *in* the story and to readers *of* the story.

Yahweh's Snares and Stumbling Blocks

The offense, the *skandalon*, of the New Testament, which manifests itself in a religious hero who calls devoutly religious, law-abiding Pharisees "hypocrites" and who calls a non-Jewish woman with a sick daughter a "dog," does not appear suddenly, ex nihilo, as a new invention of the first century C.E.; it springs directly from the Hebrew Bible. Variants of the *skandalon* are almost nonexistent in secular Greek literature. One of its rare appearances is in Aristophanes' *Acharnians*, when *skandalēthron*—a stick that sets off a trap— is used figuratively: "setting little verbal traps" (l. 687). When the Hebrew Bible was translated by Jewish scholars into the Greek Septuagint, they used the word *skandalon*, along with other words, to translate the Hebrew *moḵesh*, "snare" or "trap" (now, grimly, "explosive mine"), and *mikhshol*, "stumbling block" or "obstacle."

Thus, the meanings of the New Testament offense grew out of vivid, concrete images in the Hebrew Scriptures. In this section, I examine a series of these images, since they are essential to the existence of Jesus as *skandalon* in the New Testament. Often these Hebrew images take on the figurative meanings of "cause of ruin" and "cause of disaster" and are characterized by the elements of unexpectedness, knavery, and violence (Stählin, in Kittel and Friedrich, 7: 342). All of these elements are present in the Psalms, as the speaker expresses his sense of entrapment and pleads for deliverance:

Those who seek my life lay their snares. (Ps. 38:12)

The arrogant have hidden a trap [LXX, *pagida*] for me,
and with cords they have spread a net [LXX, *pagidas*],
along the road they have set snares [LXX, *skandalon*] for me. (Ps. 140:5)

Keep me from the trap [LXX, *pagidos*] that they have laid for me,
and from the snares [LXX, *skandalōn*] of evildoers. (Ps. 141:9)

Sometimes the speaker turns his attention away from the victim of
the trap and to the trap setter: "They hold fast to their evil purpose;
they talk of laying snares secretly, thinking, 'Who can see us?'" (Ps.
64:5). The prophet Amos uses the image of a bird to convey the
almost mysterious unexpectedness of the workings of the trap:
"Does a bird fall into a snare on the earth, when there is no trap for
it? Does a snare spring up from the ground, when it has taken nothing?" (Amos 3:5). And the Psalmist uses the same image to celebrate
joyous deliverance: "We have escaped like a bird from the snare of
the fowlers; the snare is broken, and we have escaped" (Ps. 124:7).

Bird snares convey metaphorically the sense of entrapment that
is a crucial element in the Hebrew Bible, but since the Bible represents the plight of a people to later generations, to keep alive the
memory of mistakes as well as commandments, the actual as opposed to the figurative nature of these snares is also important.
Individual people may be traps, as Moses was to the Egyptians
("How long shall this fellow be a snare to us?" Exod. 10:7), or as Saul
intended his daughter Michal to be to David ("Let me give her
to him that she may be a snare [LXX, *skandalon*] for him," 1 Sam.
18:21), or as a godless ruler is to his people (Job 34:30). Before his
death, Joshua warns the Israelites not to intermarry with Canaanites
on penalty of losing Yahweh's favor: "They [the Canaanites] shall be
a snare and a trap for you, a scourge on your sides, and thorns in
your eyes, until you perish from this good land that the LORD your
God has given you" (Josh. 23:13). Or gods may be traps: when the
Israelites disobey Yahweh by making a covenant with the Canaanites, Yahweh tells the Israelites, "I will not drive them out before
you; but they shall become adversaries to you, and their gods shall
be a snare to you" (Judg. 2:3).

It is not only, or even primarily, however, our enemies who set
snares to entrap us; it is we ourselves. Our own desires, whether for
Canaanite women, foreign gods, or gold and silver, suggest that the
enemy is within. The author of Proverbs explores the self-evident
and yet delusive quality of this trap setting through the familiar
bird-and-net image: "For in vain is the net baited while the bird is

looking on; yet they lie in wait—to kill themselves! and set an ambush—for their own lives!" (Prov. 1:17–18).

When the Israelites offer Gideon the kingship, he declines it but requires all the men of Israel to give him the gold earrings they had taken as spoils from the Midianites. From the gold of the earrings he creates an ephod, an idolatrous image. "And all Israel prostituted themselves to it there, and it became a snare to Gideon and to his family" (Judg. 8:27). The psalmist's lament, "They served their idols, which became a snare to them" (Ps. 106:36), applies to Gideon and, in continual recurrence, to the people of Israel as they are ensnared by, or fall into, idolatry. "The quintessential scandal, in the Old Testament," Girard says, "is idolatry . . . the obstacle made divine" (*Things Hidden*, 421).

While the trap or snare (*mokesh*) is the first characteristic image the *skandalon* conveys from the Hebrew Bible, the "falling into" or "stumbling" leads to the second. Here again we create the act ourselves, and at the same time we reveal ourselves to the world: "Sinners are overtaken through their lips; by them the reviler and the arrogant are tripped up" (Sirach 23:8). Such is the effect of the other form of the cause of ruin: the obstacle, the stumbling block, the *mikhshol*.

An obstacle, unlike a trap, can be seen, unless, of course, the walker is blind or it is night—both possibilities frequent in biblical imagery. But obstacles may be seen in the daylight without being seen *as obstacles*. If a person is walking, comes to a crossroad, and finds at a junction that one road is blocked, he may decide to take the unblocked road. If the unblocked road takes him to his destination, then all is well; the roadblock is no obstacle. But let us suppose that the blocked road is indeed the one that leads to his destination. If he does not know this, he probably will try the unblocked road, hoping, perhaps quite reasonably, that it is the right one, and the roadblock will at first *seem* to be no obstacle. But when he knows that he can get to his destination only by going down the blocked road, he is confronted with choices. He can remove or climb over or walk around the roadblock. But suppose the roadblock is decked out with barbed wire or a threatening sign—"Trespassers Will Be Prosecuted." The choice becomes more difficult. Is it more important to heed the authority represented by the barbed wire or sign, or to reach the destination? Since our imaginary traveler is not blind, he has no trouble seeing obstacles, but not being blind is not sufficient to allow him to know whether they are obstacles *to him*, or, if they are obstacles, to know whether they are worth overcoming; to know these things, he also must know the significance of what he sees.

Creating a gold ephod out of Midianite earrings might have seemed to Gideon and the Israelites to be a harmless, pleasurable, and perhaps even beneficent enterprise. It would be a beautiful thing in its own right, and it would celebrate both Gideon's strength, manifested in the revenge of his brothers' deaths at the hands of the Midianites, and Israel's victory. Furthermore, Gideon is not blind, either physically (indeed, the ephod will appeal especially to the eyes) or intellectually. He is wise enough to reject the people's offer to become king (even when the offer is exceptionally good, including, as it does, his son and his son's son as his successors) on the grounds that "the LORD will rule over you" (Judg. 8:23). But the gold ephod built to gratify his desire becomes a cause of disaster—a "snare" or, we might also say, an unseen obstacle, an idol blocking their view of, and obedience to, Yahweh.

Much later, Ezekiel's task is to deliver the Israelites from their idols of gold and silver. Yahweh instructs him:

> Their silver and gold cannot save them on the day of the wrath of the LORD. They shall not satisfy their hunger or fill their stomachs with it. For it was the stumbling block of their iniquity. (Ezek. 7:19)

> Mortal, these men have taken their idols into their hearts, and placed their iniquity as a stumbling block before them. . . . Thus says the Lord GOD: Repent and turn away from your idols; and turn away your faces from all your abominations. For any of those of the house of Israel, or of the aliens who reside in Israel, who separate themselves from me, taking their idols into their hearts and placing their iniquity as a stumbling block before them, and yet come to a prophet to inquire of me by him, I the LORD will answer them myself. I will set my face against them . . . and cut them off from the midst of my people. (Ezek. 14:3, 6–8)

As attractive as the objects *in front of* the people may seem to them in their delusion, they are nonetheless idols, literally "dung-balls," in one of Ezekiel's characteristically graphic images. The people continually *set* the stumbling block of *their* iniquity *before* them and still seek out the prophet, disastrously blind to the fact that there is an obstacle between them and Yahweh, separating and cutting them off from Yahweh. They do not see that their desires are dung-balls. Ezekiel must warn the people, on pain of death if he fails to warn them, to turn away from the obstacles, but the people themselves must choose how to respond to the warnings. Yahweh makes the choice clear: either "turn away your faces from all your abominations"—the obstacles in front—or keep the stumbling blocks before your faces and be cut off by them, at your choice, from Yahweh. Their doom, like their desire, will be self-inflicted: "According to their way I will deal with them; according to their own judgments I will judge them. And they shall know that I am the LORD" (Ezek. 7:27). "Therefore I will judge you, O house of Israel, all of you according to your ways" (Ezek. 18:30).

The ideal for the Israelites is clearly a world with no obstacles between the people and God or, metaphorically, a clear road, the way of the people as Yahweh's people: "It shall be said, 'Build up, build up, prepare the way, remove every obstruction from my people's way'" (Isa. 57:14). Obstacles must be removed, and none should be put in the way of the helpless. Yahweh instructs Moses to tell the congregation that "You shall not revile the deaf or put a stumbling block before the blind; you shall fear your God: I am the LORD" (Lev. 19:14). Such a world is marked by peace, love, and obedience to God. "Great peace have those who love your law," says the Psalmist, "nothing can make them stumble" (Ps. 119:165).[3]

In Ezekiel, the people transform the objects of this world into their stumbling blocks, as Gideon transforms the Midianite earrings into an ephod. And having created stumbling blocks, they must either stumble or turn. "Repent and turn from all your transgressions; so that they shall not be a stumbling block of iniquity to you. . . . Turn, then, and live" (Ezek. 18:30, 32; NRSV margin). This could be read as a plea to individuals, as is characteristic of the New Testament, but it is fundamentally a plea to the people—"O house of Israel." The nation stumbles in a kind of collective blindness, aided by its priests, the Levites, who "ministered to them before their idols and made the house of Israel stumble into iniquity" and who therefore will be punished (Ezek. 44:12).

Since the Hebrew writers are emphatic about the people's responsibility not to set obstacles before others (the blind), about the people's own responsibility in creating and worshiping idols (Gideon's ephod), and about their need to "turn, then, and live" when a stumbling block is in front of their face, the stumbling block appears to be a manifestation of evil that separates the people from Yahweh. In King Solomon's prayer, the evil may be in the form of a woman: "Keep me back from every wicked woman that causeth the simple to stumble" (Ps. Sol. 16:7; Charles, 2: 647). And in the Testament of Solomon, the instigator of stumbling is Saphthorael, the twelfth demon, who sows dissension among people and "delights to cause them to stumble" (18:16; Charlesworth, 2: 979).

But in spite of this obvious relation between the stumbling block and evil, there is nonetheless an uncanny relation between it and Yahweh. From the examples we have seen thus far, excepting possibly the non-canonical demon Saphthorael, the stumbling block may be said to be self-created; it consists of the people's desires and is the people's nemesis. But even Ezekiel, who is the most emphatic about "the stumbling block of *their* iniquity," raises its uncanny relation to Yahweh, as when he reports Yahweh's judgment: "Again, if the righteous turn from their righteousness and commit iniquity, and *I lay a stumbling block before them*, they shall die" (Ezek. 3: 20). The iniquity and the stumbling block may be said to be identical, but the same object has different sources and functions. To the people, it is a wicked thing, though they do not always recognize its wickedness; it embodies their own desires and contains attractiveness, pleasure, despair, and ruin. To Yahweh, it is what separates the people from the I AM, not simply as a result of their action but also as a result of Yahweh's own action. The very existence of Yahweh is by nature an activity; Yahweh transforms any object, including melted Midianite earrings, into a potential idol. The object— the particular manifestation of iniquity and the stumbling block— becomes an idol through both the people's and Yahweh's activity and leads to the people's fall—a metaphoric stumbling or entrapment.

Jeremiah is emphatic about Yahweh's activity in the placing of stumbling blocks and in the ensuing destruction: "Therefore thus says the LORD: See, *I am laying* before this people stumbling blocks against which they shall stumble; parents and children together, neighbor and friend shall perish" (6:21). In Isaiah, Yahweh warns his prophet *not* to "walk in the way of this people" (8:11), for there are by implication two "ways"—one for Isaiah, or anyone who walks unobstructed in the way of Yahweh, and the other for the Israelites of both houses, Israel and Judah. Yahweh manifests himself differently, depending on which way one is in. For Isaiah, Yahweh is the "sanctuary," a place where one is in the presence of holiness. For the errant Israelites, on the other hand, Yahweh is present in multiple and cumulative images of destruction—the *mokesh* (snare) and the *mihkshol* (stumbling block): "He [the "LORD of hosts," here speaking about himself to Isaiah] will become a sanctuary, a stone one strikes against; for both houses of Israel he will become a rock one stumbles over—a trap and a snare for the inhabitants of Jerusalem. And many among them shall stumble; they shall fall and be broken; they shall be snared and taken" (Isa. 8:14–15). The snare and the stumbling block are idols created by the people themselves and, at the same time, manifestations of Yahweh's activity, namely, God's laying of traps or objects in the way of people, causing them to be entrapped or to stumble. The mysterious, unfathomable name of Yahweh—I AM WHO I AM or I WILL BE WHAT I WILL BE— contains the unexpected and the contradictory, for he surprisingly *becomes* sanctuary *and* stumbling block, trap, snare.[4]

Yahweh's presence in Isaiah is not manifest in the form of burn- ing bushes, earthquakes, or whirlwinds but in the form of his peo- ple's desires. The people desire to obey Yahweh, or they desire ob- jects that defile them and obstruct them, blinding them so that they can no longer see the way of Yahweh and no longer walk in the way of Yahweh. The people create their idols. But these same blinding, defiling idols are also laid before the people by Yahweh's activity and are themselves manifestations of Yahweh, who *becomes* "a rock of stumbling to both houses of Israel."

Jesus as the Stumbling Stone

In Jesus's encounter with the Pharisees and the Canaanite woman in Matthew 15, Jesus as *skandalon* poses the possibility of offense to those who approach him. In the Hebrew Bible, the *skandalon* is any idol—not only the obvious idols, such as the golden calf constructed by Aaron and the Israelites as they waited for Moses, or the household gods Rachael stole from her father Laban, or Gideon's Midianite earrings, but rather any object of desire that stands be- tween the Israelites and Yahweh. But these idols are not at all offen- sive to the Israelites; on the contrary, they are their hearts' desires. They are offensive to Yahweh, not to the Israelites, although they *should* be offensive to God-fearing people, as the golden calf is to Moses. Jesus, on the other hand, unlike the idols, *is* offensive to those who approach him, and they *should not* find him offensive: "Blessed is anyone who takes *no* offense at me."

It would seem that something drastic has happened to the *skan- dalon* as it reappears in the New Testament. But the transformation, although striking, is not radical; it is rather an evolution of what is already contained in the Hebrew form. In the Hebrew Bible, Yahweh *becomes* (without the Israelites knowing it) the stumbling block, which is the blinding, defiling idol desired by the people; the people, if their hearts are hardened, will stumble in the darkness of not knowing Yahweh. In the New Testament, the God in the stumbling block becomes manifest as Jesus. Jesus does not embody or dwell in

the idols or desires that keep people from God but, rather, offensively challenges those idols and desires. When the rich man asks
Jesus (addressing him as "good Teacher") what he must do to inherit
eternal life, Jesus responds with a challenge: "Why do you call me
good? No one is good but God alone" (Mark 10:17–18). Then he
recites the commandments, and the man assures Jesus that he has
observed them from his youth: "Jesus, looking at him, loved him
and said, 'You lack one thing; go, sell what you own, and give the
money to the poor, and you will have treasure in heaven; then come,
follow me.' When he heard this, he was shocked and went away
grieving, for he had many possessions" (Mark 10:21–22). The rich
man is willing to keep the law to obtain eternal life, but he is not
willing to give up his possessions; he loves them more than he loves
life. To this man, Jesus poses not the offense-as-insult, as in the case
of the Pharisees and the Canaanite woman, but the offense-as-
obstacle. As Yahweh requires that the Israelites have no idols, Jesus
requires that his followers have no idols, no desires that are stronger
than the desire to come to him. The rich man stumbles not on the
commandments that Jesus recites (although it is worth noting that
Jesus leaves out the commandment "You shall have no other gods
before me"); he stumbles on his heart's desire to keep his possessions. He is blessed only if he is not offended by Jesus's requirement,
but he *is* offended; the requirement Jesus sets is the obstacle he
cannot, or will not, overcome. Like Yahweh, Jesus poses the difficult challenge. In posing it, he becomes the stumbling block.

The early Christian writers Paul and Peter both explicitly address this transformation of the *skandalon* from idol to the person of
Jesus. For Paul, eternal life or righteousness is obtained not through
works or through the law, as the rich man in Mark's story had been
counting on, but through faith. Israelites, he says, have failed to
fulfill the law "because they did not strive for it on the basis of
faith, but as if it were based on works." And, he continues, "They
have stumbled over the stumbling stone, as it is written, 'See, I am
laying in Zion a stone that will make people stumble, a rock that
will make them fall, and whoever believes in him will not be put to
shame'" (Rom. 9:32–33). Paul is here combining two passages from
Isaiah—Isaiah 8:14–15, quoted above, where Yahweh announces
that he will become a sanctuary and a rock of stumbling that "many
among them shall stumble" on and "fall" and, second, Isaiah 28:16:
"See, I am laying in Zion a foundation stone, a tested stone, a precious cornerstone, a sure foundation: 'One who trusts will not
panic.'" Paul eliminates the image of the cornerstone altogether,

substituting the image of the stumbling stone, which he identifies with Jesus, as Christ (the anointed one, the messiah). "For Christ is the end of the law so that there may be righteousness for everyone who believes" (Rom. 10:4). To have faith, to believe, or to trust (all may be used to translate the Greek *pisteuō*) is one result of encountering the stumbling stone. The alternative is to fall or to be "put to shame" in the sense of being judged by God (Bultmann, "*Aischunō*", 189).

To illustrate the fall and judgment, Paul draws on the Hebrew Scriptures again: "And David says, 'Let their table become a snare and a trap, a stumbling block [*skandalon*] and a retribution for them; let their eyes be darkened so that they cannot see'" (Rom. 11:9–10). They stumble and fall in their blindness. In the Psalm from which Paul is quoting (69:22–23), they do not see the way of Yahweh; in Paul's recension, their spiritual blindness is equivalent to not having faith in the person of Jesus.

Peter, like Paul, combines the same two passages from Isaiah, and he, too, identifies the stone as Jesus (1 Pet. 2:4–8).[5] But Peter does three things differently. First, he makes the identification much more explicit, thereby creating a new image of a "living stone"—the stone, as Jesus, takes on life. Second, he retains the image of the cornerstone, the starting place of a building, a metaphor Peter explores by imagining a "spiritual house" that the congregation he is writing to may be "built into" as "living stones" themselves. And, finally, he introduces another stone image from Psalms that makes explicit the idea of rejection always latent in the image of the idol as stumbling stone (that is, by being attracted to the idol, the Israelites reject Yahweh): "The stone that the builders rejected has become the chief cornerstone" (Ps. 118:22).

Like Paul, Peter uses faith, or belief, as the central religious concept that binds these images together and gives them meaning: "To you then who believe, he [Jesus] is precious; but for those who do not believe, 'The stone that the builders rejected has become the very head of the corner,'" and "'A stone that makes them stumble, and a rock that makes them fall.' They stumble because they disobey the word" (1 Pet. 2:7–8). Peter has used the stone imagery of Psalms and Isaiah to create an extraordinarily compact, new image of Jesus as a living stone, the cornerstone of a building where some people will find their spiritual dwelling, but a cornerstone that has been rejected by others and is therefore a stumbling stone to them, causing them to fall. But Peter, in his impressive metaphor, is fundamentally doing what Isaiah had already done when he had Yahweh say that he, Yahweh, becomes a sanctuary (the spiritual dwelling) *and* a stumbling block. The difference, of course, is that in Peter's version Yahweh is represented in sanctuary and stone by a flesh-and-blood Jesus. His Jesus, as well as the Jesus of Paul and the Gospel writers, challenges anyone who approaches him to an encounter that must lead to one of two contrary conditions, either faith or offense.

Neither biblical faith nor biblical offense can exist without the other, as Kierkegaard saw clearly. Anti-Climacus writes:

> So inseparable is the possibility of offense from faith that if the God-man were not the possibility of offense he could not be the object of faith, either. Thus the possibility of offense is taken up into faith, is assimilated by faith, is the negative mark of the God-man. . . . The person who abolishes faith abolishes the possibility of offense, such as when speculation substitutes comprehending for having faith; and the person who abolishes the possibility of offense abolishes faith, such as when the sentimental sermon presentation falsely attributes direct recognizability to Christ. But whether faith is abolished or whether the possibility of offense is abolished, something else is also abolished: the God-man. And if the God-man is abolished, Christianity is abolished." (*Practice in Christianity*, 143–44)

Jesus is the cornerstone and the stumbling stone, and as the stumbling stone he is the obstacle, the *skandalon*. Girard's penetrating analysis of the *skandalon* reveals its grounding in human desire: "Scandal always arrives through humans, and it always affects other humans" (*Things Hidden*, 424). "The scandal invariably involves an obsessional obstacle, raised up by mimetic desire with all its empty ambitions and ridiculous antagonisms. . . . The *skandalon* is the obstacle/model of mimetic rivalry" (416). In the New Testament, those who encounter Jesus often stumble over their own desires and obsessions, as in the case of the rich man who obeys the law strictly but idolizes his possessions. But Kierkegaard repeatedly calls our attention to something else: scandal is a necessary part of the New Testament drama of encountering the divine and having faith. Peter's and Paul's reinterpretations of Hebrew metaphors and Jesus's assertions insist on an essential offense embodied in Jesus: "Blessed is anyone who takes no offense at *me*" (Matt. 11:6, Luke 7:23). The Pharisees, the Canaanite woman, and the rich man encounter a stumbling block. All who approach must encounter the *skandalon* of Jesus.

3

The Offensiveness
of Offense

In associating the offense primarily with the idols that Yahweh "lays" and "becomes" in the Hebrew Bible and with Jesus in the New Testament, and in asserting, with Kierkegaard, that the offense is essential to faith, I appear to be arguing—as indeed I am—that the Bible posits the offense as both necessary and valuable. Although the offense may be seen as an obstacle that blocks the way to truth and alienates one from God, this commonsense view presents problems as soon as Yahweh or Jesus *becomes* the offense. But even where Yahweh or Jesus does not obviously or clearly constitute the offense, it is evident that in its biblical usage the offense also may lead one to "walk in the way of the LORD" (Judg. 2:22). The stumbling block is a way not only of testing the Israelites but also of revealing their hearts' desires, which may be unknown even to themselves. The revelation may or may not lead to the divine. If they desire God, they are his people. If not, their desires alienate them from God.

Jesus's offensiveness to the Pharisees and the rich man tends to harden them or to crystallize their essential opposition to him, but his offensiveness to the Canaanite woman allows her to reveal the extent of her faith: she is willing to be a Gentile dog, if Jesus says so. She does not make her willingness contingent, saying, for example, that she will be a Gentile dog *if* Jesus will hear her and heal her daughter; she simply accepts Jesus's words, manifesting her faith in him. Furthermore, it is not necessary, or even likely, that this is a revelation of something she already knows. Her willingness to be a Gentile dog picking up the crumbs from a Jewish lord is imaginable only in the context of the encounter with the Jewish lord himself.

Scurrilous insults are not, it seems safe to say, easily borne. Some of us have sufficiently fragile egos that we find it difficult to bear stinging insults from our enemies; such insults from those we admire and honor are still more difficult to bear, much less to accept without objection or recrimination. This difficult-to-bear, personal nature of an offense, its confrontational nature that makes it hard to ignore or to shrug off, its blatant attack on what we take to be our deepest selves or our strongest allegiances—these are precisely what give the offense its power. The offense has a way of bringing the individual to a moment of crisis, revealing the heart's desire.

Kierkegaard is careful to sort out the negative from the positive qualities of the offense. In *The Sickness unto Death*, Kierkegaard's narrator, Anti-Climacus, makes this observation: "That a person never once is capable of being offended by Christianity can be held against him. To speak that way implies that being offended is something good. But it must be said that to be offended is sin" (116n). We must distinguish, however, between the being offended and the offense. If being offended is sin, as Anti-Climacus says, the offense itself is the act of revelation—which may lead toward or away from God. In the *Journals*, Kierkegaard considers the act itself: "The thought that God tests, yes, tempts a man ('lead us not into temptation') must not horrify us. The way one looks upon it makes the crucial difference. Disbelief, melancholy, etc., immediately become anxious and afraid and really impute to God the intention of doing it *in order that* man shall fail. . . . The believer, however, immediately interprets the matter inversely; he believes that God does it *in order that* he shall meet the test" (2: 1401). It is worth noting that Kierkegaard is not trying to read God's mind here; he is reading the minds of humans—what the despairing person and the believer *impute* to God. His focus is psychological rather than theological, but the observation rests on two interactive theological assumptions: first, that the divine is offensive to the natural world and, second, that humans, who are necessarily part of the natural world, must encounter the offense in order to encounter the divine. The crucial thing is how the human encounters the offense. "The divine truth is 'the truth,' but in such a way that the world *takes* offense at it. It cannot be otherwise. But it cannot therefore be said that it [divine truth] *gives* offense" (my emphases; *Journals* 3: 3036).

In the Kierkegaardian view, the offense is the necessary way to truth for those who encounter it without being offended. And yet this positive quality of the offense can be grasped only by means of its contrary—the clear and direct biblical teaching against offense. The offense must exist in Jesus (and one should not be offended by him), but the offense should not exist in anyone else. Jesus says, "*Skandala* are bound to come, but woe to anyone by whom they come!" (Luke 17:1; cf. Matt. 18:7). Jesus, the *skandalon* par excellence, speaks against offense.

It is therefore understandable that some have seen the *skandalon* only as a negative, even diabolical, instrument. As I have shown in chapter 2, it is much more than that. But in Jesus's exchange with Peter in Matthew 16:13–23, and in other places as well, the most obvious offense is diabolical, although, as Girard points out, this passage (in contrast to the temptation of Christ in the desert) "deconstructs" Satan, the diabolical principle, by placing him "on the side of men" (*Things Hidden*, 419). When Peter identifies Jesus as "the Messiah, the Son of the living God," Jesus identifies him as "Peter [*Petros*], and on this rock [*petra*] I will build my church" (16: 18). Within a few sentences of this, however, after Peter rebukes Jesus for saying that he will suffer, die, and be raised on the third day, Jesus turns on Peter: "Get behind me, Satan! You are a stumbling block [*skandalon*] to me; for you are setting your mind not on divine things but on human things" (16:23).

If one wanted to speculate on why the church should find the *skandalon* a troublesome business, to be dealt with chiefly by pretending it does not exist, one might do well to start with this passage. No sooner does Jesus make Peter the rock of his church than Peter makes himself a stumbling stone to Jesus. The figurative sense of "stone" in *skandalon* stands in direct contrast to Peter as "rock" and foundation of the church (Stählin, in Kittel and Friedrich, 7: 348). No words are minced: Peter *is* Satan; he is not on the side of God. Girard has written, "From the human point of view, . . . the Passion can only be a scandal" (*Things Hidden*, 418). Paul wrote that Christ crucified, or the cross (1 Cor. 1:23, Gal. 5:11), is a *skandalon*, but Peter is chronologically the first in the narrative to be scandalized by it, and he is scandalized hard upon his being given the "keys of the kingdom of heaven" (Matt. 16:19), well before the event of the cross happens.

In Kierkegaard's terms, Peter *takes* offense at divine truth, which is in the form of a *skandalon*, Jesus. But because Peter's mind is set on human rather than divine things, he himself becomes a diabolical *skandalon*, tempting Jesus with things human. The divine offense may be received negatively (by being offended) or positively (by not being offended), but the human offense is entirely negative. Jean Bosc calls these different forms "the offense of the cross" and "the offense of the world." The offense of the cross is Jesus, who posits the possibility of offense but blesses those who are not offended. The author of this offense is Jesus himself, and its object is the human being who is in revolt against truth and love, both of which *must* be scandalous because they stand in opposition to the life of the human world apart from the spirit. The other form, Bosc's offense of the world or of the human, is the offense of the autonomous human, the human without God, the human who has succumbed to an illusion of self-sufficiency, oblivious, as Peter is, that the ostensibly well-intentioned, self-sufficient person is turned away from truth and love. The author of this second scandal is the individual person, and its object (that is, what it is directed *against*) "is always man—man considered not in his revolt and his sin but in the spiritual vocation to which God directs him" (Bosc, 672). Peter, as author of an offense of the world, tempts Jesus from his vocation. But he does this in response to an offense that has been authored by Jesus toward Peter, who, in his state of offense, is in satanic revolt against God's will.

Bosc contemplates the implications of the *skandalon* for the historical church. He charges the nineteenth-century church with having let itself become absorbed by the world and with championing the established order. But, for both Peter and the church, living in the presence of a divine offense constitutes a constant temptation to ignore the offense or to counter it with the humanly easy—and natural—offense of the world. To put this another way, the negative, human offenses are pernicious and plural, while the positive, divine offense is salutary and singular: it is the offense of Jesus himself. The terms "pernicious" and "salutary" are Wilhelm Vischer's, and his formulation is strikingly appropriate to the plight of both Peter and the church: "The pernicious scandals are products of the intention to avoid the salutary scandal. And the only way of avoiding the pernicious scandals is the affirmation of the salutary scandal" (657). This is the double bind Peter and his successors must encounter.

Jesus, then, repeatedly speaks against offense, by which he means the negative offense of the world. But there is another powerful New Testament spokesman against offense: Paul, whose theology vividly provides this contrary (but not contradictory) view of offense.[1] As we have seen, Paul reads the Hebrew Bible with the intention of showing that its stumbling block has appeared in the person of Jesus. But he is equally zealous in opposing the offense or stumbling block when it appears in anyone other than Jesus. His message is emphatic: you, the readers of the Epistles, should offend no one—not fellow Christians who are members of the same community in Rome, Corinth, or wherever; not backsliders who are drifting from the community of Christians; and not complete outsiders, the unbelievers.

As a practical man concerned about living the Christian life in this world, Paul talks about the importance of being inoffensive in the context of situations in which his readers might be inclined to be offensive. In the Roman church, there was a difference of opinion about eating meat: some felt there were no religious objections to eating meat; others felt there were. There were other disputes as well: some thought certain days (probably the Sabbath) were of special importance, and some thought Christians should not drink wine. Paul does not leave us in doubt about where he stands on these issues: scruples about meat, days of the week, and wine are scruples of the weak and have nothing to do with the kingdom of God (Rom. 14:14, 17). But he is far less interested in the doctrinal issue than in the question of how members of the community live with such conflicts.

Paul's recommended solution of these problems involves two steps. First, the Romans should not judge each other. The weak vegetarians naturally judge themselves to be superior to the meat eaters, and the meat eaters, who are strong because they are right that "the kingdom of God is not food and drink" (14:17), naturally despise the weak vegetarians. But neither is to judge the other: "Who are you to pass judgment on servants of another? It is before their own lord that they stand or fall. And they will be upheld, for the Lord is able to make them stand" (14:4). Paul conjures up a domestic scene in which the slave is judged by the master of the house. Then, by analogy, he applies the scene to the subject at hand: both the weak and the strong will be upheld by God. Only God is to judge, and meat eaters and vegetarians will both stand, even though one group is strong and the other weak, because the all-important issue is the individual's relation to God, not whether he or she eats meat or vegetables.

However, eating meat or vegetables turns out to be important after all, because weak people take the issue seriously, even though it is not intrinsically important. And if, in their misguided seriousness, they lose sight of what is important because of what another does, the other has offended and scandalized the weak: "Everything is indeed clean, but it is wrong for you to make others fall by what you eat; it is good not to eat meat or drink wine or do anything that makes your brother or sister stumble" (14:20–21). The doctrinal issue turns out to be so insignificant that the strong are advised to follow the wrong doctrine so as not to offend the weak! "Resolve . . . never to put a stumbling block [*proskomma*] or hindrance [*skandalon*] in the way of another. . . . If your brother or sister is being injured by what you eat, you are no longer walking in love. Do not let what you eat cause the ruin of one for whom Christ died" (14:13, 15).

In Corinth, the problem was slightly different. The meat sold in the marketplaces may have been slaughtered in sacrificial rites in pagan temples. Should Christians eat it? No problem and no issue, according to Paul: "We are no worse off if we do not eat, and no better off if we do." Except that what we do might offend the weak. "But take care that this liberty of yours does not somehow become a stumbling block [*proskomma*] to the weak" (1 Cor. 8:8–9). If weak Christians are scandalized by seeing you eat meat offered to idols and lose faith as a result, "you sin against Christ. Therefore, if food is a cause of their falling [literally, if food offends—*skandalizei*—the brother of me], I will never eat meat, so that I may not cause one of them to fall [*skandalizō*]" (8:12–13). The weak and the strong are so intimately connected in the Christian community that the qualities and actions of one necessarily affect the other. "Who is weak, and I am not weak?" Paul asks. "Who is made to stumble [*skandalizetai*], and I am not indignant?" (2 Cor. 11:29). Paul, who is "putting no obstacle in anyone's way" (2 Cor. 6:3), is to be the model for his readers.

Paul's position on this matter may seem like a case of strong common sense, but it must have been a highly controversial issue; it did not pass unchallenged. The author of Revelation reprimands the church at Pergamum: "But I have a few things against you: you have some there who hold to the teaching of Balaam, who taught Balak to put a stumbling block [*skandalon*] before the people of Israel, so that they would eat food sacrificed to idols and practice fornication" (Rev. 2:14). Eating sacrificial food and fornicating are themselves the offense, according to John,[2] but for Paul eating sacrificial food is not in itself offensive, though the weak brothers and sisters might (mistakenly) consider it so, in which case the stronger brothers and sisters ought not eat it, lest they offend the weaker.

The conflicting views about eating sacrificial food suggests the slipperiness of the *skandalon*. Paul thinks pragmatically about the *skandalon* in terms of responses. Even his famous reference to "Christ crucified, a stumbling block to Jews and foolishness to Gentiles" (1 Cor. 1:23) puts the focus on the responses to the cross rather than on the act of crucifying. But John in Revelation thinks about it in terms of varied, particular, identifiable acts, and most commentators and translators have followed this view. Historically, there always has been the tendency to consider the *skandalon* not only as exclusively negative but also as a particular negative act or certain kind of action that can be categorized as sin. Thus, the *Encyclopedic Dictionary of Religion* (1979) defines *scandal* as "*the sin*, contrary to charity, of occasioning another person's spiritual harm or ruin" (my emphasis; O'Brien, 3207; see also Marshall, 51).

But Jesus is even less interested than Paul in speaking about particular acts that are stumbling blocks and can therefore be called particular sins. For Jesus, the emphasis is on the activity of turning another person away from the divine and the violent results of it. "If any of you put a stumbling block before [*skandalisē*] one of these little ones who believe in me," Jesus tells his disciples, "it would be better for you if a great millstone were hung around your neck and you were thrown into the sea" (Mark 9:42; cf. Matt. 18:6, Luke 17:2). Jesus's expression of the offensiveness of offense is notable for *its* offensiveness. Some readers are scandalized by the apparently gratuitous violence of this hypothetical death by drowning. Frederick Buechner's fictional character Brownie in *Lion Country* is a parody of what some interpreters will do to avoid the offense: he argues that millstones in Palestine must have been highly porous, so that they floated in the saline waters of the Dead Sea and would function as life preservers. Thus, millstones suggest the idea of punishment but instantly eliminate the violence by the preserving grace of salvation. Brownie belongs to the tribe John Calvin complained about, those who "devise something soothing" that leads to "a watered-down and degenerate theology" (Calvin, *Concerning Scandals*, 23). Jesus's general message—do not scandalize little ones—is not in itself a theological problem, but his particular, highly offensive manner of delivering the message requires radical interpretation by the Brownies of the world in order to eliminate the offense.

Paul's version of this teaching—less violent than Jesus's—is that those in the church should not offend others in the church. But he is not content to rest his opposition to offense there: "Give no offense to Jews or to Greeks or to the church of God, just as I try to please everyone in everything I do" (1 Cor. 10:32–33). The injunction to "give no offense" is addressed to members of the Christian community, but the object of the injunction is not only the brothers, sisters, or little ones of the church but all people. The reason Paul gives is that inoffensiveness and pleasing will be to the advantage of "many, so that they may be saved" (10:33). And he concludes with the injunction, "Be imitators of me, as I am of Christ" (11:1). If Jesus was offensive, should not Paul be offensive, and thus the brothers and sisters, who are enjoined to be the imitators of Paul? Not according to Paul. To understand Paul's position, it is important to distinguish between the imitation of Christ and the imitation of the historical Jesus. Paul is urging not that the Corinthians follow Jesus's way of life or his offensiveness but that they "Let the same mind be in you that was in Christ Jesus" (Phil. 2:5). To this end, they are to imitate Paul—not his person, which is nothing, but his teaching—who imitates Christ (Conzelmann, 179–80). Paul would reject out of hand the notion that a Christian should base his or her actions on a response to the question "What would Jesus do?"

But Paul is no first-century Brownie, exuding pleasantness and conciliation indifferently. He advised the Ephesians to "Be angry" (Eph. 4:26) and proclaimed his own indignation when anyone is scandalized (2 Cor. 11:29). His advice is situational. When it is a matter of conflicting traditions or opinions among weaker or stronger brothers and sisters, all trying to glorify God, he recommends a course of action quite different from when fornication threatens the community. Furthermore, how much the people know, or what instruction they have had, must be considered part of the situation. Paul earlier had conveyed certain teachings to the Corinthians, and he expected them to follow these teachings, since they indicate how to imitate Christ. But such teaching may need to be modified, depending on circumstances: "But now I am writing to you not to associate with anyone who bears the name of brother or sister who is sexually immoral or greedy, or is an idolater, reviler, drunkard, or robber. Do not even eat with such a one" (1 Cor. 5:11). In this case they *are* to judge: "Drive out the wicked person from among you" (5:13). But they are only to judge the insiders, the brothers and sisters who threaten the community of the faithful, and to judge them only on the basis of the teachings, the practical application of the *imitatio Christi*. The outsiders, the nonbelievers, however, are *not* to be judged: "For what have I to do with judging those outside? Is it not those who are inside that you are to judge? God will judge those outside" (5:12–13). Even so, in one sense the issue of fornication is like the issue of vegetarianism: Paul is less concerned with a doctrinal or moral issue and more concerned with the community, the church. The fornicators (like the meat eaters) scandalize the weak, threatening the life (in imitation of Christ) of the individual and of the community. But fornication is different from eating ritual meat, and Paul does not recommend that the strong join the weak (to avoid offense) by becoming fornicators. In this case, the weak first must be warned, then judged, as brothers and sisters, and avoided—making them, unless they return, outsiders. But the injunction "not to associate with" (5:11, Eph. 5:7), to "keep away from" (2 Thess. 3:6), to "drive out" (1 Cor. 5:13), and to "avoid" (Rom. 16:17) applies only to errant brothers and sisters. The outsiders, Paul makes clear (1 Cor. 5:9–10), are not to be avoided by the Corinthian Christians, who are expected to live *in* the world, not separate themselves from it or reject it.

The Roman brothers and sisters who oppose Paul's teachings (in contrast to the vegetarians or teetotalers, who are trying, however misguidedly, to glorify God) are a danger to the Roman community because they "deceive the hearts of the simple-minded" (Rom. 16: 18). Hence Paul's instructions: "I urge you, brothers and sisters, to keep an eye on those who cause dissensions and offenses [*skandala*], in opposition to the teaching that you have learned; avoid them" (Rom. 16:17). The insiders-becoming-outsiders are the objects of Paul's ire and are to be avoided precisely because they are scandalizing others, in negative, pernicious, human ways, which—whether trivial or not—may lead others away from the divine. They violate Paul's consistent and emphatic injunction, which is applicable to all brothers and sisters, in spite of Jesus's example but in keeping with Jesus's teaching: do not offend.

4

Offense or Faith:
The Kierkegaardian Choice

Beguiling the Reader

In *The Sickness unto Death*, Anti-Climacus asks rhetorically how it can be explained that one never hears or reads a prayer "that in our day especially" would be appropriate. The prayer is this:

> God in heaven, I thank you for not requiring a person to comprehend Christianity, for if that were required, I would be the most miserable of all. The more I seek to comprehend it, the more incomprehensible it appears to me and the more I discover only the possibility of offense. Therefore I thank you for requiring only faith, and I pray that you will continue to increase it. (129n)

His question about why this prayer is never heard cannot be answered except by saying what Anti-Climacus is not willing to say directly, namely, that Christendom has rejected Christianity. The implication is that one ought to hear or read such a prayer repeatedly, for it contains central truths and the dilemma that faces each individual: (1) Christianity is incomprehensible, it is not a part of the category of understanding; (2) the more one tries to understand it, the more one encounters the possibility of offense; and (3) the only alternative to offense, and the only requirement for Christianity, is faith.[1] That, in a nutshell, is Kierkegaard's position, and it is the dialectical dilemma that Kierkegaard's "single individual" faces. But, alas, offense is never mentioned these days (*Journals*, 3: 3028).

Hence the absence of this prayer and the indirect judgment its absence implies.

Paul was well aware not only of the possibility of offense but also of its actuality: he preaches "Christ crucified, a stumbling block [*skandalon*] to Jews and foolishness to Gentiles" (1 Cor. 1:23). Paul's awareness of offense in itself would be sufficient to make him a figure of great influence and importance in Kierkegaard's thought. But there are also important links through Paul's suffering, his thorn in the flesh, his repeated emphasis on "fear and trembling" (1 Cor. 2: 3, 2 Cor. 7:15, Eph. 6:5, Phil. 2:12), his talk of earnestness (2 Cor. 7: 11, 8:7–8, 8:16, 8:22) and inwardness (2 Cor. 4:16–18), and his sense of being "set apart" (Rom. 1:1, cf. *Journals*, 5: 6021). When Paul tells his correspondents in the early churches to give no offense to anyone, we can be sure Kierkegaard listened.

Indeed, Kierkegaard's narrators frequently strike a distinctively, though at times slightly ludicrous, Pauline note as self-consciously careful nonoffenders. The compiler of *Stages on Life's Way*, one Hilarius Bookbinder, explains at the outset the true history of his book, lest anyone be "scandalized by the bookbinder" (*Stages*, 3). The Young Man, who speaks first at the bachelors' banquet ("In Vino Veritas"), renounces love but "without wishing either to offend or to envy anyone" (*Stages*, 45). Johannes the Seducer is equally deferential: "I offend no one" (*Stages*, 74). In "The Seducer's Diary," he claims not to be of "the aggregate of lovers who out of respect love each other, out of respect marry each other, out of respect have children together," but is nevertheless "well aware that erotic love . . . demands of the one who is its object that he not esthetically offend against morality" (*Either/Or I*, 381). Judge William professes to be "the one person who in perhaps the whole kingdom is most concerned not to give offense" on the issue of a lady's age (*Stages*, 132n) and takes care "to speak as inoffensively as possible" (135) on delicate subjects such as jealousy. Frater Taciturnus is deferential even to his own imaginary constructions, for when he makes what might be seen as a slighting comment on his professedly fictional character Quidam, he quickly adds that he does "not mean to offend that young man" (*Stages*, 403). Johannes Climacus, in the *Concluding Unscientific Postscript*, affirms that his "imaginary construction," his book, "must not offend anyone" (512). At the end of the book, however, in "A First and Last Explanation," Kierkegaard, in his own voice and over his own name, asserts that "I am not aware of any offense" but apologizes for whatever offenses his pseudonyms may have committed: "Insofar as the pseudonymous authors might have affronted any respectable person in any way whatever, or perhaps even any man I admire, . . . then there is no one more willing to make an apology than I" (625, 629).

There should be, it would seem, no call for millstones around the necks of Kierkegaard or his pseudonymous authors. And yet, with genuine trepidation and resolve, at the end of his life, when the fundamentally inoffensive pseudonymous writers had had their say and the effect of what they said was misunderstood or ignored, Kierkegaard in his own voice rejected Paul's fervent injunction not to offend. Kierkegaard became an offense and indeed a folly to the Gentiles of Christendom in an effort to awaken them, to make them aware of what it means to be an individual Christian.

However, before Kierkegaard resolved on his final, direct offensiveness, he engaged in an elaborate, multivolumed attempt to affect his readers in an indirect way, through the pseudonymous writings, as well as in a direct way, through his religious writings. The desired effect of the writings was not to provide his readers with the objective truth about the nature of humanity, world history, or God—that is precisely the Hegelian position he was arguing against—but rather to lead his readers, or each individual reader, to a dialectical truth that can never be objective without thereby becoming untruth. He was, as an author, not trying to convey doctrine but rather trying to awaken his reader, "to compel [his reader] to take notice" (*Point of View*, 34), or to help give birth to something within the reader's subjectivity. This last metaphor reappears frequently in Kierkegaard's works; like Socrates, he took upon himself the role of the maieutic teacher, the midwife. Kierkegaard did not present himself as the vessel of truth, to be poured into the receptive reader, but as the teacher, assisting in the birth of subjective truth. Naturally, it follows that this will require a special form of communication. "All the pseudonymous works are *maieutic*," he writes in *The Point of View* (148-49), though they also were accompanied by separate works written as direct communications, signed with Kierkegaard's own name.

Kierkegaard argues in *The Point of View* that the entire work, maieutic and direct, is informed by a unified idea: "the thought behind the whole work is: what it means to become a Christian" (22). This enterprise is rendered difficult because his readers believed they already knew what it meant and, furthermore, that they *were* Christian; Denmark, after all, was a Christian nation. His strategy, then, in the pseudonymous works is to "beguile" a reader "into the truth" (148) by various fictions or discourses put forth by fictitious authors. The beguiling tends to take the form of fictions within the sphere of life where a reader might feel at home, dramatically embodying the shortcomings of such a life, and contrasting it with another sphere, which is more elevated but also may have its short-comings. The narrator may or may not fully understand what he is describing, but Kierkegaard as author makes no comment; the reader must respond actively since the author makes no direct evaluations.

The spheres—or stages—of life that Kierkegaard posits are the aesthetic, the ethical, and the religious. Climacus tells us that the stages are "not abstract . . . but concrete" (*Concluding Unscientific Postscript*, 294). The aesthetic sphere is one of immediacy, in which the categories are "fortune, misfortune, fate, immediate enthusiasm, despair" (434). Judge William (an ethicist himself) says that the aes-thete "teaches 'Enjoy life' and interprets [this injunction] as 'Live for your desire'" (*Either/Or II*, 183). It is the stage of sensuous self-absorption, with no sense of the eternal, and therefore it is a one-sided, even inhuman existence, since the Kierkegaardian human is a synthesis of the temporal and the eternal, of the finite and the infinite, of possibility and necessity. Johannes of "The Seducer's Diary" (*Either/Or I*) and the other bachelors at the banquet in *Stages* are the dramatic exemplars of the aesthetic view.

The ethical sphere is embodied in Judge William, who extols (in opposition to Johannes the Seducer) the virtues of marriage. The judge's life is itself a critique of the exclusively aesthetic; he is concerned with friendship, community, and universal demands, or duty, but as temporal (rather than eternal) goals. Although his lan-guage is often religious and although he endorses a sermon (the "Ultimatum" of *Either/Or II*) by the pastor of Jylland ("In Relation to God We Are Always in the Wrong"), he is not existentially inter-ested in his relation to God, or to being in the wrong in an eternal rather than a temporal sense. He is, however, unlike Johannes, inter-ested in things beyond himself; he has an inwardness and earnest-ness lacking in an aesthete; and he chooses his actions on the basis of the universal and thereby constitutes a responsible self. The eth-icist's "movement," the judge says, is "from himself through the world to himself." "His self is . . . the goal toward which he strives," and "the individual comes to stand higher than every relationship," including (although the judge does not say this) the God relationship (*Either/Or II*, 274–75).

I leave aside for the moment the highest sphere, the religious, mindful that these thumbnail sketches, though necessary for my purpose, do not do justice to Kierkegaard's conceptions or to his ends in presenting them in his writings. Nowhere does he give a single, clear summary of them; his indirect method requires that they be presented dramatically and in some sense that they be made difficult for the reader so that the reader can find himself or herself in them and thus begin the process of being beguiled into the truth. Hence there is an inherent danger of distorting Kierkegaard's thought by systematizing it. His spheres of existence are not to be taken as "station[s] on the systematic world-historical railroad" (*Concluding Unscientific Postscript*, 67).

In truth, the use we as readers are to make of these spheres or stages of existence is ambiguous. Mark C. Taylor has pointed out four different ways of understanding them: (1) as stages of Kierkegaard's biographical development, (2) as stages of world history or the evolution of consciousness, (3) as personality types, and (4) as stages of the development of an individual's consciousness (*Kierkegaard's Pseudonymous Authorship*, 62–63). Among the pseudonymous and direct writings, one can find evidence for all of these ways, but I am primarily concerned with the fourth sense, because it is most directly pertinent to Kierkegaard's interest in affecting individual readers.

I want to remain reasonably faithful to Kierkegaard's indirect conception of offense, first, by examining Kierkegaard's manner of presenting offense in a narrative form and, second, by examining it in the dialectical context of two contrasting pairs of books, *Philosophical Fragments* (1844) and *Concluding Unscientific Postscript* (1845), both by Johannes Climacus, and *The Sickness unto Death* (1849) and *Practice in Christianity* (1850), both by Anti-Climacus. The names of these pseudonymous authors obviously link them, though not quite in an obvious way, as I shall explain below. Although the essential offense is a quality within the religious sphere, Kierkegaard introduces offense within the lower spheres (the aesthetic and the ethical), before the Climacus books were written, as an ironic and humorous preparation for grasping its importance in a higher sense. *Stages on Life's Way* (1845), in which we have already seen self-consciously inoffensive narrators, provides a glimpse of Kierkegaard beguiling the reader into the truth by dramatizing the aesthetic and ethical offense as an introduction to the religious, essential offense.

Stages on Life's Way

The biblical offense I am exploring in this book is a narrative phenomenon, and it is something more than a happy accident that the
primary explicator of the offense should undertake his explication
through narrative means. Kierkegaard is essentially a narrative philosopher; his subjects cannot be communicated solely through logical analysis or exposition. They need to be communicated indirectly, and this requires various narrative voices, speaking about the
actions of people and ideas in time, beguiling the reader through
fictions into an awakening. Thus, *Stages on Life's Way* seems closer
to the genre of the novel than to the philosophical treatise, and the
pseudonymous authors of all the indirect discourses, no matter how
logical or philosophical they may be, must always be viewed as we
view the first-person narrators of novels—perhaps reliable, perhaps
unreliable, perhaps both, but certainly not identical to the actual
author.

Kierkegaard's *Stages* consists of various narratives by various
supposed authors, or narrators. The first section, "In Vino Veritas,"
is an account of a banquet at which five bachelors speak. It is narrated by William Afham, himself not one of the speakers and a man
about whom we know nothing—"But who, then, am I? Let no one
ask about that" (86). The second section is by Judge William, "author" of *Either/Or II.* His manuscript—the second section of
Stages—was stolen from him by Victor Eremita, one of the speakers
at the banquet, and stolen from Victor Eremita by William Afham.
The third section ("'Guilty?'/'Not Guilty?'") is an admittedly fictional creation by one Frater Taciturnus, though it is sometimes
read as a purely autobiographical account of Kierkegaard's engagement with Regine Olsen. Kierkegaard no doubt drew on his own
experience to create this section, but to ignore the manner of narration (the speaking voice and point of view of Frater Taciturnus) and
to conflate the fictional character Quidam with Kierkegaard is to
misread grotesquely. The elaborate narrative construction of the
entire book serves (among other things) as a means of introducing
the offense to the reader in a beguiling way. Kierkegaard, the author-
beguiler, is palpably present but smilingly beyond our easy, officious
grasp, hidden, as he is, behind the compiler-publisher, Hilarius
Bookbinder, the various narrators, and the fictional narratives.

At the beginning of *Stages*, in the banquet scene, the inebriated
bachelors discourse on the subject of woman. The Young Man, who
speaks first, renounces erotic love, but he has the least negative

view of women. He is reflective and has some sense of the comic and the pathetic, but this leads to his erotic paralysis because of (by his account) his fear of offending a lover: "Would I not have irreparably offended the beloved[?]" (46). However, the second speaker, Constantin, has no sense of the pathetic: for him, woman is a jest. He acknowledges woman's desirability—"Beautiful is she and lovely when she is viewed esthetically" (55)—but he insists that she must be viewed ethically as well, and her ethical need for faithfulness, combined with her infidelity, confirms that she is a jest.

A third bachelor, Victor Eremita, views woman in the category of the fantastic; he rejects all aesthetic views in favor of the ideal and the infinite, to which woman can contribute only in a negative way and only assisted by fate. Another speaker, the Fashion Designer, discusses woman in ironically religious terms. Women, he says, think fashion is the sacred and the boutique a place of sacrifice. And, indeed, in his view, the "fear of God is . . . fashion," and he himself is "an emissary of the gods," though whether he is actually serving a benign god or a devil, he is not sure. The final speaker, Johannes the Seducer, is an unabashed aesthete: "I want to enjoy" (72). He rejects the positions of the previous speakers and is indignant at their treatment of women:

> I shall clothe my speech in a myth, and on behalf of woman, whom you have so unjustly offended, it will please me if the speech may pass judgment on your souls . . . because you have offended woman. Only in this way is she offended, even though she is elevated far above offense, and anyone who dares to offend in this way is punished. I offend no one. To say I do is merely the invention and backbiting of married men, inasmuch as I, on the contrary, appreciate her much more than the husband does. (74)

His myth explains how woman was created by the gods to deceive and enchant man, who is inferior to woman, and the stratagem succeeded with all except some "individual men," "devotees of erotic love," like himself, misguidedly called "seducers" by the deceived men (75). Hence deluded men, like the previous speakers, offend woman, who is a superior creature, and the offenders' souls are judged by their own offensiveness.

Johannes is aware, of course, that people, especially married, ethical folk, deem *him* an offense. One such is Judge William, the "author" of "Reflections on Marriage," which follows "In Vino Veritas." Judge William reflects on an apparently trivial problem: a young woman afflicted by nasty corns. The subject is humorous to him, but only because he is an ethicist, with his humor sustained by "marriage's sense of security." A jest on this subject in the mouth of a lover would be "utterly unforgivable." "A lover would feel offended, because this nasty corn, even after it was removed, has a most disturbing effect on an esthetic romantic view of the beautiful." Therefore, "corns should be reckoned among the infirmities one could find out about after the wedding" (129). A corn on the foot of a beautiful woman is ethically humorous but aesthetically offensive.

The judge, in his humorous way, is pursuing a serious issue, to which he later returns. The aesthetic appeal of erotic love requires an immediacy that is easily ruined by flaws that cause the lover to reflect on the object of his love. Indeed, reflection of any sort is the "destroying angel of death" to immediacy and hence to the aesthetic sphere (157). "If reflection attacks falling in love, this means that one is supposed to inspect whether the beloved meets the ideal abstract conception of an ideal. Any reflection of this sort, even the scantiest, is an offense just as it is also a stupidity." But in fact, reflection is what elevates a person from the aesthetic into the ethical; it is the difference between "falling in love" and marriage, between the aesthete's search for erotic beauty and what the judge extols as the feminine lovableness of a wife and mother. "Even if she had the face of an angel," he says, "wanting to admire this beauty is an offense" (158). There can be no fault finding (nasty corns), no calculating (the face of an angel); there can be only an individual action: "I love her" (159).

In reaching this state, the lover has leaped from aesthetic immediacy, through reflection, resolution, and action, to "a *new* immediacy," "a religious immediacy" (162), in which the confidant is God. In this process, the lover will encounter a "danger" and will make "the resolution to resolve religiously. . . . He must either let go of love—or believe in God. In this way the wonder of falling in love is taken up into the wonder of faith; the wonder of falling in love is taken up into a purely religious wonder; the absurdity of falling in love is taken up into a divine understanding with the absurdity of religiousness" (163). So rhapsodizes the ethicist, describing the state that still, in spite of the judge's high-flown terminology, is quite evidently part of the ethical, not the religious, sphere. Judge William recognizes that there is a higher state than marriage, but it involves a plunge into the abyss (171), into an abstraction (174), something "terrible, a horror" (177), requiring that one wear "the hair shirt of sufferings" (182). Indeed, Judge William would advise against such rash venturing (182–83), and its being a higher state than marriage is by no means a recommendation to pursue it.

In the last section of *Stages*, "'Guilty?'/'Not Guilty?'" an anonymous author reflects at length in his diary as he breaks off his engagement with his beloved. The diary is presented as "an imaginary psychological construction" written by Frater Taciturnus, who in the following "Letter to the Reader" discusses his hero (whom he calls Quidam) and his heroine (Quaedam). Why Quidam wants to break off the engagement is not entirely clear, but Quidam's psychological explanation is that he came to see only after his engagement that his constitutional depression made him unfit for marriage. His diary is analogous to the seducer's diary of *Either/Or I* in that it centers on his obsession with a woman and reveals his motives and guile, but he, unlike Johannes, hates seduction, he suffers rather than enjoys, and he deliberates in ethical and religious, not aesthetic, terms on his guilt, offense, and punishment (394).

During the six months when he writes in his diary, Quidam's challenge is to break off the engagement without making his beloved unhappy, trying through his treatment of her to bring her to the point where she will welcome a broken engagement or at least give him his freedom voluntarily. He fails. She clings to the engagement, changing (in his analysis) "an erotic relationship into a religious one" (393), and he, after six months, "coldly and definitely" announces that the engagement is over. The vocabulary of offense is crucial to the way he thinks about the process because he is trying to break the engagement without her feeling offended and thus unhappy. His worst fear is that she will choose decisively to be offended, perhaps by withdrawing to the country, there to nurture her status as offended woman. "Suppose she really has made a decision," he writes, "suppose she insists on being offended, wants it to be in the open, wants to despair and to have a distinctive form of desperation" (255).

Quidam's fear is that his beloved might become insane from "an offended feminine pride over being rejected, which, despairing of taking revenge, inclose[s] itself with itself until it los[es] its way" (271). But he thinks this not probable since, he believes, she is not sufficiently reflective and since "a woman rarely has much dialectic" (274). Despair, anguish, and suffering are states he wants to shield her from, though he himself feels them all in his belief that "it is spirit that gives life" (396). His is finally a religious quest, but he acknowledges that "it would have been greater if my spiritual existence had countenanced everyday use in a marriage" (396). That, however, he cannot manage.

The uncertainty—and it is never resolved in the diary—is what *she* will do, whether she will fall into a state of offense ("bleed[ing] to death in a futile passion" of withdrawal or madness) or be "saved by a help that . . . comes close enough when it is needed." "If she helps herself in some other way"—as, in fact, Regine Olsen did by marrying her former suitor when Kierkegaard broke off their engagement—"that is superfluous" (396–97). The non-superfluous choice for the beloved, Quaedam, is either offense or salvation, though not of the religious variety. She, according to both Quidam and Taciturnus, exists in the sphere of the aesthetic, while Quidam exists in the ethical-religious. Indeed, this difference is the source of their comic and tragic misunderstanding: "The tragic is that the two lovers do not understand each other; the comic is that two who do not understand each other love each other" (421). The comedy-tragedy turns on the misunderstanding of offense: "She believes that he has insulted and offended her by breaking the relationship, and yet he has offended her only by beginning it" (434).

Frater Taciturnus, in his discussion of his "imaginary construction," is aware of the danger of publishing a book "without a result" (441)—and indeed he expects that he has no readers by the end—but he tells us the result of the story: Quaedam, "of course," does not die, go mad, or retire to the country; she "changes her mind" about Quidam and finds another lover (430). This to Quidam's chagrin, however, since he did not really want to give her up. Her value, according to Taciturnus, is "that the girl is helpful in getting him out upon the deep" (473), that is, in driving him inward, to guilt and suffering, where he is venturing out toward the religious, the subjective, or what Kierkegaard called the seventy thousand fathoms of water, where danger exists, far from human help. "On the whole," Taciturnus tells us, Quidam's "concern for the girl is sheer enthusiasm, in itself ludicrous, tragic because of his suffering, comic because he does the most foolish things" (429). But he is an interesting case to his constructor because he is "a demoniac character in the direction of the religious—that is, tending toward it" (398).

This way of seeing is precisely to Taciturnus's liking, for he is an observer of life, a kind of "street inspector," as he calls himself (456), and "an enthusiast of the understanding" (428), who views life as "the unity of the comic and tragic" (463). He is also interested—only as an observer—in the religious, making it quite clear that he is not religious himself. He knows, more clearly than Judge William does, that there is a leap to the religious that he is not willing to make. Few are willing to make it, in his view, and few have any notion of the difference between wading in shallow water and venturing out into seventy thousand fathoms. Thus, Taciturnus is a useful part of Kierkegaard's pseudonymous guile in that he explains human behavior by the common category of the understanding. Without claiming to be extraordinary himself, Taciturnus can see clearly what constitutes the extraordinary, thereby awakening the reader to it.

Taciturnus distinguishes between people (such as Heine and Feuerbach) who are "well informed about the religious," "know[ing] definitely that they do not want to have anything to do with it," and the systematicians (presumably such as Hegel) who do not know "where the religious really is located" but "take it upon themselves to explain it." Even though people in the first group are "offended by the religious," they can be "just as well informed about it as the believer." Indeed, "we must always be pleased to have a few really clever ones who are offended." For his own part, however, Taciturnus is neither "a rigorous believer" nor "an offended nonbeliever" (452). He can understand that the religious posits "the individual himself—this particular individual placed in his relationship with God under the qualification: guilty/not guilty," but he quickly adds, "I do not see it this way. . . . I am not an offended person, far from it, but neither am I religious" (463). And though he is not offended, he knows that he is an offender, since his view of life as a balance in the unity of the comic and the tragic is, he says, "an offense against the holy passion of the religious" (486).

Thus, Taciturnus, Quidam's constructor and explicator, is highly knowledgeable but existentially uncommitted. His construction, Quidam, on the other hand, is unknowledgeable about the religious (because of his obsession with the woman and because he suffers rather than knows) but committed. He is, Taciturnus says, at "the crisis prior to the religious" (430), while Taciturnus himself is in "the metaphysical," which *is* but does not *exist*. It is not one of the three existence spheres: the aesthetic, or sphere of immediacy; the ethical, "which is only a transition sphere"; and the religious, or "the sphere of fulfillment," which involves "the religious contradiction: simultaneously to be out on seventy thousand fathoms of water and yet be joyful" (476–77). The religious is indifferent to the realm of immediacy and to the external and, instead, "lies in the internal" (441) or the subjective. Its outcome is "faith," "the absurd"

(442, 440). And the only way to faith, as Taciturnus may know metaphysically, but does not say, is through the possibility of offense. He comes close to saying it, however: Quidam, he points out, "must be able to grasp the ethical with primitive passion in order to take offense properly so that the original possibility of the religious can break through at this turning point" (430). Without taking offense "properly," one cannot make the leap to the religious.

Climacus on the Non-understandable

Taciturnus, an "enthusiast of the understanding," does not see things from the religious point of view and confesses that he does not understand the religious (*Stages*, 428, 463, 435). However, Johannes Climacus, the pseudonymous author of *Philosophical Fragments* and *Concluding Unscientific Postscript*, writes his "thought-project" and his "mimical-pathetical-dialectical compilation" (his descriptions of the two works) from what he calls a religious point of view, although it might better be described as a psychological view. He exists, he tells us, within the boundaries of religiousness A (*Concluding Unscientific Postscript*, 557), where the single individual exists before "the god" (as Climacus usually refers to the deity) who is immanent but not transcendent. The other form of religiousness he refers to as B, dialectical religion, paradoxical religion, or Christianity. Climacus is clear about what he is ("a humorous, imaginatively constructing psychologist"; 483) and what he is not ("I . . . do not even pretend to be a Christian"; 466). He is an "outsider" who, "without having comprehended Christianity" (16), is passionately engaged in a problem: to "find out where the misunderstanding between speculative thought [Hegel] and Christianity lies" (241).

But in Kierkegaard's dialectical project of indirect communication, Climacus's position as outsider suggests the need for a counterpart, namely, Anti-Climacus, author of *The Sickness unto Death* and *Practice in Christianity*. Anti-Climacus is a pseudonymous ideal, a corrective or supplement to, rather than a contrary of, Climacus. Kierkegaard described the two narrators in his journal:

> Johannes Climacus and Anti-Climacus have several things in common;
> but the difference is that whereas Johannes Climacus places himself so
> low that he even says himself that he is not a Christian, one seems to
> be able to detect in Anti-Climacus that he regards himself to be a
> Christian on an extraordinarily high level. . . . I would place myself

higher than Johannes Climacus, lower than Anti-Climacus. (*Journals*, 6: 6433)

Both speak on the subjects of the existing individual, speculative philosophy, and religion, but both are poetic constructs, speaking from different points of view—one a humorist and the other an ideal Christian. As a pseudonym, Anti-Climacus may reasonably be seen as an ideal, reliable spokesman for Kierkegaard, who nearly published *The Sickness unto Death* under his own name (see Hong and Hong's introduction to *Sickness* for an account of his wavering). But Climacus, Judge William, Johannes the Seducer, and the other pseudonyms are not always, or even essentially, reliable; indeed, they live in a state that Kierkegaard would like to awaken the reader out of.

The reader of the earlier pseudonymous writings (*Either/Or* and *Stages*) has been beguiled by Kierkegaard into thinking that offense and not giving offense are matters of some importance. I say "beguiled" because almost all of the offenses the earlier pseudonyms understand are of relatively little importance. It is true, as Anti-Climacus says, that the offense is "Christianity's crucial criterion" (*Sickness*, 83), but the earlier pseudonyms do not exist in the religious sphere and therefore do not know or care about this. Anti-Climacus says that what many call offense is "merely a provisional category" (*Practice*, 111), and the non-Christian Climacus sees the chasm between what is commonly taken as offense and what is the essential offense:

> Christianity is the only power that truly can cause offense, because hysterical and sentimental spasms of offense over this and that can simply be rejected and explained as a lack of ethical earnestness that is coquettishly busy accusing the whole world instead of itself. For the believer, offense comes at the beginning, and the possibility of it is the continual fear and trembling in his existence. (*Concluding Unscientific Postscript*, 585)

Such a dismissal of the ordinary offense might seem odd in light of the dramatic energy Kierkegaard has devoted to portraying petty offense in the pseudonymous works, but this is a sign of the importance he attached to what he thought of as "awakening" the individual reader through narratives to what is interesting in his or her sphere and then leading beyond that to issues of true decisiveness. The discourse on offense by the pseudonymous writers before Anti-

Climacus constitutes "negative preparation" (to borrow a notion from Mark Lloyd Taylor's argument about *Fear and Trembling*, 44): the reader is shown what the essential offense is *not*.

Offense "over this and that" is a "provisional category" of one who is not qualified by the spiritual (i.e., who does not exist "before God"). It may be trivial, like the suitor's offense at nasty corns, or it may be a matter of life and death: Abraham's "whole task of sacrificing Isaac for his own sake and for God's sake is an offense to esthetics" (*Fear and Trembling*, 112). Any such offense is in fact a state that needs to be remedied, whether the offended knows it or not, and the remedy can be found only through the offense in the essential sense. "Not until Christianity recommends the remedy against it [offense as a provisional category] does the possibility of offense come into existence, for in the relation to this remedy lies the decision: to become a Christian or to be offended" (*Practice*, 111).

Having reached the religious sphere, however, does not mean a reader can simply be given an explanation of the offense, as if it were a simple, or even complex, matter for the understanding, since the difficulty—and the simplicity—of the offense is precisely that it is contrary to the understanding. Thus, Climacus backs into his subject through a narrative mock conflict with his reader. First he dramatically portrays the paradoxical difficulty of the god who becomes flesh—divine and full of love yet fearful that he will offend and therefore full of sorrow:

> Look, there he stands—the god. Where? There. Can you not see him? He is the god, and yet he has no place where he can lay his head, and he does not dare to turn to any person lest that person be offended at him. He is the god, and yet he walks more circumspectly than if angels were carrying him—not to keep him from stumbling, but so that he may not tread in the dust the people who are offended at him. . . . Such a life—sheer love and sheer sorrow. To want to express the unity of love and then not to be understood. . . . Thus does the god stand upon the earth, like unto the lowliest through his omnipotent love. . . . Oh, to sustain heaven and earth by an omnipotent "Let there be," and then, if this were to be absent for one fraction of a second, to have everything collapse—how easy this would be compared with bearing the possibility of the offense of the human race when out of love one became its savior! (*Philosophical Fragments*, 32)

Thus, Climacus, speaking as "the poet," carries on in his prose poem, which is a pastiche of passages from the Gospels about the suffering of Jesus and the response of those who encounter him.

But the imagined reader, as Shandean character, interrupts and accuses him angrily of "the shabbiest plagiarism." The poet at first defends himself by saying that he is not stealing from a single poet but as if from a proverb which "all humanity had composed"; however, his own defense undermines his case. Yes, he acknowledges, in a sense he "robbed the deity"; he, "a shabby thief . . . blasphemously pretended to be the god." And with this he is persuaded by the reader: "Now, my dear fellow, I quite understand you and understand that your anger is justified." But no sooner is the poet-narrator penitent than a "new amazement" grips him: a human being might imagine himself as a god, but how could it occur to him to imagine a god poeticizing himself in the likeness of a human, and furthermore of needing the human? This is something human thought cannot think, yet it is a thought, or more precisely a wonder. The poet penitently asks the accusing reader to "forgive me my curious mistaken notion of having composed it myself"; instead of being offended, the reader is invited to join the poet and "stand here before *the wonder*" (*Philosophical Fragments*, 35–36). The wonder of this curious drama is highly improbable: it is the god become man, a paradox, and the Kierkegaardian response to the paradox is faith— or, alternatively, offense, the possibility of which anyone must encounter before being able to stand before the wonder.

In this beguiling little episode, we have no sense of whether the Shandean reader has the inwardness or subjectivity to encounter the paradox. But by imagining a reader offended over this and that (here, offended by an author who plagiarizes from the Gospels) and by imagining a poet imagining a God-man, Climacus suggests to the actual reader what is involved in a coming to faith, namely, something wondrous that does not fit the category of human understanding and something that contains the possibility of offense.

But *the* offense, as opposed to offense over this and that, is far more momentous than this mock-offensive narrative can suggest, for it is not light-minded or poetic but involves "the most terrible decision" (*Philosophical Fragments*, 34), which is the choice between offense and faith. Kierkegaard wrote in *The Point of View* that his entire work, pseudonymous and direct, was written to explore what it means to be a Christian (22). Although Climacus is no Christian himself, his part of Kierkegaard's work in this task is to explain the difference between the speculative view, which is based on the category of understanding, and the Christian view, which is based on the category of spirit. "To become a Christian," as Climacus sees it from the outside, "becomes the most terrible of all decisions in a person's life, since it is a matter of winning faith through despair and offense (the Cerberus pair who guard the entry to becoming a Christian)" (*Concluding Unscientific Postscript,* 372). This, not the provisional this and that, is the only kind of offense that matters. According to Climacus, "Christianity is the only power that truly can cause offense," and offense can be aroused only in the single individual (585).

Kierkegaard's distaste for the crowd is well known; any person whose identity is found only through a crowd or race or through values common to a time or an environment cannot attain human individuality, which depends on an existential God relationship. Each human is potentially the synthesis of the animal and the spiritual, of time and the eternal, of possibility and actuality, but each person can live strictly in the temporal, or in the realm of physical probability, which means living within Kierkegaard's aesthetic stage, always concerned with the immediate and relating the self "absolutely to relative [or temporal] ends" (*Concluding Unscientific Postscript,* 432). The single individual, by contrast, lives as an individual "before God," relating himself or herself absolutely to the eternal and only relatively to the temporal. By existing "before God," the individual becomes less a member of a crowd or race and more an eternal self that binds the dialectical elements of one's humanity into a synthesis.

In Climacus's terms, existing "before God" places one in the stage of religiousness A. But an outside observer can never know whether another exists "before God" since the relationship is in no way objective, only subjective. It is a product of an inwardness that has no necessary external manifestations. From the outside it might be hard to distinguish Johannes the Seducer from Quidam, but in some respects they are opposites. Johannes understands human psychology, knows his will and pleasures, and knows how to obtain his pleasures; Quidam, however, ventures toward an unknown where his will and the probability of pleasure are uncertain. The person who ventures toward Christianity, the dialectical religion of paradox, leaves probability, proof, and objectivity increasingly behind and ventures into the seventy thousand fathoms of water. He or she exists inwardly, in the subjective self, "before God," who may uphold as water upholds the individual when there is no solid ground. Such is the state of freedom, but it is a terrifying, fearful freedom, full of risk.

According to Climacus, Christianity "requires that the individual, existing, venture everything," but paganism can require the same thing. Christianity, however, requires that "the individual also risk his thought, venture to believe against understanding," which is its dialectical quality. Christianity is "the absolute daring venture" (*Concluding Unscientific Postscript*, 429). One might think that Jesus, as God become flesh, and the written Gospels, proclaiming the good news of a God-man, should make Christianity relatively easier, but in fact they make it more difficult—which lies at the heart of the Kierkegaardian offense and, I will argue, of Gospel narratives.

The single individual who ventures forth will, by venturing, encounter the moment, a dialectical ambiguity that, viewed "pathetically," may be a single second full of infinite value, or, viewed "comically," may be part of ten thousand years that is a mere trifle. The moment comes into existence when time and the eternal make contact. "Nature does not lie in the moment," but "as soon as the spirit is posited, the moment is present" (*Concept of Anxiety*, 88–89). Climacus in the *Philosophical Fragments* says that the moment is "short and temporal . . . yet it is decisive, and . . . filled with the eternal" (18). The moment is "the point of departure for the eternal" (59); it is "the paradox" (51), which is Christ, the contradictory God-man.

We will return to the question of how Christ is a contradiction and a paradox, which is explained more fully by the ideal Christian, Anti-Climacus. The non-Christian Climacus is more expert in tracing the juxtaposition in other terms, as when he says that "the understanding and the paradox happily encounter each other in the moment" (59). The word *happily* is crucial here. Although the understanding cannot understand the religious paradox—since the paradox is the object of faith, not of the senses, logic, or probability— the understanding and the paradox are capable of encountering each other happily in the moment, just as the dialectical oppositions of the temporal and the eternal come together in the moment. But if the understanding refuses to acknowledge the existence of the paradox, then the paradox thrusts the individual away "and he takes *offense* or is scandalized" (*Philosophical Fragments*, 196; *Journals*, 3: 3082). In this case the relation, Climacus says, "is unhappy, and the understanding's unhappy love, if I dare call it that . . . , we could more specifically term *offense*" (49).

Climacus's explanation of the relation among the understanding, the offense, and the paradox is difficult but worth pondering. In an appendix to a section called "The Absolute Paradox" (i.e., "the god"), Climacus discusses "Offense at the Paradox (An Acoustical Illusion)." The heading of the appendix indicates that offense at the god is like an echo (an acoustical illusion), real enough to be heard but real only in relation to something else, the original sound (or, in this analogy, the god), before it re-sounds as an echo. In this section, Climacus explains that the offense is always a suffering. The offended person may appear to suffer passively (as the passive verb form—*to be offended*—itself suggests) or may appear to be active (e.g., through mockery or active aggression), but even the activity is a form of suffering or passivity, like "someone with a broken back," Climacus says, "which does indeed give a singular kind of suppleness" (50).

When the understanding cannot exist in a happy relationship with the paradox, the understanding's self-love results in offense, which the understanding develops, actively or passively, but always with suffering. The offense is discovered not by the understanding but by the paradox. Just as truth is the criterion of itself and of its opposite—falsehood—so the paradox is the criterion of itself and of offense. Thus, the suffering offense appears to sound from the understanding, because the offended person clings to the understanding and rejects the paradox, but in fact it is "an acoustical illusion," as it seems to the one offended, a sounding from the understanding. The offense is a *resounding* of the paradox, an echo of the unknown, "the god." Or, to put it another way, the offense is a kind of caricature of the paradox. "The one offended does not speak according to his own nature but according to the nature of the paradox, just as someone caricaturing another person does not originate anything himself but only copies the other in the wrong way" (51).

The offense, then, does not come from the understanding. "No, the offense *comes into existence* with the paradox; if it *comes into existence*, here again we have the moment, around which everything indeed revolves." The offense occurs in the moment, when the eternal touches the temporal, in an unhappy relationship of the understanding and the paradox. "All offense is in its essence a misunderstanding of *the moment*, since it is indeed offense at the paradox ["the god"], and the paradox in turn is the moment" (*Philosophical Fragments*, 51).

This "explanation" of offense has become difficult to understand, to say the least. But the *Philosophical Fragments* is not meant to be a didactic work of direct communication. In the *Concluding Unscientific Postscript*, Climacus comments on a review of *Philosophical Fragments*, and he is quite perturbed that the reviewer treats the earlier book as a doctrinal work, ignoring its audacity, its irony, its parody, its satire. In truth, Climacus says, *Philosophical*

Fragments was written not to inform people; rather, it was written for people who already know too much. It communicates by *taking away* what they know. "Because everyone knows the Christian truth, it has gradually become . . . a triviality," incapable of stirring any passion (*Concluding Unscientific Postscript*, 275n). When Climacus "explains" offense as a "misunderstanding," the knowledgeable reader wants, of course, to understand the misunderstanding, but Kierkegaard, the ironist behind Climacus, wants us to know less by realizing that understanding/misunderstanding is the wrong category for offense. Offense is an action, or reaction, that comes into existence (and is not merely an illusion), but it does so only outside the understanding.

Even Climacus, our non-Christian narrator, makes it clear that the essential offense is religious. "One who has no religiousness at all," Climacus says, "certainly cannot be offended" (*Concluding Unscientific Postscript*, 439n). He himself is not offended, but that is because "in Religiousness A, offense is not at all possible" (585); only when one encounters the dialectical paradox, at the beginning of Christianity, is the offense possible.

When one encounters the offense, the result is a Kierkegaardian either/or: either faith or offense. If one is offended, this state of being offended will take one of two forms:

(1) *The offense that suffers.* This suffering, weak, passive offense is what Anti-Climacus calls "negative" offense and takes "the form of being acted upon." The individual approaches the paradox in earnestness but does not dare to believe and cannot leave Christ alone.

(2) *The offense that mocks.* This "active" offense manifests itself in defiance, in the will not to believe; it "derides the paradox as foolishness." Anti-Climacus calls it "positive" offense; it actively denies all that is essentially Christian and is "sin against the Holy Spirit." It adopts the mode of jest, the dialectical contrary of earnestness (*Concluding Unscientific Postscript*, 585; *Philosophical Fragments*, 50; *Sickness unto Death*, 130–131).

Both types require passion—the first in the form of religious inwardness (such as the New Testament Jews have) and the second in the form of intellectual inwardness (such as the Greeks have; *Concluding Unscientific Postscript*, 293). But Climacus argues that the Hegelian speculative philosophers have neither religious nor intellectual passion and that "perhaps it is preferable by far to be someone who takes offense but still continually relates himself to Christianity" instead of a speculative philosopher who "has understood it" (216). Still, "the only unforgivable high treason against

Christianity," in Climacus's view, is to take it for granted, as a matter of course (16). Climacus's fundamentally un-Christian view is evident here in his idolatry: the true Christian would be concerned with Christ, the offensive God-man, not with the Christianity (Hartshorne, 37). But even self-proclaimed Christians engage in the same idolatry, which is what led Kierkegaard eventually to his direct attack upon Christendom.

Anti-Climacus's Dialectics[2]

In *The Sickness unto Death*, Anti-Climacus distinguishes between the two major types of the divine offense on the basis of how one receives the possibility of offense: offense toward faith and offense away from faith.

The first major type Anti-Climacus describes in this way: "offense as annulled possibility is an element in faith" (116n). Kierkegaard's frequent phrase "the *possibility* of offense" is a repeated reminder that offense only becomes *actual* when a single individual is offended (122). It is a basic premise in all of Kierkegaard's writings that existing as a single individual, as opposed to a member of a crowd or race, is a good thing. Yet "offense is the most decisive qualification of subjectivity, of the single individual, that is possible" (122). The good is not mere individuality, or subjectivity, but to arrive in the moment of offense at this most decisive qualification and to annul the possibility of offense; this is offense toward faith.

In the second major type, the possibility of offense is actualized; the individual is offended and either suffers or mocks. These two major types of offense explain why Anti-Climacus talks about it as "the crossroad, or . . . like standing at the crossroad": one encounters here the decisive choice, "either to offense or to faith" (*Practice*, 81). Hence the "terrible" nature of it. "For the believer, offense comes at the beginning, and the possibility of it is the continual fear and trembling in his existence" (*Concluding Unscientific Postscript*, 585). *The Sickness unto Death* is Anti-Climacus's treatise on offense away from faith, exploring as it does the relationship between offense and sin. ("Despair of the forgiveness of sins is offense. And offense is the intensification of sin"; 124.) *Practice in Christianity* is his treatise on offense toward faith.

The moment, the offense, and the paradox in Kierkegaard's thought are distinguishable but not separable. We find Climacus saying "the paradox . . . is the moment" (*Philosophical Fragments*, 51) and "the moment is the paradox" (58); "the paradox resounds

. . . in it [the offense]", yet "the offense remains outside the paradox" (51–52), "offense is . . . a misunderstanding of *the moment*" (*Philosophical Fragments*, 51), and "the absolute paradox [is] . . . an offense to the Jews, foolishness to the Greeks, and the absurd to the understanding" (*Concluding Unscientific Postscript*, 219). Similarly, from a religious point of view, these three terms coalesce in the figure of Christ. In the journals, Kierkegaard says, "the paradox is the God-man" (*Journals*, 3: 3074). Climacus, although without calling him Christ, says that "the teacher," who "must be the god, and . . . he must be man"—and hence a "contradiction"—"is in turn the object of faith and is the paradox, the moment" (*Philosophical Fragments*, 62).[3] And Anti-Climacus calls Christ "the sign of offense and the object of faith" (*Practice*, 35).

Christ, then, is at the center of Kierkegaard's use of the terms *offense, faith, moment,* and *paradox;* Christ is the sign of offense, the object of faith, the moment when the eternal touches the temporal, and the paradox "that God has existed in human form" (*Concluding Unscientific Postscript*, 217). Christ is the essential offense in two ways, each of them separately and both together embodying the dialectical nature of Christianity that is at the heart of Kierkegaard's understanding of it. "Essentially," Anti-Climacus says, "offense is related to the composite of God and man, or to the God-man. . . . The God-man [Christ] is the unity of God and an individual human being" (*Practice*, 81–82). Calvin had made the same point: those who find Christianity absurd "are offended by the fact that in Christ divinity is united with humanity in one person. Let us realize that those people are offended precisely because they have absolutely no fear of God, and so have no taste for spiritual teaching" (*Concerning Scandals*, 21).

The first essential offense of the God-man is his loftiness. When, for example, a surgeon acts with such power, authority, and grandeur that we suspect him of confusing himself with God, we might be offended. We might suffer in our offended state, or we might make fun of him (the offense that mocks). Or, to move to the other end of the social spectrum, when a petty criminal justifies his acts by calling himself God, we might respond with anger or laughter, if we were able to consider the claim in anything approaching earnestness or jest. That any individual human being should claim to be God is the offense of loftiness.

However, if we accept the claim that Jesus is the God-man, in spite of its offensiveness, a new offense immediately rises from the other side. How is it that God—presumably the all-powerful, the creator, the eternal—appears as a lowly human being, Jesus, consorting with the likes of fishermen and lepers and suffering a painful, humiliating death? The very idea of God as human is an offense; the idea of God as this particular human is particularly offensive. This is the second essential offense, the offense of lowliness (*Practice*, 82).

If a person is able to avoid the possibility of offense in one form, because of (for example) a peculiarly childlike way of thinking, he or she will then stumble on the other form. The offense is necessary in Christianity because the divine is other than man "by the most chasmal qualitative abyss" (*Sickness*, 122). In the non-Christian religiousness A, where the divine is thought to be immanent, there is no infinite difference or otherness between the human and the divine. In Christianity, this infinite difference creates and perpetuates the offense. "The existence of an infinite qualitative difference between God and man constitutes the possibility of offense, which cannot be removed" (*Sickness*, 127). The opposite side of the coin, however, is that annulling the possibility of offense (the offense toward faith) is joy, or the equivalent of entering into "life" in the Gospel sense. Anti-Climacus explains this in a section entitled, in Jesus's words, "Blessed is he who is not offended at me":

> Christianity places infinite emphasis upon entering into life, upon eternal happiness as the absolute good, and thus in turn the infinite emphasis upon avoiding offense. Therefore that which is really the occasion for offense is the infinite passion with which eternal happiness is comprehended, which corresponds to the infinite fear of offense. It is precisely this that is the occasion of offense to the natural [or aesthetic] man; the natural man does not have and does not want such a conception of eternal happiness, and therefore has no conception of the danger of offense either. (*Practice*, 111)

We have seen that when the aesthetic person, such as Johannes the Seducer, speaks of offense, it is not the essential offense he refers to, for he is too far from the moment of the eternal to experience true offense. But without having a conception of the infinite passion of faith or the infinite fear of offense, the aesthetic person is offended by the infinite passion and the infinite fear that he or she cannot experience. Thus, the aesthetic person misses the joy associated with the moment but also misses the suffering that is dialectically joined to it: the fear and trembling that come from knowing that faith is contained in the possibility of offense (*Practice*, 76).

Johannes the Seducer and Judge William alike are spared the terrors of the seventy thousand fathoms of water and of the essential offense. Instead, they write about their offense "over this and that." It is left to the reader who has been beguiled into an awareness of the moment, the paradox, and the offense, and who has ideally been left at sea, over seventy thousand fathoms of water, to note well, in full awareness, the comfortable plight of both Johannes and Judge William. What remains for such a reader is a choice: either offense or faith.

Offending the Establishment

I have been arguing that throughout most of his career Kierkegaard earnestly and jestfully presented the concept of offense to his readers in an inoffensive way, through fictional narratives involving aesthetic and ethical characters and through expositions by pseudonymous writers with differing points of view, as well as through his direct writings, such as the *Eighteen Upbuilding Discourses* and *Works of Love*. Although his manner was not that of Paul, whom he called simply "the apostle," the content is thoroughly compatible with Paul's concept of the offense: Christ is the stumbling block or offense; the cross is an offense to the Jews and folly to the Gentiles; and those who follow the pattern of Christ must take care not to give offense, even though Jesus frequently did. On this last issue, however, Kierkegaard changed his own personal stance radically near the end of his life. The death of Bishop Mynster in 1854 caused him to reject Paul's advice and to become himself highly offensive.

This radical change was almost entirely a change in manner; the content of his final attack on the dead bishop (Mynster), on the new bishop (Professor Martensen), on the priests in the Danish church, and on all Christendom is suggested or implied, although in an inoffensive way, in the earlier works. But as long as his father's and his own friend, the old bishop, was alive, Kierkegaard held out the hope that the bishop and the established church would acknowledge the truth that Kierkegaard wanted to make known—that what it meant to become a Christian was altogether different from what was proclaimed within the church throughout Christendom.

Practice in Christianity was intended to be the work that would bring Mynster to realize that "the Establishment is, Christianly, indefensible," so that he would use his power to acknowledge the true Christian requirement. He had thought, he wrote, that Mynster must do one of two things: *either* declare himself decisively for the book [*Practice*], venture to go with it, let it count as the defense which would ward off the accusation against the whole official Christianity which the book implies poetically, affirming that it is an optical illusion, "not worth a sour herring"; *or* attack it as decisively as possible, brand it as a blasphemous and profane attempt, and declare that the official Christianity is the true Christianity. He did neither of the two, he did nothing; and it became clear to me that he was impotent. (*Attack upon "Christendom,"* 54–55)

After his death, this "impotent" bishop was extolled from the pulpit by Martensen as "the genuine witness to the truth," and it was this debased use of a profound phrase that initiated Kierkegaard's attacks on official Christendom in the periodicals *The Fatherland* and *The Instant* (or *Moment*) (1854–55).

In a series of thirty-three articles, Kierkegaard under his own name directly attacked Mynster, Martensen, and the whole "clerical gang of swindlers" (*Attack*, 117), the one thousand Danish priests paid by the state—all "parasites" (142), "quacks" (140), "counterfeiters" (151), "cannibals" (268), "knavish tradesmen" (282), etc. Christianity, he announced, "does not exist" (29); it has been replaced by Christendom, a "rotten, nauseating" thing (88), "a prodigious illusion" (97). "When scandal has been given, a scandal must be raised against it, and one must not complain that the step I have taken has unfortunately aroused so much scandal. No, it has not yet aroused scandal enough in proportion to the scandal of representing from the pulpit Bishop Mynster as a witness to the truth" (22), though the larger issue was, of course, that "the official Christianity is aesthetically and intellectually a laughingstock, an indecency, in the Christian sense a scandal" (48). The difference between "true," "primitive," or "New Testament" Christianity on the one hand and Christendom on the other is precisely what Climacus and Anti-Climacus had earlier set forth: "'Christendom' . . . takes away from Christianity the offense, the paradox, etc., and instead of that introduces probability, the plainly comprehensible"; it is "exactly the opposite" of Christianity (162–63). As a result, being a Christian in the official sense is easy and pleasant; a bishop enjoys admiration, success, comfort—the reverse of the supposed pattern, Christ—as did, only to a lesser degree, the one thousand priests paid by the state. "According to the New Testament," Kierkegaard asks, "what is it to become a Christian? Whereto the oft repeated warnings not to be offended? Whence the frightful collisions (hating father, mother, wife, child, etc.), in which the New Testament lives and breathes? Surely both are accounted for by the fact that Christianity knows well that to become a Christian is, humanly speaking, to become unhappy for this life. . . . He [Christ] makes thee unhappy, but he does it out of love—blessed is he who is not offended!" (189–90).

One might argue that Kierkegaard is not, after all, unlike Paul in his wrath. Paul himself had a Swiftian genius for scathing abuse, as when he attacks the Gentile idolaters as "gossips, slanderers, God-haters, insolent, haughty, boastful, inventors of evil, rebellious toward parents, foolish, faithless, heartless, ruthless" (Rom. 1:29–31). But the most dangerous people in Paul's view were those in the church who did not love God. Kierkegaard, likewise, was attacking those in the church. And there was no longer any need to heed Paul's counsel not to offend the faithful within the church or the nonbelievers outside the church because of this bizarre situation: there were no faithful people within the church, and virtually everyone was within the church. "Christianity does not exist" (29), but the church thrives—a state noted by a man who was to become the dean of St. Patrick's Cathedral in Dublin, Jonathan Swift, in "An Argument against Abolishing Christianity," more than a century before Kierkegaard. Kierkegaard stopped his lifelong habit of attending services, but he did not claim that he was the sole existing Christian: "I do not call myself a 'Christian' (thus keeping the ideal free), but I am able to make it evident that the others are that still less than I" (283).

Only by proclaiming Christianity to be dead could Kierkegaard avoid the charge that in his offensiveness he rejected Paul's admonitions. But there is no evidence that he was worried in the least about disregarding Paul. One reason might be that he considered the decay of Christianity into Christendom to have begun with Paul: "As early as 'the apostle' [Paul] the scaling down process begins, and it seems as if the natural man gets off a little easier in becoming a Christian." In this degenerative view of the history of religion, as more and more people flocked to Christianity, the definition of it changed until "nowadays whole countries and kingdoms are called Christian" and "millions of natural men [are] disguised as Christians" (*Journals*, 3: 2921). In spite of his great admiration for Paul and his writings, Kierkegaard saw him also as the harbinger of things to come.

A second, and more certain, reason for Kierkegaard's readiness to offend his contemporaries lay in his understanding of the historical offense, or the offense against the established order, in contrast to the essential, divine offenses of loftiness and lowliness. In the

Gospels, the historical offense is manifest when Christ as a mere man comes into collision with the established order as represented by the scribes and Pharisees (*Practice*, 83–94). This offense has nothing to do with Christ as God-man but only with Jesus as man. The established order "wants to be a totality that recognizes nothing above itself" and tends to deify itself, even though, Kierkegaard notes, "the deification of the established order is the secularization of everything" (91). When Jesus as man challenges the scribes, Pharisees, or temple tax collectors, he is an offense in the historical, nonessential way, but this offense can occur only in his actual presence. It "vanished with his death [and] existed only for his contemporaries in relation to him, this individual human being" (94), and in this the historical offense is unlike the essential offense, which is always a possibility.

This offense against the established order is the scandal Bakhtin finds repeatedly in Dostoyevski's work, and in Menippean satire generally, which he traces back to the Gospels. Unlike the essential offenses, it does not require a God-man; therefore, even though Jesus can no longer be an offense in this sense after his death, others can be. As Kierkegaard noted in his journal when he was writing his attacks on Christendom:

> Act just once in such a manner that your action expresses that you fear God alone and man not at all—you will immediately in some measure cause a scandal.
> The only thing that manages to dodge scandal is that which out of fear of men and deference to men is completely conformed to the secular mentality. (*Journals*, 3: 3679)

Kierkegaard admired Luther as an offense in this sense and had little regard for Mynster because, as a person of no courage and as the representative of the established order, Mynster could not abide any kind of offense. A journal entry from 1850 contrasting Luther and Mynster is worth quoting at some length:

> Mynster is an intelligent, circumspect man who shrinks from nothing, nothing, more than he shrinks from scandal. . . .
> But what is essential Christianity! From first to last it is scandal, the divine scandal (*skandalon*). Every time someone risks scandal of high order there is joy in heaven, for only the divinely chosen instrument achieves a scandal of high order.
> What is Luther's greatness? His writings will perhaps be forgotten, even his opposition to the pope (although that was indeed scandal enough) will very likely vanish—but at the peak of the mentality of

the middle ages to dare to marry, himself a monk, and with a nun! O, God's chosen instrument! By this act the biggest scandal ever raised in Christendom is reserved for you! First of all comes the introduction of Christianity into the world, when Christ and the apostles proclaimed it: this in itself was the divine scandal. But next, and in Christendom, Luther takes the prize for having raised the biggest [historical] scandal.

And now Mynster with his—Christian—dread of even the slightest scandal [of either kind]! And he and others are inspired by Luther! All is vanity, declares the Preacher. (*Journals*, 6: 6651)

In the remarkable exuberance of this entry, I fancy I hear Kierkegaard, the opponent of Mynster, taking positive pleasure in his brotherhood of scandal with Luther. Far from feeling fear and trembling over rejecting Paul's admonition, he seems to feel that his attack on Christendom, in progress while this entry was written, is a venturing, a risk of high order, perhaps even a joy in heaven. And he—no apostle, to be sure, and no sublime producer of scandal on the order of Luther—may nonetheless be a divinely chosen instrument.

Given the state of Christendom in his own time, "offense," he wrote in 1848, "cannot become more than a kind of awakening" (*Journals*, 2: 1958). Kierkegaard wanted to awaken individuals to the Christianity of the New Testament. Not to the Christianity of Mynster and Martensen—that was the established order, the scandalous other to the New Testament—and not to Christianity as any set of doctrines—"Christianity is not a doctrine," Climacus writes (*Concluding Unscientific Postscript*, 379)—but to Christianity as a paradox, expressed as dialectical communication, and written down in the form of narratives that themselves embody what Anti-Climacus calls "Christianity's crucial criterion: *the absurd, the paradox, the possibility of offense*" (*Sickness*, 83). Narratives of the absurd—not, certainly, a common way of viewing the Gospels, but in the Kierkegaardian sense in which the absurd is embodied in the improbable and unnatural paradox of the God-man who cannot be encountered without the possibility of offense, the Gospels are such narratives.

Like Kierkegaard, the Gospel writers chose to write about the truth not in systematic philosophic discourses, not in theological disquisitions, not in poetry, but in narratives. And at the heart of the Gospel narratives is what Kierkegaard calls the divine *skandalon* and the historical offense: Jesus. Readers or hearers of the Gospels must encounter the possibility of this offense, but in Kierkegaard's view such readers or hearers must be single individuals, not members of a race, crowd, or church, and they must be willing to venture out into the seventy thousand fathoms, encountering the absurd and the paradox in the nontemporal moment. Kierkegaard's task was to awaken single individuals, through narratives and expositions, to the possibility of offense that Christendom had obliterated.

II

OFFENSE IN GOSPEL NARRATIVES

The fact that the Son of God, who is life eternal, is de-clared to have put on our flesh and to have been a mortal man, the fact that we are said to have procured life by his death, righteousness by his condemnation, salvation by the curse he bore—all that is so greatly out of step with the common outlook of men that the more intelligent a man is the quicker will he be in repudiating it.

JOHN CALVIN, *Concerning Scandals*

Why did they spread this scandalous document [the Bible] before our eyes? If they had read it, I thought, they would have hid it.

ANNIE DILLARD, *An American Childhood*

5

Parabolic Lies,
Parabolic Truth

Parables as Obstructions and Revelations

One of the most difficult problems concerning the understanding of parables is raised in the Gospels themselves by Jesus's comment about parables in response to the disciples' puzzlement over parables in general and over the parable of the sower in particular. In Mark's Gospel, Jesus says to the disciples, "To you has been given the secret of the kingdom of God, but for those outside, everything comes in parables; in order that 'they may indeed look, but not perceive, and may indeed listen, but not understand; so that they may not turn again and be forgiven'" (Mark 4:11–12; cf. Matt. 13:11, 13–15, Luke 8:10). Versions of this saying are repeated in all the synoptic Gospels, though Matthew "softens" (as Fitzmyer says in the Anchor *Luke*, 708) the "so that" (or "in order that") by substituting "because" (or "the reason . . . is that").

Parables, according to Jesus's comment, would seem to obstruct understanding. Mark's *"in order that* 'they may indeed look, but not perceive'" (or Luke's *"so that* 'looking they may not perceive, and listening they may not understand'") implies obstruction, although scholars have tried to find ways to make the sense of this passage more reasonable and beneficent. Some scholars argue that not perceiving and not understanding are the result, not the purpose; in this case, Mark's *hina* ("so that"/"in order that") means something

71

close to Matthew's *hoti* ("because"/"the reason is that"). Without trying to resolve arguments about the force of these terms, I want to
explore what is clearly stated in all three of the synoptic Gospels:
that parables do obstruct understanding in the normal sense. I will
also argue that they make possible a positive transformation of another kind, but I first want to take the synoptic Gospels seriously
when, through "so that" and "because," they link parables with non-
understanding. This is the obstructive effect of parables, whether
the obstruction is a result or a purpose.[1]

Much current scholarly opinion readily acknowledges the elements of obstruction, obscurity, and opacity in Mark, though not
in Matthew. Frank Kermode, in *The Genesis of Secrecy*, finds in
Mark's opacity the secrecy of all great narratives, which is that they
allow, at best, a momentary radiance, perhaps delusive, before the
door of disappointment is finally shut. Paul Ricoeur calls this a
"second opaqueness," intended "to increase perplexity and to call
into question the reader's understanding" (*A Ricoeur Reader*, 460,
298). Robert Fowler discusses the obscurity of Mark by contrasting
it to the "clarity and straightforwardness" of Matthew, who misreads
Mark in order to eliminate puzzles and opacity (238–39). Fowler
represents a prevalent critical tendency to elevate Mark at the expense of Matthew: "Matthew is uncomfortable with all kinds of
opacities, solves riddles implied by metaphors, dismantles dramatic
ironies, and so forth" (224–25).

Matthew, however, in spite of his softened "because," elaborates
the obstructive view of parables most fully. Matthew's Jesus begins
by emphasizing the non-understanding as a result of the crowd's
own failure ("The reason I speak to them in parables is that 'seeing
they do not perceive, and hearing they do not listen, nor do they
understand'"; 13:13), and he continues to recount their failures by
quoting Isaiah from the Septuagint. He is not in a soft or compromis-
ing mood as he speaks to the disciples: "With them [the crowd]
indeed is fulfilled the prophecy of Isaiah that says: 'You will indeed
listen, but never understand, and you will indeed look, but never
perceive. For this people's heart has grown dull, and their ears are
hard of hearing, and they have shut their eyes; so that they might
not look with their eyes, and listen with their ears, and understand
with their heart and turn—and I would heal them'" (Matt. 13:14–15;
cf. John 12:40). In contrast to the disciples, to whom "it has been
given to know the secrets of the kingdom of heaven," the crowd has
not been given to know the secrets. They do, however, get parables.
But in light of Jesus's hard saying, "from those who have nothing,

even what they have will be taken away" (13:12), the parables and the prophecy are distinctly ominous.

After relating four parables, however, Matthew interjects another, very different reason for Jesus's telling of parables, this reason also to fulfill "what was spoken by the prophet"—not Isaiah this time but the singer of Psalms: "I will open my mouth to speak in parables; I will proclaim what has been hidden from the foundation of the world" (Matt. 13:35). This is the revelatory effect of parables: they obstruct, but they also reveal what has been hidden.

Parables as Lies

If we do not attend to Matthew's dual effects of parables—that they both obstruct understanding and reveal what has been hidden—we inevitably fail to see the paradoxical nature of them. Matthew's playing with different kinds of seeing and hearing (literally, "seeing they do not see, and hearing they do not hear") establishes a duality that is readily observable in the parables themselves—the kingdom of heaven on one hand and the man or grain or leaven compared to it on the other hand, the wheat and the weeds, the mustard seed and the tree, the good fish and the bad fish, and so on.

The duality of parables is built into the word itself. *Parable* comes from a Greek word meaning something thrown (*bolē*) alongside (*para*); the parable is literally a throwing of something alongside something else. It is usually assumed that the purpose of this throwing alongside is to represent, to illuminate, to allow understanding of something else, which Matthew calls "the kingdom of heaven." But this is at best a half-truth, if we acknowledge the obstructive as well as the revelatory function of parables, and at worse a delusion, if we take "understanding" to be a gaining of factual knowledge about the "something else." Parables, like other *skandala*, can be stumbling blocks that stand in the way of seeing the truth, the kingdom, or life (which I take to be synonymous in the Gospels), or they can be occasions that lead one to see, hear, and understand—in the active and transformative sense of being at one with—the truth, the kingdom, or life.

In Jesus's disparaging characterization of the crowd, the crowd sees something, but it does not see the truth. Insofar as parables obstruct the truth (or, less purposefully, are obstructions standing in the way of the truth), they are lies. I do not wish to attach moral opprobrium to parables; rather, I want to use the word *lie* to distinguish one kind of understanding—understanding about sense objects—from another: understanding about what Matthew calls the kingdom of heaven, which cannot, in fact, be understood in the usual sense, though it can be encountered and in some way even "seen" and "heard."

In positing the truth as ultimate reality, or *life* in the biblical sense of the word, or the embodiment of godhead (as in Jesus's statement "I am the way, and the truth, and the life"; John 14:6), and contrasting it with the lie, which includes all objects, facts, or thoughts that are detached from the godhead, I am exploiting a distinction made in another context by the psychoanalyst W. R. Bion, who argues that "the lie requires a thinker to think. The truth, or true thought, does not require a thinker—he is not logically necessary" (102). Bion continues:

> Nobody need think the true thought: it awaits the advent of the thinker who achieves significance through the true thought. The lie and its thinker are inseparable. The thinker is of no consequence to the truth, but the truth is logically necessary to the thinker. His significance depends on whether or not he will entertain the thought, but the thought remains unaltered.
>
> In contrast, the lie gains existence by virtue of the epistemologically prior existence of the liar. The only thoughts to which a thinker is absolutely essential are lies. Descartes's tacit assumption that thoughts presuppose a thinker is valid only for the lie. (103)

I am using *lies* in a still more radically uncommon way than Bion, however, since in my usage the speaker may be saying what is factually true though separated from God. If I say, "My car is blue," I state a true fact, but in my special sense the fact is a lie if I speak, as I do, of my car as an object unrelated to the godhead. (If this sounds absurd, consider the extraordinary significance some of us attach to the make, model, and appearance of our automobiles, or consider television ads for automobiles, with their appeals to power, beauty, personal fulfillment, and even transcendence, in the light of the second commandment.)[2] Thus, to someone for whom everything is separated from God—in my admittedly curious usage of *lie*— everything, including all true facts and all real objects, is a lie. I want to insist on this odd usage not because I expect to alter the way auto dealers, consumers, and politicians use the word but because I want to reanimate, for the purposes of my exposition, the biblical meaning of lying, which is intimately tied to the biblical concept of understanding. In John, Jesus says to a group "who had believed in him":

Why do you not understand what I say? It is because you cannot accept my word. You are from your father the devil, and you choose to do your father's desires. He was a murderer from the beginning and does not stand in the truth, because there is no truth in him. When he lies, he speaks according to his own nature, for he is a liar and the father of lies. But because I tell the truth, you do not believe me. Which of you convicts me of sin? If I tell the truth, why do you not believe me? Whoever is from God hears the words of God. The reason you do not hear them is that you are not from God. (John 8:43–47)

Hearing the truth depends on being "from God"; likewise, seeing and understanding. The alternative, in the New Testament world of radical dichotomies, is hearing lies and existing by nature in lies. The liars, of course, do not think of themselves as liars (any more than I think of myself as a liar when I say that my car is blue); on the contrary, in John's story they reject the label, call the labeler a crazy half-breed, and begin collecting stones to throw at him. The lie, then, is not limited to the realm of thought (or, even more restrictively, of facts); it has, as Bion says, "its counterpart in the domain of being; it is possible to be a lie and being so precludes at-one-ment" in truth, ultimate reality, or the godhead (104).

A lie presupposes a liar, and my argument seems to be drifting toward the scandalous assertion that Jesus is a liar. But parables, as paradoxes, are revelatory as well as obstructive, and the effect of parables depends not on the teller but on the listener—whether the listener hears or does not hear, sees or does not see, understands or does not understand. In Jeremiah 6:21 (discussed above, in chapter 2), Yahweh says, "I am laying" stumbling blocks before the Israelites, and in Isaiah, Yahweh says that Yahweh will become "for both houses of Israel . . . a rock one stumbles over. . . . And many among them shall stumble" (8:14–15). Likewise, Jesus puts stumbling blocks in the form of parables (as well as in sayings, proclamations, and actions) in front of those he encounters. They may stumble on them by hearing them as lies (hearing they do not hear), but that is not the only alternative.

Parables reveal desires. In Matthew 13, immediately after Jesus's assertion "Let anyone with ears listen!" (13:43), he tells the parables of the treasure and the pearl, which are parables about selling and buying to get valuable treasures. We may well hear these parables as the expression of a desire for unexpected wealth, which may be a genuine and even justifiable desire. But in hearing the parable in this way, we expose our lying nature, in the biblical sense. The reader/hearer makes the parable into a lie and stumbles on it, making it into an obstruction standing in the way of the kingdom, ultimate reality, the godhead.

The parable of the vineyard laborers (Matt. 20:1–6) is sometimes interpreted, by enthusiastic capitalists, as an apology for free enterprise. The householder, in this view, performs a valuable service by providing work to people standing idly in the marketplace; he fulfills his promise by paying the first group according to contract, and he pays the others generously when there was no contract. As owner of the capital, the godlike householder may choose to pay as he pleases, and he pleases to be generous to some and fair to others. I consider this to be a perfectly legitimate interpretation of the parable, because it reveals the desires of the interpreter, which is what parables as *skandala* exist to do. It is also in biblical terms a lie, in that the interpreter has incorporated the parable into the scheme of his own desires, without encountering any collision with the truth that, as Bion puts it, requires no thinker to make it truth.[3]

Parables as Transforming Acts of Truth

Parables are lies (in the special biblical sense of alienation from God), *and* parables reveal truth, which is hidden from normal seeing, hearing, and understanding. The qualities of the latter function are not easily characterized, but they are essential to the *skandalon* that leads toward, rather than away from, faith. The parable of the vineyard laborers provides a useful illustration of the three qualities I want to call attention to in this form of the *skandalon*.

The first is activity. The parable begins, "For the kingdom of heaven is like a landowner who went out early in the morning to hire laborers for his vineyard" (Matt. 20:1). The analogy is not: the kingdom of heaven is like a landowner. The analogy is: the kingdom of heaven is like a landowner who engages in certain actions. More specifically, the kingdom of heaven is like a landowner who goes out, hires laborers and sends them to work, goes out again and hires and sends more, and again, and again, and who pays them equal amounts in reverse order, and who responds to grumblers. The kingdom of heaven is like a series of acts.

The second quality is truth. Bion's truth seems to be an isolable thought, discrete from the thinker. But Bakhtin's notion of truth as a "live event," existing on the boundaries between the self and other (or Other, as in Buber's I-Thou relationship), does not involve logical entities but rather dialogic persons and therefore comes closer to the spirit of parables, as well as of proclamations, hard sayings, and

Gospels. I take the kingdom of heaven in Matthew to be a symbol of a divine truth that is not isolable or explainable in rational, factual terms that we associate with matter-of-fact human understanding. In the parable, this divine truth is said to be like a series of acts that involves an unconventional, unworldly choosing and giving. There are two kinds of choosing in the parable. First, the choice of which laborers are hired. In the story, those who are hired at about the eleventh hour (about five P.M.) have been standing in the market all day; they were presumably there early in the morning, at six A.M., available to be hired, but the landowner chooses to hire others in the early morning, others later, and only near the end of the day some who had been waiting all day. It is clear that the laborers have to be in the marketplace to be hired, but beyond that they have no say in the matter; the choice of laborers is up to the landowner. The second choice is how much and in what order to pay the laborers. The last hired are paid first, and all are paid the same amount—a denarius, one full day's wages. Those who worked one hour at the end of the day are paid the same as those who worked twelve hours in "the scorching heat." The landowner's truth (which offends those who have worked twelve hours) seems in his mind to be bound first to his choosing (how much and to whom to give money) and second to his giving (which he calls his generosity or goodness): "I choose to give to this last [group who worked one hour] the same as I give to you [who worked twelve hours]. Am I not allowed to do what I choose with what belongs to me? Or are you envious because I am generous [literally, is your eye evil because I am good]?" (Matt. 20:14–15).

It is certainly easy to share the point of view of the twelve-hour laborers, to whom this truth must appear to be a perversion of free choice, justice, and generosity or goodness. The payment is, relatively, ungenerous to those who worked twelve hours, unjust except in a legalistic, contractual way (did you not agree to work all day for a denarius?), and a species of free choice that bears marks of deliberate upending of normal and reasonable expectations ("the last will be first"). The content of the landowner's truth is not accessible as communicable information; we can only say that it is related to an unorthodox choosing and giving and that it collides with normal expectations.

The third quality is transformation. There are two transformations to consider: first, of the characters in the parable and, second, of the hearer/reader of the parable. Within the parable, idleness is emphasized: the landowner "saw others standing idle in the marketplace," and, coming back later, he says to others, "Why are you standing here idle all day?" Idlers are transformed into workers. But the ones asked about their idleness are chosen to be first in receiving their pay equal to the others. The unexpected transformation of order among the laborers through the unorthodox pay system is crucial to the action and is summarized in the last line: "So the last will be first, and the first will be last." The transformation of idlers into laborers is a simple economic act: unhired, they are idle; hired, they are laborers. The transformation of the last as the first, and vice versa, is a simple but unexplained choice by the landowner: it might be a whim, it might somehow be rational, or it might be deeply, and perhaps irrationally, wise. We do not know. But among the characters there is a potentially more significant transformation which is left unresolved. I refer to the twelve-hour workers who are transformed into grumblers, offended at what they perceive to be unjust treatment. "These last worked only one hour," they say, "and you have made them equal to us who have borne the burden of the day and the scorching heat." They receive an explanation, likely to be unsatisfactory, told to "Take what belongs to you and go," and left with the choice of being envious because of the landowner's generosity (seeing self-proclaimed goodness with an evil eye) or not. They may choose to remain offended or not, but the reasons offered for not being offended are, by normal standards, not compelling.

What of the hearer's/reader's transformation? I cannot say. Negatively, my argument is that the hearer/reader, like the twelve-hour laborer, might be offended by the landowner's odd distribution of wealth; or (as in the case of the "free enterprise" reading) the hearer/reader may actively try to avoid that offense by interpreting the parable, making it a lie by incorporating his or her own desires into the interpretation. In this case the parable will function as another offense, a stumbling block that obstructs the kingdom. But, positively, if the parable is to act as an offense that leads to faith, no interpretation will suffice. A close hearing or reading, which pays attention with what Kierkegaard calls "a passionate concentration" (*Journals*, 3: 3130) on the story, its characters, and its details, is certainly essential. But if the likeness—the kingdom of heaven is like a landowner engaging in these actions—is to reveal something significant, it can do so only by presenting a *skandalon*, which may turn the hearer to faith, which is itself the revelation. The turning to faith can occur only if the hearer encounters the real possibility of offense in the narrative (the potential for injustice, lack of generosity, and perversion of free choice) but transforms this possibility into the contrary of offense, faith.

Can the parable of the vineyard laborers possibly be a *skandalon*? There is certainly a *skandalon* confronting the twelve-hour laborers within the parable. To them, the landowner is unfair and unjust, and his question—"Or are you envious because I am generous?"—is offensive because the so-called generosity is (to them) partial and arbitrary, which is not (they might argue) the true nature of generosity. Furthermore, the proposition addressed to the hearer of the parable—"the last will be first, and the first will be last"—is offensive. Human institutions are posited on the reverse: the first will be first, and the last, last. It is common sense, it is the way things are, it is the nature of the verb *to be*. But the kingdom of heaven that Jesus (who in Matthew is a man and also the Christ, Son of God) is talking about has nothing to do with common sense; nothing to do with the ordinary way things are on earth, though everything to do with the way things are or shall be in the kingdom of heaven; nothing to do with grammatical forms of *to be*, though everything to do with a transformed "being."

If the parable is encountered as an offense away from faith, it becomes an obstruction and a lie. If the parable is encountered as an offense toward faith, it becomes a transforming act of truth, which necessarily involves a collision.

Collision and Crisis

The twelve-hour workers in the parable are offended at being paid last and the same total amount as the one-hour workers; it is for them a matter of no small importance. Yet, in Kierkegaardian terms, theirs is an offense "over this and that" rather than the essential offense. Like any offense, however, it involves a collision between two different realms—in this case, between their sense of work, fairness, and generosity and the radically different sense of the landowner. This collision leads to a challenge and rebuff, but it is not resolved in the narrative. We do not know whether the twelve-hour workers continue to grumble, try to argue, contemplate revenge, simply depart as they are told to do, or something else. They are suspended in the narrative in a state of offense.

The landowner says their offense takes the form of an evil eye that is the direct result of his goodness or generosity ("Is your eye evil because I am good?") and that their alternative is to accept his goodness (allow him to do as he chooses with what belongs to him). There is something fascinating about this self-assured, persistent, unconventional landowner. His scandal calls forth the evil eye of the all-day workers, and it may call forth the evil eye of readers or hearers. But few people who see through an evil eye know that their eye is evil. As Samuel Johnson was fond of saying, hypocrisy is an uncommon vice; humans who hold to selfish, greedy, vicious positions are usually convinced that they are in fact justified. In this case, the workers with the evil eye might argue quite credibly that they are not being selfish at all; they just want to be treated fairly. They are angry but also fascinated by this man; their eye is evil. (*Fascinate* derives from *fascinum*, the evil eye.)

The workers have collided with this unconventional, powerful, and persistent man who proclaims his own goodness. They have literally wrecked their way of seeing. The collision is unwanted and unplanned; it is incomprehensible to the workers' normal ways of thinking and doing. And yet the ruinous effects we normally associate with a collision are not unavoidable: the landowner gives them a choice of ways of seeing, though both choices have as their given his goodness. The incomprehensible goodness may be seen through an evil eye or through some other, better eye. Which eye they see it through will be their—the workers'—doing. But it will be the result of the landowner's goodness, since it caused the collision.

The disciples, as hearers, or Matthew's readers have various options: they may side with the workers or the landowner; they may be uninterested in the whole business, curious, puzzled, and so on; and, quite possibly, they may find themselves in a collision of their own. An engaged hearer or reader may have difficulty *not* being fascinated by this landowner's unconventional actions. Will this fascination lead him or her back to the root sense of the word—to the evil eye? The *skandalon* provokes to a collision, and the result of that collision may be that the hearer or reader comes to see evilly, to see and not perceive. But the parable does not insist on that result. As a *skandalon* it provokes to a collision without determining a result.

Explaining what that collision might be is as difficult, perhaps as impossible, as explaining what faith is. Kierkegaard provides a way of pointing to, though not explaining, the phenomenon when he describes the collision as the act in that state of risk that accompanies the possibility of offense and that may lead to faith. Faith is, according to Kierkegaard's experimenting psychologist, Johannes Climacus, "the highest passion of subjectivity" (*Concluding Unsci-*

entific Postscript, 132); it discovers "improbability, the paradox" (233); it is "the objective uncertainty with the repulsion of the absurd, held fast in the passion of inwardness" (611); it is "the contradiction" and "the truth" (204); and it is possible only when the existing individual is at risk, venturing out over seventy thousand fathoms. It is contrary to the category of understanding, not amenable to explanation. It happens when the single individual collides with the unexplainable.

The prospect of a collision is attractive to few sane and healthy people, conjuring up as it does images of smashed windshields, mangled bodies, hospitals, lawyers, and wrecked lives. No one ought to be expected to choose or want a collision. And yet—though it is something we reasonably shun—Kierkegaard's collision is necessary for life, for life, that is, if it is to be lived "before God."

For Kierkegaard a collision is prompted by the coming together of two incommensurate spheres. Since the human is a synthesis of the physical and the spiritual, the temporal and the eternal, the probable and the necessary, collisions play an inevitable and essential role in existence. But if one does not venture out into the religious, one will not experience a collision with the spiritual. This, for Kierkegaard, constitutes the wasted life. "Only that person's life was wasted who went on living so deceived by life's joys or its sorrows that he never became decisively and eternally conscious as spirit, as self, or, what amounts to the same thing, never became aware and in the deepest sense never gained the impression that there is a God and that 'he,' he himself, his self, exists before this God" (*Sickness*, 26–27). Such a person lives in a realm where he or she may be offended at this or that but not at the essential.

To become conscious, to become a self, to become aware requires the presence of the absolute other, God. Becoming conscious is therefore not contingent merely on participating in life's joys and sorrows, or in following a safe, accustomed course, or by remaining a member of an institution, crowd, or group. It requires that an individual exist in contradictions. "Consciousness emerges precisely through the collision. . . . Ideality and reality . . . collide—in what medium? In time? That is indeed an impossibility. In eternity? That is indeed an impossibility. In what, then? In consciousness—there is the contradiction" (*Philosophical Fragments*, 171).

The essential offense can occur only when the temporal encounters the eternal, at which moment the paradox and the understanding meet in the happy passion Climacus eventually names "faith" or in the unhappy suffering he calls offense. And, as we saw in chapter 4, since the offense is an "acoustic illusion," it can be discovered only in the presence of the paradox ("the god"). As Kierkegaard wrote in a draft of *Philosophical Fragments*, "If the learner does not collide in *the moment* in the collision of understanding, . . . then the paradox thrusts him away, and he takes offense or is scandalized" (*Journals*, 3: 3082).

The phrase "collision of understanding" illuminates Matthew's emphasis on the crowd's non-understanding and his obstructive explanation, "so that they might not . . . understand with their heart" (13:15). They can understand with their heart only by experiencing a collision with their normal understanding. As members of a crowd, as institutional beings, or as merely natural humans, they can never experience the collision. Their not understanding in Jesus's sense is perfectly natural, since they are confronted with an improbable narrative told by a God-man. But however natural the failure may be, the stakes are high; in Jesus's terms, the alternatives are spiritual blindness versus knowing what has been hidden since the foundation of the world, offense versus faith, death versus life. As Climacus says in the *Concluding Unscientific Postscript*, "that collision of the infinite and the finite . . . is precisely a mortal danger for one who is composed of both" (233). Only the individual who exists before God experiences the collision.

The hearer who sees, hears, and understands a parable uttered by the God-man (who is himself an offense) is engaged in an encounter with the improbable and the spiritual, both of which are an offense to the natural human.[4] Hence the collision. The result of the collision will be either faith (itself the revelation offered by the God-man, hidden since the foundation of the world) or offense. A hearer might be indifferent and therefore not apparently offended at all, but only when the possibility of offense exists will the possibility of faith exist. "And blessed is anyone who takes no offense at me," Jesus says (Matt. 11:6), but the person who is offended is closer to this strange blessedness than the person who is indifferent, because the person essentially offended by Jesus (and not offended "over this and that") has experienced a collision.

The term *collision*, like Bakhtin's *crisis*, is misleading insofar as it suggests an inevitably dramatic, outward encounter, like that of the high priest who "tore his clothes" and spoke of "blasphemy" at Jesus's response during the trial before the council (Matt. 26:65). The collision is indeed an action but not necessarily dramatic in the spectacular sense. The rich young man who was told to sell what he had and give to the poor simply "went away grieving" (Matt.

19:22). And the Canaanite woman who had been a positive nuisance, "crying after" the disciples, responded to Jesus's offense with an apparently quiet affirmation, "Yes, Lord, yet . . ." (Matt. 15:27). But most of the collision narratives in the Gospels do not even record a response. Like the grumbling twelve-hour workers in the vineyard, they are suspended in the moment of collision, narratively frozen in what is for them the eternal moment.

To experience the collision of offense, either away from faith or toward faith, is to experience a *skandalon* posited by Jesus. This experience is not the content of the parable; it is an action on the part of the reader. The referent of the parable ("the kingdom of heaven is like . . .") is finally unknowable in any ordinary sense; the kingdom may be mysterious or absent, but it is never within the merely sensory or intellectual range of seeing, hearing, or understanding. The Gospel writer, of course, can assert that the kingdom is truth, but only through the *skandalon* can the Gospel writer's truth (or Jesus's truth enacted within the Gospel) become the reader's or hearer's truth. And even then, this truth cannot be communicated as propositional content since it is, in Kierkegaard's terms, contrary to the understanding. It is instead an action, a changing and becoming, that the Gospel writers refer to as faith. But a transforming act of truth is only one alternative; the other is that the scandalous parable may become the reader's or hearer's lie.

Toward Reading Parables as Scandals (A Critical Addendum)

The Gospels record the difficulty the disciples—those simple fishermen, innocent of hermeneutics—have as they try to decipher Jesus's parables, even in his presence. And, in truth, reading parables is no easy task for sophisticated readers. In the scholastic tradition of the Middle Ages, the art of interpreting parables allegorically was refined with extraordinary subtlety, though not with unanimity. In the parable of the vineyard laborers, for example, the five times of day when the householder hired the laborers were usually interpreted in one of two ways: first, as historical ages, with the early morning covering the time from Adam (or Abel) to Noah, the third hour from Noah to Abraham, and so on, up to the present age; second, as the human life span, with some workers being called in childhood, some in adolescence, and so on. But other interpreters viewed it as a moral allegory: the vineyard is justice, and in it grow the individual vines of kindness, chastity, patience, and so on; the idle workers are those who have omitted good works, but if they have been called to the vineyard (by grace), they receive the same reward. The denarius usually was said to represent eternal life, with some interpreting the denarius's ten units as the Ten Commandments.[5]

In these various interpretations, the offense is eliminated, ameliorated, or displaced away from the interpreting community. For example, "But many that are first will be last, and the last will be first" is sometimes interpreted to mean that the last called are the first to come to the last judgment.(ameliorating the offense by reducing it to a longer wait for some than for others but with the same reward in store, ultimately, for all) or to mean that even though the Jews came first, the Christians replaced them (displacing the offense away from the interpreting Christians). The grumbling or murmuring by the twelve-hour workers proves to be a more difficult issue, since some who have the denarius/eternal life are grumbling in a distinctly human and unheavenly vein. Gregory the Great solved the difficulty by ignoring verse 15 ("Are you envious?"; literally, "Is your eye evil?") and arguing that the murmuring was not of envy, or anything malicious, but of longing. Innocent III took the grumbling to be a hypothetical, not an actual, evil, but most commentators saw it as an evil associated with the Jews or the early church. In the most extreme reading, Geoffrey Babion interpreted "Take what belongs to you and go" as a damnation of the Jews, who get their literal denarius but no allegorical salvation (Wailes, 139–44).

Reading allegorically in this fashion requires the discovery of a message through the equivalencies that parallel the narrative. These messages do not necessarily eliminate the *skandalon* (though there is a distinct tendency in that direction), nor are messages necessarily limited to allegorical interpretations. It is not my intention to survey the complex field of parable criticism,[6] but a brief overview and a selective look at several approaches will indicate how modern critics have handled the issue of parables-as-message, which I take to be a centuries-old stumbling block. This is a lively and ongoing debate, and I want to address it directly, if only sketchily, to indicate where the *skandalon* fits into the controversy.

When Jülicher initiated modern parable criticism with his attack on allegorical interpretations, he argued that parables work as similitudes or exemplary tales, that their truths are not hidden or esoteric, and that they convey clearly one point. They convey instruction, but not through obscure allegories. The allegorical interpretations within the synoptic Gospels are not the words of Jesus,

Jülicher argued, but of the early church. Much of what Jülicher argued has been accepted by later critics such as C. H. Dodd, though with significant modification. Dodd, for example, followed Jülicher in rejecting allegorical interpretation, but he did not accept the notion of one broadly applicable, essential point. Instead, Dodd argued that parables must first be viewed in the context of Jesus's *Sitz im Leben*, or setting in life, especially the historical situation of Jesus's attempt to bring his contemporaries to the recognition that the kingdom of God had arrived with Jesus. Later generations could find meaning in the parables as well, in Dodd's view, but interpretation should start with the historical situation. Unlike Jülicher, Dodd did not find one moral point in each parable, but the parables embody in themselves Jesus's message of a realized eschatology: the kingdom has now come. The parables "represent the interpretation" Jesus offered of his own ministry (158) — a ministry that "caused scandal." To the scandalized ones who raised "objections Jesus appealed in parables with an ironical point" (161). Thus, though the point of parables is far from the simple moral with the broadest possible application, as Jülicher saw it, it is a message about the realized kingdom. Parables make points (see 127), they invite interpretation, they tease the mind into active thought (5). (Dodd's definition of parable is deservedly famous: "a metaphor . . . leaving the mind in sufficient doubt about its precise application to tease it into active thought.") They also have, for Dodd, a powerful existential effect on individuals of different times and in different situations.

Joachim Jeremias continued the work of Jülicher and Dodd by reconstructing the parables as they were originally told by Jesus, trying to eliminate what Matthew, Mark, Luke, and other members of the early church had added to them, including the allegorical interpretations. Much of his book is organized around the messages embodied in the parables — messages rather different from the ones Jülicher found — and although Jeremias is probably the most influential modern scholar in parable studies, Norman Perrin's critique of his method reflects a new way of thinking about parables. After commenting that Jeremias's messages look "very much like a summary of a rather conservative Lutheran piety," Perrin continues: "What is important is that the very nature of the parables of Jesus as texts forbids the reduction of the message to a series of general moral principles, or to a series of rubrics. Parables as parables do not have a 'message.'" Perrin's formulation of what parables do instead gives a new twist to Dodd's formulation. "They tease the mind into ever new perceptions of reality," Perrin says; "they startle the imagination; they function like symbols in that they 'give rise to thought'" (106).

Perrin's turn toward symbols reflects the influence of critics such as Ricoeur, Crossan, and Funk, who place much more importance on symbol and metaphor than their predecessors and less on ideational content, points, messages. Robert Funk allows that a parable may have "as many points as there are situations into which it is spoken" (*Language*, 151), but he insists, with Ernst Fuchs, that "the parable is not meant to *be* interpret*ed*, but to interpret. The parable keeps the initiative in its own hand. Therein lies its hermeneutical potential." The parable is, above all, metaphor, and "the metaphor must be left intact if it is to retain its interpretive power" (152), a power that depends on the participation of the hearer or listener, who is not a receiver of messages. "The metaphor, like the parable, is incomplete until the hearer is drawn into it as participant" (143).

John Dominic Crossan's definition of parable—"a metaphor of normalcy which intends to create participation in its referent" (*In Parables*, 15–16)—indicates his emphases on metaphor ("verbal symbol," 21) and on something radically different from conveying messages: creating participation.[7] In parables he finds the advent of new world, the reversal of normal reality, and action—an "empowering to life" (36). Part of the process of reversal involves a "shattering" of world as a necessary prelude to participation. "When a metaphor contains a radically new vision of world it gives absolutely no information until after the hearer has entered into it and experienced it from inside itself. In such cases the hearer's first reaction may be to refuse to enter into the metaphor and one will seek to translate it immediately into the comfortable normalcy of one's ordinary linguistic world" (13). Information is contained within the vision, within the metaphor, but it is secondary to the participatory vision. Later, after Crossan had read Derrida, there is no more talk of information: "Metaphor or symbol does not so much have a 'surplus of meaning,' in Ricoeur's phrase," Crossan writes in *Cliffs of Fall*, "as a *void of meaning* at its core. Like a Rorschach, it can mean so many things and generate so many differing interpretations because it has no fixed, univocal, or absolute meaning to begin with" (10).

To clarify my own position vis-à-vis Crossan's, I would agree with his emphasis on creating participation, on radical new vision (the New Testament "life"), and on the possibility of the hearer to refuse to enter the metaphor, preferring comfortable—or even uncomfortable—normalcy (which I have called, following Kierke-gaard, the offense away from faith). I also agree with Crossan's later position that there is no "information" to be gained from the parable and that it can generate numerous differing interpretations (depend-ing, as I will argue, on the hearer's desires). But instead of a "void of meaning at its core," I am arguing that what is at the core is "the way, the truth, and the life," the God-man, the Absolute Other, which—though not meaning-as-information—is meaning of another kind. The Rorschach readings are the result not of a void of meaning at the core but of the reader's offense away from faith.

Of course, modern parable criticism is by no means a mono-lithic and consistent movement away from parables as informative containers of messages to visionary containers of the void. Scholars such as Bernard Brandon Scott continue to work in the tradition of Dodd and Jeremias, trying to determine the original meaning of parables as told by Jesus, although Scott, as a reader-oriented plural-ist, never insists on a single correct meaning. Others, such as J. D. Kingsbury, look for the meanings of Matthew's parables within the context of the early church, and Dan O. Via has written from a literary and existential point of view, with very little interest in the historical Jesus or the early church. Girard finds specific parabolic meanings that reveal something about violence and sacrifice (*Things Hidden*, 185–90). But with the increasing emphasis on parable as metaphor and symbol, there has been a clear tendency away from viewing parables as containing codifiable messages.

Another tendency in parable criticism that is relevant to my argument about the double-sided offense may be seen in Ernst Fuchs and his American successor, Robert Funk. Fuchs emphasizes the importance in the parable of a call to decision. His teacher, Rudolf Bultmann, had written that Jesus's message about the kingdom of God "demands . . . decision" (*Jesus and the Word*, 35); Fuchs simi-larly states that "Jesus' parables summon to decision. . . . Like the man who found the treasure, or the pearl merchant who found the one pearl of great price, the hearer must stake all on one thing— that he can win the future which Jesus proclaims to him" (220). The parable, by portraying Jesus's understanding of his situation, allows the hearer to share it or to stand in opposition to it. About the vineyard laborers, Fuchs writes, "The parable itself tells us that Je-sus . . . solicits understanding by giving us to understand his [Je-sus's] conduct as God's conduct. *It is up to the person who under-*

stands the parable to give the verdict on the truth of Jesus' claim. It is the person who understands who has to decide" (37; Fuchs' emphasis).

Funk follows Fuchs closely in this regard: parables are "language events in which the hearer has to choose between worlds. If he elects the parabolic world, he is invited to dispose himself to concrete reality as it is ordered in the parable, and venture, without benefit of landmark but on the parable's authority, into the future" (*Language*, 162). This emphasis on decisive effect on the hearers or readers leads Funk to notice that, in what he calls parables of grace (including the vineyard laborers and six or seven others), the parables "invariably cause offense to [Jesus's] opponents (usually designated as scribes and Pharisees)" (*Language*, 14).

No one, to my knowledge, has come closer to the notion that the offense is crucial to parable than Paul Ricoeur, who raises this possibility in *Biblical Hermeneutics*: "It seems to me that its [the kingdom of God's][8] role in eschatological proclamation, proverbs, and parables is to make us see a modality which logic tends to pass over in silence, the logical *scandal*. In effect, 'oddness' says too little; only 'scandal' fits. . . . The function of the qualifier is to disorient [our discourse and our action], to upset them, in short, to introduce paradox and scandal into them" (121, 124). In spite of his saying that "only 'scandal' fits," Ricoeur usually uses the word *extravagance* or *paradox*. "Paradox," he writes, "disorients only to reorient"; it is "the eruption of the unheard in our discourse and in our experience." Behind this eruption—the moment I have called collision or crisis— is one of the three essential elements in his understanding of parables. "The parable," according to Ricoeur, "is the conjunction of [1] a *narrative form* and [2] a *metaphorical process*," along with "a third decisive trait," which he identifies as "the *extravagance* [oddness, logical scandal] of the dénouement and of the main characters" that provides the specific "religious" trait of the parable, pointing toward the meaning "kingdom of God" (*Hermeneutics*, 30–33).

Ricoeur does not, however, link this extravagance or scandal with the biblical *skandalon*. In a later work, he associates "scandal" with proverbs and continues to use "extravagance," "paradox," or "the fantastic" to characterize parables. "The parable surprises, astonishes, shocks, provokes: exposing such and such a prejudgment (an opinion or belief imposed by the milieu, one's education, or the epoch), it obliges one to reconsider things, to come to a new decision" ("The Kingdom," 166). The critical element that causes surprise is extravagance:

We touch here on the paradox of the parable: it begins in an ordinary manner, only to turn to the fantastic, but to a fantastic that remains a fantastic of the everyday, without the supernatural, as it appears in fairy tales or in myths. The extraordinary in the ordinary, that is what baffles one and leads one to ask: Why is this story told? It certainly isn't told in order to teach gardening, sheep-rearing or domestic economy! But if it is not told for the sheer pleasure of the story, then it must be that the story, under the appearance of banality, speaks about something else. This "drift" [*dérapage*] of the story is the secret of the parabolic genre. The parable signifies the Kingdom, precisely by means of this trait of extravagance that causes it to burst out of its framework.

For Ricoeur, the parable "disorient[s] existence with a view to reorienting it." Extravagance is "the instrument of this disorientation" ("The Kingdom," 168).

What Ricoeur refers to as the extravagant, odd, fantastic, scandalous instrument is, however, as we have seen, no oddity in the Bible: it is the *skandalon* of Yahweh in the Hebrew Bible and of Jesus in the New Testament. In the parables, it is the *skandalon* of Jesus's word—the word as utterance and as action, linking speaker to listener in such a way as to bring God's kingdom or reign into collision with the listener's reality, forcing the listener into the moment of crisis, where one's eye may, or may not, be evil.

6

Training the Scribes
of the Kingdom

Substance versus Response

The argument that parables are the scandalous word of Jesus, that they constitute a collision between the world and the kingdom, and that they bring the reader to a threshold experience, may, I am well aware, seem to violate common sense. Some readers of Crossan's *In Parables* found his arguments that a parable "shatters world" (26–27, 114–15) unconvincing, perhaps because they had read parables for years without the reading ever having been accompanied by anything resembling a shattered world. Experientially, it seems more sensible to look for, and find, meanings in these utterances. Parables seem to cry out for explanations. Why not respond with explanations? Many, perhaps most, hearers or readers feel that the role of interpreter, looking for codifiable meanings, whether through allegorical, exemplary, or metaphorical readings, is a reasonable role to assume. It even has a biblical basis: parables are told by Jesus to (among others) twelve chosen disciples who want to know what they mean, and Jesus, as teacher, explains them, asking the disciples whether they understand them and sometimes reprimanding them for their slowness in understanding. In such a context, it is little wonder we should keep asking, "What do they *mean?*"

And yet parables are above all narratives, not assertions, and as narratives they hold a place of honor as the distinctive speech genre of the teacher and hero in a text full of narratives. Jesus seems disinclined to speak in terms of theological or philosophical meanings and naturally inclined to speak in narratives. "Jesus told the crowds all these things in parables," Matthew tells us; "without a parable he told them nothing" (13:34).

But Jesus also, in the narrative and as part of it, interprets his parables allegorically. If Jesus, why not us? It is almost too compelling a model to resist, and it seems safe to assume that there will always be allegorical interpreters, following the model of the synoptic Gospels' Jesus and following the implicit invitation to allegorize Mark's vineyard parable (12:1–12). Some will even feel they can reach certainty in interpretation, allegorical or otherwise, but the certainty is by no means unanimous. Where two or three like-minded individuals are gathered together to interpret, there may be unanimity, but where two or three other individuals or groups interpret, there are likely to be two or three different interpretations. What Wayne Booth says about critical responses to Henry James's stories — "The critical disagreement revealed to anyone who compares two or three critics on any one story is a scandal" (315) — is applicable to many biblical stories. The salutary drift, though not the only current, of recent criticism is that parables and Gospels not be interpreted as containers of meaning, which might seem to minimize the scandal of multiple interpretations. But parables offer us the possibility of interpreting our desires (which, of course, multiplies interpretations), while at the same time they — the parables and indeed the Gospels as well — offer another scandal, this one within the text: parables and Gospels are themselves occasions for offense.

In observing that Gospel narratives are occasions for offense, I include the narratives of interpretation, in which Jesus interprets his own stories. Since the beginning of this century, scholars have increasingly considered Jesus's interpretations of parables to be historically inauthentic. Many scholars now take it as a given that Jesus's allegorical interpretations as recorded by Matthew, Mark, and Luke were inventions of the early church and have no basis in Jesus's utterances.[1] But the general twentieth-century movement away from allegorical interpretation has not hindered scholars and other readers from searching for meaning. The meanings have become more and more indeterminate, as in Bernard B. Scott's recent book, where he argues that "The parable suggests, but it leaves to its hearer the responsibility for meaning" (280). The search for meaning may be displaced into multiple responses, but the search continues.

Matthew 13 contains the largest group of Matthew's kingdom of heaven parables, but when readers attempt to understand them, they usually fail to notice that the parables are themselves part of a larger narrative that is driven by the issue of understanding.[2] Attending to the dramatic representation of understanding in the larger narrative — involving Jesus, the crowd, and the disciples — raises questions about the kind of understanding appropriate to parables. Early in the narrative, our usual notions of understanding are challenged by what I have called the obstructive function of parables: "The reason I [Jesus] speak to them in parables is that 'seeing they do not perceive, and hearing they do not listen, nor do they understand'" (Matt. 13:13). Non-understanding is one function of parables. But the other function is not normal understanding; it is rather the transformation of the whole person, including the way a person sees. This has something to do with understanding, of course, but it is not what we normally mean by understanding. Matthew 13 dramatizes the problem of understanding parables.

Matthew 13 is a single narrative unit even though it is set in two places and has two different groups of characters. Within the narrative unit we find eight parables — the parables of the sower, the planted weeds, the mustard seed, the leaven, the treasure, the pearl, the fishnet, and the master of the household. Verses 1–53 constitute one continuous action, beginning by the sea, with Jesus leaving a house to sit by the sea. When a large crowd gathers, Jesus distances himself by getting into a boat, from which, still sitting, he begins to tell parables to the people who are listening as they stand on the beach. A principle of separation is established: Jesus sits, the crowd stands; Jesus is in a boat, the crowd is on the beach. At the end of his talk — which consists of a short narrative, the parable of the sower — Jesus says to the listeners, "Let anyone with ears listen!" (13:9), but we soon gather that the crowd has not heard ("hearing they do not listen, nor do they understand" 13:13).

The disciples then come out to Jesus, who is presumably still in the boat, and begin a private conversation with him, out of earshot of the crowd. Although they, too, have not understood or "heard" the parable, as we later realize, they do not hazard the question they may have wanted to ask: What does the parable mean? (In the comparable passage in Luke, they go straight to the point: the "disciples asked him what this parable meant"; Luke 8:9.) Instead, they ask a question about method rather than meaning: "Why do you speak to them [the crowd] in parables?" Jesus's answer seems to establish their separateness by attributing extraordinary gifts to the disciples. They, Jesus says, have been given to know the secrets of the kingdom of heaven, whereas the crowd has not; the disciples have blessed ears to hear and eyes to see things that not only crowds but many prophets and righteous men have not heard or seen (Matt. 13:11, 16). But seeing and hearing are not always what they seem to be. It is worth remarking that although the disciples are told that the secrets have been given to them, it is nowhere said that they have received or appropriated the gift.

In spite of his apparently flattering assessment of the disciples' gifts and blessedness, Jesus clearly assumes that the disciples have not "heard" his parable, since he then goes on to explain it, without their having to ask directly for an explanation. "Hear then," he says, and he explains the parable of the sower as an allegory about hearing and understanding. The seeds that are sown, he tells them, are the word of the kingdom of heaven. The rocky ground is the person who receives it with joy but does not allow it to take root; the seed/word survives for a short time, and when trouble or persecution comes, the person "falls away" (NRSV margin: "stumbles") or is offended (*skandalizetai*, 13:21). And the interpretation continues.

Jesus then turns to the crowd again (13:24), and the disciples continue to listen. They hear another parable about seeds—a man sows good seeds, an enemy comes along and sows weeds, and the man decides to let both grow together until harvest, when he burns the weeds and gathers the grain into his barn. Then comes a short parable about a mustard seed and another about leaven hidden in flour. Matthew then tells us that all of this is revelatory, fulfilling the words of the prophet: "I will open my mouth to speak in parables; I will proclaim what has been hidden from the foundation of the world" (13:35). Matthew says that through parables things hidden have been "proclaimed"; he does not assert that they have been "heard," or understood.

In fact, they have not, even by the disciples. After Jesus leaves the crowd and goes into the house, the disciples come to him again to continue their search for meaning. Given the context, their request—"Explain to us the parable of the weeds of the field" (13:36)—may seem odd. They have been given the secrets of the kingdom; they have blessed ears and eyes; they have had a private explanation of one parable; and they are now faced with an apparently simpler parable that can be accounted for relatively easily by the same principles as the first parable. But, in spite of these extraordinary advantages, they still do not understand. Jesus's dramatic response to their request—whether surprise, disappointment, quiet acceptance, or

whatever—is not related. We hear only his answer, again as an allegorical explanation: he who sows the good seed is the Son of Man;
the enemy who sows the weeds is the devil; the weeds are *skandala*—offenses, "causes of sin" (NRSV)—and evil-doers, which are
thrown into the furnace of fire, "where there will be weeping and
gnashing of teeth"; the wheat is the righteous. He ends by telling
the disciples what he previously told the crowd: "Let anyone with
ears listen!" (13:43). In repeating this, he now associates the disciples, as hearers, with the crowd that does not see and does not
hear—a much less flattering address than his previous assurances
that they have been given secrets and have been blessed with eyes
and ears beyond the prophets and certainly beyond the crowd.

He then tells two apparently simple parables and ends with a
still simpler one about fishing with nets, which the disciples might
be expected to find easy to understand, since it fits the pattern of the
second parable that Jesus explained and since it relates so directly to
their own knowledge as fishermen. But, in a third explanation, Jesus
spells out a meaning, apparently gratuitously, since this explanation
is in the same words as the previous explanation. With assurances
of blessed eyes and ears, a patient tutor, and solicitous explanations,
the disciples seem to be in the best of all interpretive worlds. Indeed,
Jesus's tutoring seems as much an exercise in building the disciples'
self-esteem as in training their interpretive abilities.

The teacher, however, has not finished his tutoring; he is still
solicitous. "Have you understood all this?" he asks them (13:51).
Understanding is, of course, the crucial issue. Jesus uses this verb
three times in as many verses (13:13, 14, 15) when explaining his
use of parables with the crowd, who will not understand. And when
the disciples come to him later, saying, "Explain this parable to us,"
he responds, "Are you also still without understanding?" (15:15–
16). After the fishnet parable, however, the disciples think they do
understand "all this": when Jesus asks, "Have you understood all
this?" Matthew tells us, "They answered, 'Yes'" (13:51). The instruction has apparently been successful. If the narrative concluded with
this, it would have a happy ending, denoting successful teaching
through patience and repetition to willing, if slow, students. But
there are two narrative elements that merit our attention. First,
Matthew does not affirm that the disciples understood "all this"; he
reports that they say "Yes," indicating only that they think they
understand. The narrator takes no position on the actual fact of
understanding. Second, the narrative does not end here. The story
continues, undercutting the happy ending: "And he said to them,

'Therefore every scribe who has been trained for the kingdom of heaven is like the master of a household who brings out of his treasure what is new and what is old.'" And with that, "he left that place" (13:52–53).

These proud students, so slowly and solicitously brought to apparent understanding of how to hear or read parables as simple allegories, must react with puzzlement—or perhaps astonishment—to this far from simple "therefore" followed by a new and uninterpreted parable that seems to have little in common with the earlier interpreted parables.[3] Given their problems in understanding the previous parables, it seems highly unlikely that they will know what to make of this new one. Who are the scribes? Does Jesus want the disciples to see themselves as scribes? Are the disciples being trained for the kingdom of heaven? This would seem plausible, since what has preceded this has been training in the interpretation of parables, but calling them scribes is a curious surprise. Why are they, who have left their jobs, families, and homes, compared to the master of a household? What treasure is Jesus referring to? And what is the difference between the old and the new treasure? Alas, the answers to these questions do not follow readily—or at all—from Jesus's instructions about how to hear and understand the three parables he glossed for them.

Matthew has presented the reader with a carefully crafted narrative, displaying an apparent movement of the disciples from ignorance to understanding, and back suddenly and inexplicably to the surprising possibility of ignorance once again. Most commentators and other readers do not even notice the highly dramatic role of the disciples in the context of these parables, perhaps because our attention, like the disciples', tends to be riveted on the eight parables that seem to cry out for interpretation. Matthew's readers, as readers, have not here been given secrets of the kingdom (since Matthew does not say what the secrets are) or blessed with eyes and ears beyond the prophets, but they find themselves in the position of the disciples, wondering what these parables mean and why Jesus is speaking in parables. As the disciples are puzzled and slow to learn, so are the readers; as the disciples are eager to proclaim the "Yes" of understanding in the face of repeated, simple explanations, so are the readers. As they confront a baffling new parable, recalcitrant to the easy explanations that seemed to open up the earlier parables, their presumed sense of bafflement may be the readers'. The disciples, in their dramatic context, are uncomfortably situated: theirs is no longer simple ignorance but ignorance in the face of knowledge that they have been given secrets without knowing what secrets, and that they possess blessed eyes and ears without knowing what they have seen or heard. Matthew's readers, trying to follow the disciples in their search for the meaning of the apparently simple yet enigmatic parables, are in deeper trouble, for they have not received from the text assurances of secrets or blessedness—whatever these assurances may mean—in the way the disciples have.

How do the disciples react in the face of this last, puzzling parable that does not yield its meaning readily—or in the face of the other non-interpreted parables? The narrative responds with silence. We are told that Jesus departs and goes to his hometown, Nazareth, where he continues to teach and people respond. In the Nazarene passage, however, we hear nothing about the substance of Jesus's teaching and much about the response to his teaching:

> When Jesus had finished these parables, he left that place.
> He came to his hometown and began to teach the people in their synagogue, so that they were astounded and said, "Where did this man get this wisdom and these deeds of power? Is not this the carpenter's son? Is not his mother called Mary? And are not his brothers James and Joseph and Simon and Judas? And are not all his sisters with us? Where then did this man get all this?" And they took offense at him [*eskandalizonto en autō*; literally, "they were offended in him"]. (13:53-57)

The contrast between these two sections is striking—the stuff of the training dramatized in the first, but with almost no response, and the substance of the response to, but no substance of, the teaching (only he "began to teach the people") in the second. At the end of the first passage, we have a dramatic gap: we do not know, and cannot know, what the disciples think or feel. As readers who share the disciples' puzzlement, we must enact some response ourselves. We must try to "hear," as the disciples try, and we must try to make use of Jesus's explanations, as the disciples must. A possible response to the puzzling parables for the disciple and reader is to react as the Nazarenes do—to be scandalized. The disciples and readers are looking for meaning, for explanations, for clarity, and what do they get? Little narratives or images, with realistic yet surprising and enigmatic substance and no clear meanings. And when interpretive aids are provided, offering interpretations of three parables, the aids prove not to be readily transferable, leaving disciples and readers as puzzled as before. Being offended is not a necessary reaction, but it is a possible one, as the Nazarenes dramatically attest. Teaching can be offensive business.

Meir Sternberg distinguishes Hebrew narratives from Gospel narratives by observing that "the poetics of maneuvering between the truth and the whole truth," characteristic of Hebrew narratives, is "foreign to the either/or spirit of elitism that informs the gospels" (56). In making this distinction, he is referring to the insiders and outsiders, those who are given the secrets of the kingdom (the disciples as well as Jesus) and those who are excluded (the crowd). Sternberg refers to Jesus's separation from the crowd, sitting in his boat in the sea, as "an unintentional yet deeply revealing irony" (49). This "elitism," however, has a different irony: the supposed elite—the disciples—have been given secrets but have quite evidently not received them, the extraordinary gift not generating extraordinary understanding. The disciples are in as much danger of being scandalized by the enigmatic parables as is the crowd. But, still, Sternberg is correct in a different sense about the distinction between Gospel and Hebrew narratives. The Gospel narratives are not based on a poetics of "maneuvering between the truth and the whole truth" but rather on a poetics of maneuvering between lies (as alienation from God) and truth, between offense and faith, which is indeed an either/or. It is not, however, an either/or settled once and for all: as the disciples discover, it continually repeats itself in encounters with the person or the stories of Jesus.

Interpreting the Householder

It is the nature of offense or scandal to act quickly. Consider Jesus's explanation of part of the sower parable: "As for what was sown on rocky ground, this is the one who hears the word and immediately receives it with joy; yet such a person has no root, but endures only for a while, and when trouble or persecution arises on account of the word, that person immediately falls away [*skandalizetai*: "he or she is offended"]" (13:20–21). In the rocky ground passage of the sower parable and in Jesus's explanation of it, one Greek word for "immediately" or "quickly" is used three times (13:5, 20, 21). The Nazarenes waste no time in being offended: "they were astounded," they name his relatives—ordinary folk, presumably, not the sort to be related to a truly extraordinary teacher—and "they took offense at him" (13:54–57). If the disciples choose to be scandalized by the eight parables—or, more particularly, by the parable of the master

of the household, which is somehow conclusive ("therefore . . ."), as
well as the surprise ending of the training session—they will be
scandalized immediately, only to be (in the eyes of the readers) in
the company of the scandalized Nazarenes, who are scandalized in
spite of, and because of, their closeness to Jesus ("in their own country and in their own house"; 13:57). The Nazarenes, who might
expect to be insiders, are offended. Like the crowd, they hear but do
not understand and are therefore outsiders.

Let us assume the readers do not know the secrets of the kingdom, since Matthew has not stated them explicitly. Even so, instruction in hearing parables has been explicit; the readers of Matthew 13, unlike the crowd, know as much about understanding
parables as the disciples in the narrative. What can we—or the disciples—make of the last, unexplained parable on the basis of Jesus's
instruction? "Therefore every scribe who has been trained for the
kingdom of heaven is like the master of a household who brings out
of his treasure what is new and what is old" (13:52). Jesus's method
of training in Matthew 13 is based on establishing one-to-one allegorical correspondences. In the first parable, the parable of the
sower, the unnamed seed (actually, *a* [some] and *alla* [others]) corre-
sponds to "the word of the kingdom" (13:19) as taken in by different
kinds of people (the seed in different soils). In the second interpreted
parable, the parable of the planted weeds, the good seeds "are the
children of the kingdom," whereas the "weeds" (the bad seeds) "are
the children of the evil one" (13:38). The terms seem to have shifted
here, but in fact they have not. The good seeds planted in good
soil in both parables are the same: "one who hears the word and
understands it" (13:23), which, in the plural, we may reasonably
suppose to be related to "the children of the kingdom." Unfortunately for the interpreters—disciples and readers—of the uninterpreted parable of the master of a household, there are no seeds and
no soil in it.

If we look at the second and third interpreted parables (the parables of the planted weeds and the fishnet), we see that although
there is no correspondence between the first terms (seed, enemy,
fish, etc.), there is correspondence between the second terms, those
of the interpretation. In the parable of the planted weeds, the reapers
who sort the weeds from the wheat are angels; in the parable of the
fishnet, the fishers who sort the bad from the good fish are also
angels. The angels gather out "*skandala* [causes of sin, NRSV] and
all evil-doers" in the second interpretation (13:41), and "evil" in the
third (13:49). The place where the weeds are burned is "the furnace

of fire, where there will be weeping and gnashing of teeth" (13:42); the place where the bad fish are thrown is "the furnace of fire, where there will be weeping and gnashing of teeth" (13:50).

Central to all three interpreted parables is a division into two basic categories: bad and good. The seed on the path, on rocky ground, or among thorns fails to produce fruit; the seed on good soil bears fruit. The weeds are burned; the grain is harvested. The bad fish are thrown away; the good are put in baskets. In the first, the causes of the bad are made explicit: lack of understanding (13:19), trouble or persecution, which lead to someone being scandalized (*skandalizetai*; 13:21) by the word, and cares of the world and lure of wealth (13:22). In the second and third interpretations, there is no particularity, just offenses (*skandala*) and evil-doers (13:41) and evil (13:49). An enemy has performed a scandalous action by sowing weeds in the field, but the wise sower is not scandalized; he will protect the good and have the scandalous separated from the righteous at the close of the age. The evil consequences in the first interpretation take the form of devouring or being snatched away; withering or being scandalized; and choking or unfruitfulness. In the second and third, the *skandala* are consigned to fiery furnaces, with weeping and gnashing of teeth.

All of this, however, is of very little help when it comes to interpreting the final parable. There are no divisions that invite us to attach the terms *good* and *bad*. There are no seeds or fish to help us launch an interpretation from Jesus's instructions, and there are no immediate interpretive precedents for most of what *is* here: scribes, training, treasure, new, and old. For one term there is an equivalent: "master of a household" reappears from 13:27 (where it is translated "householder," but it is the same Greek word). He is the man who sowed good seed in his field, later identified as "the Son of Man" (13:37). This is hardly a connection that leaps out at a hearer, however. Although it is a key term in the final parable ("every scribe . . . is like the master of a household"), it is buried in the middle of the earlier parable and not repeated in the interpretation ("The one who sows the good seed," not "the householder," is "the Son of Man").

If the disciples—whose training has not included the repetition of key, or less than key, terms—have a slim chance of making this connection, Matthew's hearer or reader, who has the advantage of repeated readings, is possibly in a better position. In the absence of other connections, this appears to be significant: if every scribe is like a householder, who has earlier in the instruction been identified as the Son of Man, then every scribe may be in some sense like the Son of Man. But then what? With no other clear connections in the interpreted parables, the reader might look to the parables Jesus did not interpret and take hope from the reappearance of treasure, which was found (in 13:44) even though hidden, responded to as a source of joy, and covered up again. What is new might recall the new tree, from the mustard seed, or the leavened flour, emerging from what had been hidden. What is old might recall something very old indeed—namely, "what has been hidden since the foundation of the world"—as well, perhaps, as the treasure in 13:44, which is old enough not to be known about by the present owner, who, if he only knew, would certainly not sell. And the householder bringing things out might recall other bringings-out—of fruit and grain to be harvested, the hospitable tree to be the home of birds, the leavened dough, a treasure, a pearl, and some fish.

There are, upon inspection—and, to be sure, the kind of inspection the immediate hearers, the disciples, can scarcely be expected to make—a sufficient number of correspondences here to give one hope. And yet there is a certain straining in all of this: the correspondences are not the sort to fall immediately into place in a neat one-to-one ratio to allow us to emulate the interpretive skills of Jesus. They are suggestive rather than definitive (like seed = word), forcing us back to the parables and back to our attempts to read without the help of the meanings already offered.

Finally, there is no helpful hint whatsoever for the scribes. Scribes are certainly relevant to the plight of the disciples, for it is a scribe's job to interpret—and that is precisely what they, and the readers, are left to face in the parable Jesus has left with them, as he, the master interpreter, departs to offend (as it turns out) the Nazarenes. But the disciples are not scribes in the usual sense—not experts in the law; not interpreters of the law or teachers of the law; not, certainly, professional lawyers or high-ranking members of the establishment. And not even, perhaps, writers at all, in the most literal sense of the word—not literate, not scribblers, much less scribes. But the disciples have certainly just been through "training"—albeit dubiously successful—on the subject of the kingdom of heaven (this being the seventh mention of the term within this narrative and the ninth if we count two appearances of "kingdom" by itself). "Every scribe who has been trained for the kingdom of heaven" could conceivably apply to a disciple, though it would require a radical transformation of how a disciple thinks about himself and what he is. Radical transformations do seem in order in this narrative. Consider the surprising transformation of the flour into leavened bread (did the woman really think she could hide the leaven there?); or of the insignificant grain of mustard seed into the amazing tree—host, destination, and home to birds. With these correspondences, the reader may be better situated to hear the parable but still will not be in a position to assign one-to-one, allegorical meanings, in the manner of Matthew's Jesus.

The nonscholastic reader, trained only by the master interpreter, might be led, albeit uncertainly, to possibilities raised by these correspondences. Perhaps every scribe (transformed disciple? transformed reader?) who has been trained (as interpreter? as "hearer"?) for the kingdom of heaven (which we are told—if we will only "hear"—is like a man who sowed, a grain of mustard seed which a man sowed, leaven which a woman hid, hidden treasure which a man found, a merchant in search of pearls, and a net which men throw into the sea) is like a householder (like the Son of Man, Jesus himself?) who brings out of his treasure (hidden but regarded with joy?) what is new and what is old (as new as fresh dough and as old as the foundation of the world?). Perhaps. But the master interpreter has left, and readers and disciples are on their own. If we are honest about our ability to apply the training offered in Matthew 13, we must confess that without the master interpreter, we are left in some uncertainty and doubt.

Jesus's allegorical interpretation of the three parables does not explain the parable of the master of a household or the other parables Jesus does not interpret. These uninterpreted parables are stumbling blocks (*skandala*) to the interpreter. This may seem to be an unduly pessimistic conclusion, calling into question both Jesus's abilities as teacher and ours as learners. A non-allegorical, deconstructionist reading of Matthew 13 arrives at an apparently happier conclusion. "Matthew 13 is a manual for scribal or interpretative self-development, a working template of how to be a competent scribe oneself; it is a text that leads to the production of the reader by showing narratively the way Jesus spoke and the way Matthew the narrator speaks" (Phillips, 136). There is certainly something to be said for competence: the householder whose field was perniciously sown with weeds is, like the Son of Man, competent; the angels who sort the good from the evil are competent; and we trust that Jesus is a competent interpreter of the parables he chooses to interpret. But to see Matthew 13 as a "manual" for attaining competence, given the ending of this narrative and given the disciples' later lack of competence, seems a curious sort of deconstruction.

These parables and this narrative—in spite of our heartfelt desire for competence—speak of something quite different. The three interpreted parables contain scandals—the rootless receiver of the word is scandalized in the first, the enemy performs a scandalous act in the second, and the place where scandals are thrown is identified in the second and third. The other five parables become stumbling blocks themselves insofar as they cannot be explained by Jesus's "method." Jesus forces the disciples—and Matthew forces the readers—back into the realm of non-method and non-system when confronting the other parables. Our natural, human desire for knowledge with which to interpret and for a system by which to interpret is thwarted; our yearning for kernels of meaning is undermined. If we are to "hear," we must do it without a method, without a system, without a master interpreter always providing authoritative glosses, but rather in the presence of stumbling blocks, which confront us as an offense—either away from faith or toward faith.

Interpreting Desire

I said at the outset that parables seem to cry out for explanations. Jesus, teaching the disciples, and Matthew, teaching the reader, have offered a system or method of interpretation that does not work with any certainty on the uninterpreted parables, so that the disciples and readers, at the risk of being scandalized, will be forced to something beyond method, system, or master interpreter, to "hear" the parables. What we hear will vary according to what we bring to the parable and what we encounter in the moment of the parable. What we often bring to our encounters are desires. Parables force us to enact our desires, or they allow us to "hear" and "see." In parables we confront not a message, with a neatly codified meaning (although there is a long, continuing tradition of wanting, and finding, meaning), but a story, an image, or a symbol. Consider the fifth parable in Matthew 13: "The kingdom of heaven is like treasure hidden in a field, which someone found and hid; then in his joy he goes and sells all that he has and buys that field" (13:44). This parable likens the kingdom to an unspecified treasure that is found, hid, and bought. What is hidden is revealed, only to be hidden again. The syntactic emphasis is on the treasure, but what is subordinate syntactically becomes of primary interest, partly because of the action itself but partly, too, because of the shift from past into present tense, conveying a sense of immediacy: after he found and hid (past tense) the treasure, the finder joyfully goes, sells all he has, and buys the field, all in the present tense. No motivation is given (was the man looking for treasure?); no explanation of the nature of the treasure (money? valuable minerals? artifacts?); no description of what he might do with the treasure (hoard it? sell it for a profit?); no exploration of potential ethical issues (should he inform the owner of the field of his treasure? is his purchase unscrupulous?);[4] or of the nature of the joy (allied to a desire for wealth or greed? joy untainted by desire?) The hearer is forced to fill in enough gaps to make this into a story. At the very least, the reader has to imagine why the finder covered up the treasure (e.g., we may assume that he did so to prevent the owner from knowing why he wants to buy the field, but there might be other reasons as well) and what kind of joy he feels. Without filling these minimal gaps (which is part of the act of reading), the story remains unread.

A reader must create the story and may do so in any number of ways. For example, a reader may imagine that the finder is like people we know (including perhaps ourselves) who would be overjoyed at sudden wealth; the joy of the finding exposes in the finder a latent, or not so latent, desire for wealth or treasure. The desire, projected into the narrative, is so great that the finder is willing to sell everything to obtain what is worth far more than he now possesses. On the other hand, a reader might imagine an entirely different scenario: the hidden treasure is not something ever desired or ever known about before; it is entirely new to the finder. So entranced with this discovery is the finder that he covers it up, to prevent the possibility of losing it and (without any intention to deceive the present owner, since he thinks only of his discovery and his joy), he sells everything (without considering how he is to live in the future) so that he may have the treasure—not in order to do anything with it, and not for any external end. And so on. There are many possibilities and permutations that this one-sentence anecdote may call forth from a hearer or reader.

However, one might ask, should we not be looking for allegorical equivalences instead of contemplating these as narratives, imitating Jesus's interpretive training by trying to match elements of the story with meanings? It is not, in fact, difficult to concoct a plausible allegorical interpretation of this parable, starting with the field, which Jesus said in the parable of the sower represented the world (13:38). The treasure might be the word of the kingdom (as the seed is in the parable of the sower); the covering up of the treasure might be the secrecy Jesus sometimes required from people who knew his power; the buying might be the person's acceptance of the word (salvation); and the selling might be the giving up of all worldly goods, the price of salvation.

Such a reading cannot be rejected out of hand, given Jesus's interpretations. But two things must be remembered. First, confidence in accurate interpretation came slowly—and ultimately not at all—to the disciples. They are never shown practicing accurate interpretation, and when they think they have got the rules, they discover real and formidable difficulties, and a short time later they are "still without understanding" (15:16). With the same instruction, though once removed from the scene of instruction, how can we be confident that the treasure is the word of the kingdom rather than something else? As Aquinas observed, "This treasure can be explained in many ways" (Wailes, 118). Since the disciples can never interpret allegorically themselves but have to rely on the master interpreter (who suddenly absents himself), does this not give us dramatic pause about employing the allegorical method as a way of explaining meaning, and is not this pause the appropriate effect of Matthew's dramatic narrative? Second, even if we insist on interpreting allegorically, we still have to read the parable as narrative. In order to arrive at the proposed allegorical reading above, I still had to imagine a narrative; I simply chose to alter some of the elements given in the realistic form of the narrative. Instead of a field, I had to imagine something vast and general, the world; I had to imagine an owner (God) who would not be cheated by the man's appropriation of the treasure; I had to imagine a non-greedy motivation, a non-rapacious joy, and so forth. Narratives interpreted allegorically do not cease to be narratives.

Readers, like disciples, want an easy method of interpretation, or they want somebody to do it for them. Jesus's easy method, which proves to be full of frustrations, difficulties, and inescapable uncertainties, is his potentially offensive way of teaching the disciples and readers that there is no easy method. This anti-message is itself a stumbling block. When finding the right equivalences proves hopeless, we are left with the injunction—"listen!"—and with the parables themselves.

Consider the sixth parable: "Again, the kingdom of heaven is like a merchant in search of fine pearls; on finding one pearl of great value, he went and sold all that he had and bought it" (13:45). Unlike the previous parable, which moved from past to an immediate present, this one begins in the apparent present, only to fall into the past. This fluctuation of tense—which continues in the next parable (past tense, but followed by Jesus's interpretation in the future tense)—has a disorienting effect: the parables are never quite predictable, and the hearers' or readers' attempts to systematize them, to reduce them to a single, manageable method, are subtly undermined.

But there is clearly continuity between the substance of these two parables, since both deal with treasure—the second specified as a pearl—and both involve the same actions of selling all and buying the treasure. Both play on the worldly desire of the tenth commandment without necessarily dramatizing that desire. The parable of the pearl could portray obsessive desire for fine pearls as objects, apart from their monetary value (the merchant forgoing desire for money because of his desire for the best pearl); or, it could portray the ultimate business transaction (the merchant seizing on what he sees as the chance of a lifetime, willing to sell all to make a potential killing); or it could portray a radical transformation (the "merchant in search" ceases to sell, ceases to search for goods, and gives up all when he finds the one thing *only* that is precious beyond all other goods); or whatever the reader imagines. The parable is an invitation to the reader or hearer to imagine an action that is like the kingdom of heaven and thereby to reveal not the kingdom of heaven but himself or herself. A reader devoted to the world in a certain way will imagine an action much like the world's actions, for the world is what fulfills that reader's desire. The lack of conclusion in this parable—exultation over possessing the pearl of his dreams? visions of great wealth to be gained through the pearl? deliverance from the search and from the world of buying and selling?—invites the hearer to imagine a conclusion to his or her heart's desire. As Ernst Fuchs has pointed out, we do not interpret the parable, the parable interprets us (*Studies*, 212).

The final parable of the scribe who has been trained for the kingdom is another matter, however. It does not so much invite revelations of desire as frustrate the potential interpreter, especially since the master interpreter has departed. Readers and disciples are left to their own devices and a handful of correspondences to work with. We do not know how the disciples responded to the interpretive challenge left them by their teacher at the end of this tutoring session. Matthew later relates, however, how the disciples acted during the events preceding the crucifixion. Like the Nazarenes, they were scandalized by Jesus and abandoned him in his passion. As Jesus predicts—"You will all become deserters [*skandalisthēsesthe*] because of me this night"—and in spite of Peter's scandalized protests—"Though all become deserters [*skandalisthēsontai*] because of you, I will never desert you [*skandalisthēsomai*]" (Matt. 26: 31–33)—all of the disciples are offended. They, like the Nazarenes, reject the prophet in their midst.

In Matthew 13, Jesus has left the disciples with a *skandalon* or, more precisely, with a series of *skandala*, in the form of parables. And Matthew has placed the reader in the same interpretive position as the disciples. If we are looking for codifiable meanings, perhaps the first message we should find in this narrative is that reading for codifiable meanings, and under a master tutor, will not provide us with what we need in order to "hear" parables.

Parables assert no messages. It is true that we find messages. The plants that grow up on rocky soil only to wither away under the scorching sun, when taken figuratively, convey a message—and (like other scandals) it ought to be a profoundly discomforting one. But it is nonetheless true to say that parables assert no messages. Messages of various kinds may be formulated by an interpreting reader or provided by a narrator after the end of the parable. The parable itself is a narrative, an action—not a vehicle to carry messages.

Unlike *Pilgrim's Progress, Candide, Animal Farm,* and other narratives whose characters and actions are invented and arranged to convey formulable meanings, parables are not organized to convey information or to express propositions. Parables do not "contain" knowledge; they cannot be understood as we understand a moral tale, an argument, or a statement. Parables precipitate internal action, forcing the hearer or reader to a crisis or collision that requires movement, which in New Testament terms is an either/or: either stumbling or changing-and-becoming, either enacting a lie that we desire or being transformed. And it should be said that the second alternative—changing-and-becoming, transformation, the offense toward faith—would, in Kierkegaardian terms, be a matter not simply of joy but also of fear and trembling in the seventy thousand fathoms of water.

7

The Offensive and Inoffensive Jesus

Writers, Readers, and Contexts

If Jesus was suggesting that his disciples were somehow scribes being "trained for the kingdom of heaven" (Matt. 13:52), they were not the only scribes to encounter difficulties. In his novel *If on a winter's night a traveler*, Italo Calvino relates a brief tale:

> Once—the biographers of the Prophet tell us—while dictating to the scribe Abdullah, Mohammed left a sentence half finished. The scribe, instinctively, suggested the conclusion. Absently, the Prophet accepted as the divine word what Abdullah had said. This scandalized the scribe, who abandoned the Prophet and lost his faith.
>
> He was wrong. . . . He lost his faith in Allah because he lacked faith in writing, and in himself as an agent of writing. (182)

To his credit, the scribe was capable of being scandalized; to his discredit, he lacked faith, including faith in writing. Jesus's non-metaphorical scribes were Matthew, Mark, Luke, and John. Whoever they may have been, however they understood their tasks, and in whatever order they may have written their narratives, they had an extraordinary faith in writing and in themselves as agents of writing. They were scribes of the God-man, not only telling his story but putting words into his mouth. They ran the risk of the scribe Abdullah, but they kept the faith in their subject and in themselves.

If the reader of their Gospels is spared Abdullah's offense of writing the divine word, he or she nonetheless must encounter a risk in hearing it. The Gospel narratives presuppose readers who are capable of being offended. When that capability is suppressed— whether by getting and spending, by a conviction that knowledge is empirical data, by Kierkegaard's Christendom, or whatever—the reader is not "wrong" as Calvino's offended scribe is, but rather the reader is metaphorically, in the terms of the Gospels, dead—dead in not being able to see the Light or hear the Word, dead to Truth, dead to Life. In the Gospels, the Light, Word, Truth, and Life are embodied in the person of Jesus, who poses, because of what he embodies, the possibility of offense to the reader. But the presence of Jesus, either in the narrative (to characters who encounter him) or as the narrative (to readers who encounter his story), does not determine or guarantee any particular response, whether of faith, offense, or indifference. That depends on the individual character or reader. If the response is to be faith or offense, the narrative requires a single individual, encountering the God-man in a moment of crisis like that of Calvino's scribe.

All readers select as they read. Some readers of the Gospels go to the extreme of selecting a Jesus who is essentially, or even exclusively, peaceful, loving, and gentle. They ignore, minimize, or interpret in beneficent ways the Jesus of the hard sayings ("Do not think that I have come to bring peace to the earth; I have not come to bring peace, but a sword[,] . . . to set a man against his father, and a daughter against her mother"; Matt. 10:34–35), the Jesus of violent images (people thrown "where there will be weeping and gnashing of teeth"; Matt. 8:12 and five other places in Matthew), the Jesus of violent action ("he overturned the tables of the money changers and the seats of those who sold doves"; Matt. 21:12). And some readers minimize or subordinate the Jesus who weeps, has compassion, loves the weak and the outcast (a potential scandal in itself), and celebrates the meek.

William Blake reads the Bible through his principle of Contraries: "Attraction and Repulsion, Reason and Energy, Love and Hate, are necessary to Human Existence" (*The Marriage of Heaven and Hell*, plate 3). Jesus is the Lamb of Innocence ("For he calls himself a Lamb: / He is meek & he is mild, / He became a little child"; *Songs of Innocence and of Experience*, plate 8) *and* the Wrath:

Thunders & lightnings broke around
And Jesus voice in thunders sound

Thus I seize the Spiritual Prey
Ye smiters with disease make way . . .
And bursting forth his furious ire
Became a Chariot of fire
Throughout the land he took his course
And traced diseases to their source
He cursd the Scribe & Pharisee
Trampling down Hipocrisy.
>   (*Poetry and Prose*, "The Everlasting Gospel," 515)

Blake's Jesus is an oxymoron, a spiritual body, an embodiment of Contraries: "I am sure This Jesus will not do / Either for Englishman or Jew." (*Poetry and Prose*, "The Everlasting Gospel," 796)

Blake's way of proclaiming his vision of Contraries is "by printing in the infernal method by corrosives, which in Hell are salutary and medicinal, melting apparent surfaces away, and displaying the infinite which was hid" (*Marriage*, plate 14). The salutary and medicinal corrosive is literally the acid working on the copper plates of his engravings, but it is also the scandal of his Contraries, which requires that both the Prolific and the Devourer be celebrated: "whoever tries to reconcile them seeks to destroy existence. Religion is an effort to reconcile the two. Note. Jesus Christ did not wish to unite but to separate them, as in the Parable of sheep and goats! & he says I came not to send Peace but a Sword" (*Marriage*, plates 16–17). Blake's illuminated works have much in common, as he views them, with parables: they are scandalous revelations of the infinite, which has been hidden.

But the method of the Gospels is not Blake's method of lyrical and dramatic poetry, engraved with corrosives; the Gospels proclaim a scandalous Jesus through narratives. The narrative forms are essential in the Gospels for holding what Kierkegaard called the "frightful collisions" (*Attack*, 190) of Jesus, who exists in narratives not to be interpreted partially, systematically, or at all, but who is proclaimed in order to provoke response, specifically a response away from faith or toward faith.

When Gospel narratives, including Jesus's parables, are removed from their contexts, the grounds for response are removed. This happens most obviously in the liturgy and in biblical criticism that takes the pericope—a selection or extract, something cut out of its context, literally "a cutting around"—as its basic unit of investigation. Of course, it will be argued that selection is a pragmatic necessity, and I confess that it is hard to say how worship or scholarship is to take place without it. But it is worth remembering that the

Gospels were not written for worship, as we normally understand the word, or for scholarship and that the loss of narrative context carries serious risks. Parables, especially, are victims of their own success. They are good stories in their own right, apart from their teller or their audiences within the Gospels. They take on lives of their own, the same parable sometimes sloughing off entirely different contexts in different Gospels.

All parables, not just those of Matthew 13, depend on contexts. Originally, they were part of an oral context that is now altogether irrecoverable: the tone of Jesus's voice; the place of the parable within Jesus's whole discourse (what the parable follows and precedes); the mood, character, and receptivity of the audience, and so on.[1] Assuming that the parables were actually spoken by the historical Jesus, each telling of a parable would have had a different context, and the parable itself—even if told in exactly the same words—would be a different thing on each occasion because of the differing contexts and audiences and manners of speech. In contrast, the *literary* contexts crafted by the authors of the Gospels replace the ever-changing oral contexts with something much more static. The words are frozen on the page, and the cast of characters, the actions, and the ideas exist only through these words embedded in their never-changing contexts. But readers or listeners will nonetheless "hear" them differently, and it is only through reading or listening that they are brought to life. The life of any one of the Gospel parables now necessarily depends on its situation within the Gospel. Written parables are not separate, isolated units; their effects—different though they will be for different readers—depend on their literary contexts.

In order to illustrate the interactions within narrative contexts, and the ways in which context controls response, I have selected—and, yes, cut out from its context—a passage, Matthew 17:22–18:35, that includes various smaller narratives. The entire passage includes two important parables—the parables of the lost sheep and the unforgiving slave—as well as important appearances of *skandalon*, the meaning of which also depends on context, and an important discourse on the kingdom of heaven, or "life," which is the central subject of most parables.

Jesus's audience in this passage is the disciples; there are no crowds and no Pharisees present, unlike the story in Matthew 15 that we considered in chapter 2. But within this passage, the audience shifts—from all the disciples to one (Simon Peter), back to all, and finally to one again, this time with the others present as auditors. As readers outside the narrative action, we, too, are members of the audience — Matthew's audience. We listen to Jesus along with the disciples, but we observe, rather than participate in, the drama of Jesus's interaction with the disciples. As observers, we are in a sense more privileged than the disciples: we may see connections among the various concepts woven into the entire passage — concepts of community ("two or three . . . gathered in my name") and isolation (the lost sheep or brother); of "life" (the kingdom of heaven) and death (drowning with a millstone around the neck, or Gehenna — hell — the place of fire[2]); of offending and not offending; and of forgiving and not forgiving. As we observe the larger narrative involving the tax collectors, Jesus, and the disciples, we are less likely to find Jesus (or Matthew) building a system, argument, or doctrine than if we limited ourselves to one pericope. Instead, the interactions among the various parts suggest problems, contradictions, and possibilities of offense that are characteristic of Jesus's way of teaching.

I quote the passage in full in order to call attention to the appearances of the Greek *skandal-* as well as to prepare the way for exploring the interactions within this part of Matthew's Gospel:

As they [the disciples] were gathering in Galilee, Jesus said to them, "The Son of Man is going to be betrayed into human hands, and they will kill him, and on the third day he will be raised." And they were greatly distressed.

When they reached Capernaum, the collectors of the temple tax came to Peter and said, "Does your teacher not pay the temple tax?" He said, "Yes, he does." And when he came home, Jesus spoke of it first, asking, "What do you think, Simon [i.e., Simon Peter]? From whom do kings of the earth take toll or tribute? From their children or from others?" When Peter said, "From others," Jesus said to him, "Then the children are free. However, so that we do not give offense [*skandalisōmen*] to them, go to the sea and cast a hook; take the first fish that comes up; and when you open its mouth, you will find a coin; take that and give it to them for you and me."

At that time the disciples came to Jesus and asked, "Who is the greatest in the kingdom of heaven?" He called a child, whom he put among them, and said, "Truly I tell you, unless you change and become like children, you will never enter the kingdom of heaven. Whoever becomes humble like this child is the greatest in the kingdom of heaven. Whoever welcomes one such child in my name welcomes me.

"If any of you put a stumbling block [*skandalisē*] before one of these little ones who believe in me, it would be better for you if a great millstone were fastened around your neck and you were drowned in the depth of the sea. Woe to the world because of stumbling blocks [*skandalōn*]! Occasions for stumbling [*skandala*] are bound to come, but woe to the one by whom the stumbling block [*skandalon*] comes!

"If your hand or your foot causes you to stumble [*skandalizei*], cut it off and throw it away; it is better for you to enter life maimed or lame than to have two hands or two feet and to be thrown into the eternal fire. And if your eye causes you to stumble [*skandalizei*], tear it out and throw it away; it is better for you to enter life with one eye than to have two eyes and to be thrown into the hell [NRSV margin: "Gehenna"] of fire.

"Take care that you do not despise one of these little ones; for, I tell you, in heaven their angels continually see the face of my Father in heaven. What do you think? If a shepherd has a hundred sheep, and one of them has gone astray, does he not leave the ninety-nine on the mountains and go in search of the one that went astray? And if he finds it, truly I tell you, he rejoices over it more than over the ninety-nine that never went astray. So it is not the will of your Father in heaven that one of these little ones should be lost.

"If another member of the church [NRSV margin: "If your brother"] sins against you, go and point out the fault when the two of you are alone. If the member listens to you, you have regained that one. But if you are not listened to, take one or two others along with you, so that every word may be confirmed by the evidence of two or three witnesses. If the member refuses to listen to them, tell it to the church; and if the offender refuses to listen even to the church, let such a one be to you as a Gentile and a tax collector. Truly I tell you, whatever you bind on earth will be bound in heaven, and whatever you loose on earth will be loosed in heaven. Again, truly I tell you, if two of you agree on earth about anything you ask, it will be done for you by my Father in heaven. For where two or three are gathered in my name, I am there among them."

Then Peter came and said to him, "Lord, if another member of the church [NRSV margin: "if my brother"] sins against me, how often should I forgive? As many as seven times?" Jesus said to him, "Not seven times, but, I tell you, seventy-seven times.

"For this reason the kingdom of heaven may be compared to a king who wished to settle accounts with his slaves. When he began the reckoning, one who owed him ten thousand talents was brought to him; and, as he could not pay, his lord ordered him to be sold, together with his wife and children and all his possessions, and payment to be made. So the slave fell on his knees before him, saying, 'Have patience with me, and I will pay you everything.' And out of pity for him, the lord of that slave released him and forgave him the debt. But that same slave, as he went out, came upon one of his fellow slaves who owed him a hundred denarii; and seizing him by the throat, he said, 'Pay what you owe.' Then his fellow slave fell down and pleaded with him, 'Have patience with me, and I will pay you.' But he refused; then he went and threw him into prison until he would pay the debt. When his fellow slaves saw what had happened, they were greatly distressed, and they went and reported to their lord all that had taken place. Then his lord summoned him and said to him, 'You wicked slave! I forgave you all that debt because you pleaded with me. Should you not have had mercy on your fellow slave, as I had mercy on you?' And in anger his lord handed him over to be tortured until he would pay his entire debt. So my heavenly Father will also do to every one of you, if you do not forgive your brother or sister from your heart."

Meanings in this passage do not become static teachings or doctrines. The reappearances of the same things—money (in the temple tax and slaves' debts), violence (in the prophesied death of Jesus, the millstone, and the torture of the debtors), and concern for others (tax collectors, children, lost sheep, brothers, slaves in debt)—interact in this narrative to unsettle teachings, lest they become objective doctrines, and to provoke listeners to listen with ears that hear, or do not hear.

Offenses from Within and Without

Some scandals in this passage are marked by a form of the Greek *skandal-*, and some exist only in the dramatic action. The first one signaled by the Greek term concerns the annual temple tax. When confronted by the collectors of the temple tax, Peter gives an inoffensive answer to their question about whether Jesus will pay. "Yes," he says, though it turns out that he is speaking without authority and that the proper answer—following Jesus's line of argument about the children of kings—ought to be "No." But, as it happens, Jesus rejects the line of his own argument; he, like Peter, does not want to offend the tax collectors. To avoid offense or scandal, Jesus will pay for himself and for Peter, but it will in fact cost them nothing, since the required coin will be provided in the mouth of a fish. Jesus deliberately chooses the role of an inoffensive, non-scandalous Jewish male, willing to support the temple by paying money, even though by some logic he could be considered free from the taxation. In refusing to scandalize the collectors and temple authorities, he affirms Peter's initial, inoffensive response to the collectors.

Having established dramatically his own opposition to being offensive, Jesus reinforces his opposition by denouncing those who scandalize "little ones" and by generalizing about offenses ("Woe to the world because of *skandala*!"; 18:7). Part of the teaching is that scandals are necessary, with the implication that the misery associated with them (the "woe") is inevitable. There are, indeed, some forms of misery within this passage. In 17:23, the disciples are distressed to hear Jesus's prophecy of his death and his rising (Paul's scandal of the cross in Gal. 5:11); and in 18:31, the fellow slaves are distressed when the unforgiving slave puts his debtor in jail (which the fellow slaves find offensive, leading them to report it to the king). In both cases the same phrase is used, "They were greatly distressed," thus bracketing the discourse on offense by dramas of distress. In these dramas, the disciples and the slaves recognize a scandal when they see one; they are not blind or unfeeling. Within their respective communities, of Jesus and the king, they acknowledge the "woe" that is inevitable by seeing a scandal and being distressed over it. They are not themselves the primary actors in the offenses, and they do not stumble, but they are participants, part of the misery that scandal can and will bring.

Although Jesus deliberately avoids scandalizing the authorities by paying the temple tax and claims that it is better for a person to drown with a millstone around the neck than to scandalize little ones, he is himself the source of offense. In one of the most notoriously offensive passages in the New Testament, Jesus discourses on offense, specifically on offending oneself: "if your hand or your foot causes you to stumble [or "offends you"], cut it off and throw it away."

Offenses of the world are created by individuals and responded to by individuals. In the case involving the person who deserves the millstone and the little ones who are scandalized, the offender and the offended are different individuals. But this is not always so. We have observed (in chapter 2) the phenomenon of the offended being also the offender. Jesus's discourse in Matthew returns to this idea. Our own hand, our foot, and our eye may scandalize us, ourselves; that is, what we do, where we choose to go, and how we see (which will determine what we see) may be our self-created and self-determining scandals. When this happens, we are confronted (whether we are aware of it or not) with the choice of "life" or the Gehenna of fire (18:8–9). The choice, when presented this way, is clear enough: "life," even if we are physically maimed in a gruesome way, is infinitely preferable to the Gehenna of fire. To "enter life" (18:8, 9) is clearly something other than being born into physical life; the "life" one enters is identified in 18:3 as the kingdom of heaven (literally "heavens"). The relationships among entering life, bringing *skandala*, encountering *skandala*, and responding to *skandala* are the subjects of Jesus's discourse to the disciples.

Jesus's talk about cutting off the hand or foot or tearing out the eye is sometimes cited as the prime example of the inhumane, indeed monstrous, logic of a Christian teaching of brutality and masochism. It is indeed a violent and scandalous series of images. Whether we stumble over it depends on how we read it. In the context of Jesus's teaching about transformation ("unless you change and become like children"; 18:3) and about not scandalizing and being scandalized in a world where scandals are inevitable (18:7), we are confronted with various possibilities. First, we might read the passage as saying that the proposed maiming, terrible though it is, is the authorized teaching, in some sense deserved (because of the sins of the hand, foot, or eye), and therefore acceptable. Or, second, we might reject the passage as a monstrous and offensive teaching that any right-thinking, decent person ought to be scandalized by. Third, we might consider that in its hypothetical literalness, it is a form of the Hebrew stumbling block—idolatry—that is not to be stumbled over. And, finally (though other alternatives exist), we can escape all of the above choices, and the offenses they entail, through a figurative interpretation that substitutes another, less offensive, object for foot, hand, and eye.

Interpreting this passage has significant consequences. People do maim themselves on the basis of these words, and people are offended, put off, turned off. Accepting my first, apparently literal, alternative has the built-in problem of requiring a kind of idolization of the foot, hand, and eye—that is, investing them with extraordinary powers that they do not by themselves possess. In the preceding verses, the cause of stumbling is a person ("If any of you put a stumbling block . . ."; 18:6); here, however, the cause has been hypothetically reduced to one part of the offended person's own body. If the reader takes this in the most literal way, he or she may say that the foot literally causes one to stumble by bumping into a rock or going into a hole. Does the foot itself cause the stumbling or do the offending? As expert as many of us are at disengaging ourselves from responsibility for error, we do not usually find it convincing to blame our right foot for pressing too hard on the accelerator when we get a speeding ticket. To take offense at the foot requires granting the foot the power of intentionality. The isolating of the foot can be done, to be sure, by cutting it off (as the teaching appears to recommend), but in that case it ceases to be even a minor part of a person's intentional activity. But people do read the passage in this way, and when they act on it, with bloody consequences, they invariably succeed in scandalizing people, violating Jesus's and Paul's injunction (discussed in chapter 3): do not offend.

Accepting the second alternative—that this is a monstrous and offensive teaching—is a more attractive alternative because of its commonsense shunning of the fanatical. And yet to be offended by this patently scandalous saying is to be so in the midst of a passage that dramatically opposes scandalizing or being scandalized.

A third alternative is to recognize the scandal and not be offended ("And blessed is anyone who takes no offense at me"; Matt. 11:6). A careful literal reading will pay attention to the hypothetical *if*: *if* the hand itself offends or causes the scandal, cut it off. But this will happen only if we miss the mark widely, perhaps insanely, by idolizing the hand as an independent member. And, by implication, if the hand (or foot or eye) does not offend or cause the scandal, do not cut it off.[3] The hypothetical violence invites the reader to recognize the crucial choice—the choice of life as opposed to the Gehenna of fire—by acknowledging that grotesque physical maiming is far preferable to spiritual death. But at the same time it posits the possibility of idolizing a physical object (hand, foot, or eye). The same possibility of offense that exists in Isaiah and Ezekiel reappears in Matthew.

A fourth alternative is to interpret the hand, foot, or eye as a reference to something else, as Origen, for example, years after his self-castration (following Matt. 19:12), interpreted them to refer to separate individuals, offensive members of the church, who should be "cut off" by being driven out of the church.[4] We have seen Paul giving similar advice in a direct, literal way: "Drive out the wicked person from among you" (1 Cor. 5:13). And, indeed, we find Jesus saying something similar a few sentences later, in a figurative way, about the "member of the church" or "brother" ("Let such a one be to you as a Gentile and a tax collector"; Matt. 18:17). A figurative application is certainly plausible and appealing. But, in contrast to a more literal reading, Origen's figurative reading removes the offense from oneself and attaches it to another, and it therefore carries little offensive power. The weakly offensive reading stands in striking contrast to Jesus's offensiveness. It robs the text, which is asserting the inevitability of scandal, of its dramatic *skandalon*.

Jesus, deliberately inoffensive toward the temple tax collectors, then inoffensive toward the disciples, becomes decidedly and notoriously offensive to the disciples and, through Matthew's story, to the readers of the Gospel. Clearly, choosing not to offend is only one strategy in the world; choosing to offend is another, at least for Jesus. But his aim is not to teach the disciples to live inoffensively or to live offensively; it is to bring them to live. And they cannot live, or enter the kingdom, without encountering the offense. Nor can Matthew's reader.

Luke's question, "How do you read?" (RSV, Luke 10:26), is always pertinent in the Gospels. Or, to pose the question in the terms of this passage, "What do you think?" (or, literally, "How does it seem to you?"), as Jesus asks twice, first of Simon Peter (17:25) and next of all the disciples (18:12). It is entirely possible that Jesus (or Matthew, as scribe) may offend some little one, and the offense might be away from faith, which is the contrary of the other, "blessed" alternative, toward faith. Jesus is like the one who deserves a millstone around the neck in that he, too, brings offenses, but he differs importantly in that his offenses are necessary in order for a person to turn toward faith. Jesus's offenses are made offensive not by Jesus but by the stumbler. The stumbler's fall will come about, in the presence of an offense, because of what he thinks of it, or what it seems to be to her, or how the reader reads. It is not in this passage a matter of knowledge or teaching or doctrine but of transformation: to "change and become." Changing-and-becoming is not the assimilation of doctrine in this passage; it is nothing less than entering life.

Thus, several principles about the *skandalon* are established in these passages: scandals are necessary and inevitable; scandals cause misery; the bringer of scandals is the object of misery; and scandals of the world come from oneself as well as from others. Jesus teaches, by example and precept, that individuals should not bring scandal to others (here, tax collectors, little ones, and brothers) or to themselves. And he seems also to do what he condemns: he brings scandal to his disciples (as Matthew does to the reader), but with the hope that the individuals who encounter the scandal will not be scandalized.

Curiously enough, Matthew is not content with only one version of this scandal. The offensive passage about hand, foot, and eye in 18:8–9 is a modified repetition of a similar passage in 5:29–30, which is about the "right eye" and "right hand" but contains much of the same language ("tear it out and throw it away . . . cut it off and throw it away") and is equally scandalous. The eye is the primary part in Matthew 5 because Jesus is redefining adultery: "But I say to you that everyone who looks at a woman with lust has already committed adultery with her in his heart" (5:28). As in the earlier cases of Israelite idolatry, the object of desire is the *skandalon*, and it comes from within. Jesus makes this clear (through the phrase "in his heart") at the same time as he posits, hypothetically, a cause of stumbling in the right eye or right hand. In both Matthew 5 and 18, the stumbling block is posited in a way that can cause stumbling; the *skandalon* scandalizes.

It is tempting to wish these scandals away. The notes to the *Jerusalem Bible* assert that the scandalous sayings in 18:8–9 "have been inserted into this passage at the expense of the context," but I see no sign of a dozing editor at work here. The stumbling blocks or offenses *within* oneself are entirely relevant to the subjects that immediately follow these verses: the person who despises little ones, the sinning church member or brother, and the unforgiving slave. All three are subject to offenses from within rather than offenses from some other individual who causes them to stumble.

How Does It Seem to You?

In the temple tax episode, Jesus says that "the children [of kings] are free" from taxation, and he implies that he should be free. "However," he adds enigmatically, "so that we do not give offense to them," he will not press publicly the issue of whether he is the child of a king. He will pay, and avoid scandal. The reasoning that would offend the tax collectors is not made explicit to them or to Simon Peter or to the reader, thereby leaving us in doubt about who are children of kings and who are not. We know only that the children are free in (obscure) theory but not, in this case, in practice.

There is a strong implication here of what Kierkegaard calls the essential offense of loftiness, of Jesus claiming to be the God-man and thereby offending the tax collectors. But Kierkegaard refers to this particular moment as the nonessential offense against the establishment, what he calls the historical offense. The basic issue, he says, is whether Jesus as mere man will collide with tax collectors, who represent the established order. The hidden, analogical reasoning behind his decision not to offend, however, hints at the essential offense, and his way of paying the tax—taking the coin out of the mouth of a fish—carries with it a possibility of essential offense. As Kierkegaard observes, "He does, to be sure, pay the tax, but he procures the coin by means of a miracle, that is, he shows himself to be the God-man" (*Practice*, 93). Of course, the tax collectors do not know of the unorthodox source of the coin and that the tax costs Jesus nothing at all.[5] But Peter, who must have been shocked by the uncanny timing of Jesus's question about taxes ("And when [Peter] came home, Jesus spoke of it *first*"; 17:25), is now sent on the bizarre errand of fetching a certain coin from the mouth of a fish in the sea, which is apparently waiting uncannily for Peter's hook. And Matthew's readers know the source of the coin as well; for us, unlike the tax collectors, the possibility of essential offense is flagrant.

Abruptly, with the tax issue resting in its uneasy stasis as an offense to avoid offense, Jesus is presented with a question from all of the disciples: "Who is the greatest in the kingdom of heaven?" The disciples are slow to learn that the important thing is *being* in the kingdom of heaven and that to worry about degree in the kingdom (who is the greatest?) can only be a stumbling block to entering. Jesus tries, once again, to teach them, this time by dramatically setting a child in their midst and telling them, "unless you change and become like children, you will never enter the kingdom of heaven." Only then does he answer their question: "Whoever becomes humble like this child is the greatest in the kingdom of heaven." To enter, you must be like children, and if you are like this child (a generic but particular child, with no distinguishing characteristics), you will be the greatest. The formula makes the degree meaningless; the only thing is to enter into the kingdom, to live. Their question itself is a stumbling block for the disciples, but Jesus refrains, once again, from giving offense. He might have chided them for their obtuseness, as he does on occasion—"Do you still not perceive?" (Matt. 16:9)—which would be like saying to the temple tax collectors, "Do you not perceive that I, as the son of a king, do not need to pay the tax?" Both the disciples and the collectors would probably have to respond, "No, we do not." But in this case, instead of challenging, provoking, or offending, he answers the misguided question in an inoffensive way, rendering the issue of degree meaningless and showing (as well as saying) something quite different about the kingdom of heaven.[6]

In adopting an inoffensive stance toward the disciples, Jesus is trying to bring them to life by making certain distinctions and breaking others down. His habit of saying that x is like y, which we often see in the parables, is a way of breaking down useless, possibly pernicious distinctions and thus opening the possibility for his disciples, and Matthew's readers, to perceive in a different way. In this passage, Jesus breaks down the distinction between children and disciples (or "whoever"; 18:4). He then proceeds to break down the distinction between himself and children ("Whoever welcomes one such child in my name welcomes me"; 18:5). "Little ones" becomes Jesus's referent not only for the actual child who has been dramatically pulled into their midst but also for "whoever becomes humble like this child" and for people of whatever size or age "who believe in me" (18:4, 6). Both disciples and readers know the difference between child and adult, but now they are invited not to know the difference and to be like little ones in order to enter the kingdom of heaven. This does not involve knowing or grasping or understanding concepts; it involves an action. The disciples must "change and become like children."

Enacting, however, cannot exist apart from seeing, hearing, and responding. Hence Jesus's question that is repeated twice in this passage, first to Peter about the temple tax and then to the disciples about the lost sheep: "What do you think?" or, more literally, "How does it seem to you?" Sometimes when Jesus asks a question, he pauses for an answer—as with Simon Peter, who does indeed provide an answer (right in theory but wrong in practice) about the temple tax. In asking the disciples about the one sheep out of a hundred that goes astray, however, Jesus does not pause for an answer. He answers himself, though again in the form of a question: "Does he [the shepherd] not leave the ninety-nine on the mountains and go in search of the one that went astray?" The grammatical form in the Greek presupposes an affirmative answer, but surely the prudent response of a person who cares about sheep might be to ask more questions. Is this shepherd tending all one hundred sheep by himself? If he leaves the ninety-nine spread over mountains (note the alarming plural), is there a chance that he may lose some or many of the ninety-nine sheep while he is looking for the one? If so, might not a shepherd reasonably consider the option of not going, or of seeking help before he goes? Jesus's own answer contains problems of theory and practice about saving lost sheep or lost little ones.

Jesus himself raises the problem inherent in his answer through the phrase "if he finds it" (18:13). Finding the lost sheep is not guaranteed; the shepherd indeed may not find it, in which case there will be no rejoicing. If the shepherd leaves ninety-nine sheep on the mountains for a time, he may return to even more distress. This parable of apparent losing, finding, and rejoicing has, within its narrative, a shadow side. How does it seem to you? It may seem like an entirely happy story, but only if you are not willing to encounter potential offense. The good news is stated negatively: "So it is *not* the will of your Father in heaven that one of these little ones should be lost" (18:14). The bad news is not stated at all, but it is a corollary of the negation: it is not the Father's will, but it may happen anyway. The narrative makes it clear that God's will does not determine the outcome. In the following actions in the chapter, the sinning brother may choose to listen or not, the king may choose to forgive or not, and the slave likewise.

The parable of the lost sheep, like the hand, foot, and eye passage, is a kind of snare or trap. It offers a straightforward assertion that disciples and readers can ignore only at risk of life ("do not despise one of these little ones"), but the narrative—with its questions ("What do you think?" "does he not leave . . ."), its hypothetical qualifier ("if he finds it . . ."), and its negations ("does he not leave . . . it is not the will . . .")—supports the assertion at the same time as it raises unsolved problems about the practice and effects of not despising, which are themselves vitally important to life.

These problems, it is true, are buried under apparent rejoicing. But if it seems simple—a matter merely of seeking, finding, and rejoicing—read on in the Gospel. The buried problems become explicit in the following passages and downright disturbing to Peter.

The Sublime and the Bathetic

In the passage about the sinning brother (Matt. 18:15-17),[7] Jesus continues to develop the idea of the broken community—of going astray, which for humans, unlike sheep, involves scandals. To this he, as speaker (or Matthew, as author), adds the issue of forgiveness, which he will develop through the rest of the chapter. Moving from the lost sheep to the sinning brother is an appropriate next step in the exposition. Jesus has talked about scandalizing little ones, about scandalizing oneself (a potential little one), about sheep and little ones going astray, and now about "your brother"—another potential little one—going astray. The implicit uncertainty about whether the sheep will be found is here explicit. Given that he has gone astray, the question is, what can be done to regain him as a brother, as part of a community? The progressive steps—talk to him alone, with one or two others, and finally with the church—offer three opportunities for the lost brother to listen. You can regain him as a brother only if he chooses. You can provide the opportunity by telling him his fault, but only he can decide to become a "brother," which will then be your gain (18:15). Just as the disciples must change and become like children, he must change and become a brother. If he refuses three times, "let such a one be to you as a

Gentile and a tax collector," that is, perhaps, as a foreigner and someone who exploits and abuses you (Patte, 253), or as outsiders, though it should be noted that we have just witnessed a dramatic example of how Jesus decides to treat tax collectors—inoffensive-ly—and, in Matthew 5:43–47, Gentiles and tax collectors are Jesus's illustrations for his hard saying, "Love your enemies and pray for those who persecute you." The effect of this apparently formulaic procedure is a binding (gaining a brother, who becomes part of a gathering) or a loosing (letting him go as an outsider). The effect is more complex than that of the parable of the lost sheep because there is a new element for the strayer: choice.

With the binding and loosing theme (18:18), Jesus returns to and develops the obscure, truncated reasoning about earth and heaven of the temple tax episode. What is bound or loosed on earth (as a result of the brother's decision) will be bound or loosed in heaven (or, more accurately, "will be what has been" bound or loosed). Fur-thermore, "if two of you agree on earth about anything you ask, it will be [what has been] done for you by my Father in heaven." There is no conclusion to the discourse about the sinning brother, but the possibility is raised that he could choose to become a brother within a gathering—two or three people or a church. In such a gathering, agreement and asking are associated with activity "by my Father in heaven." Human agreement is intimately bound with God's activity. The obscure logic of the temple tax narrative and Jesus's identifica-tion of binding and loosing as the same on earth and in heaven begin to demolish the distinctions between earth and heaven as separate places. And the third assertion continues the demolition: "For where two or three are gathered in my name, I am there among them" (18:20)—a statement that can only jolt the hearer out of an ordinary sense of location.[8]

In order to teach the disciples about the kingdom of heaven, Jesus had brought a child "among them" (18:2). Having identified the disciples and then himself with this child, he now generalizes to all gatherings that constitute the kingdom of heaven. Like the actual child now among them, Jesus will be present in the gathering, and his Father will have made what the gathered (little ones, or brothers) have agreed on and asked for into divine enactments.

The narrative has arrived at a profound moment: Matthew has woven together Jesus's actions, statements, and metaphors into a teaching about "life" that transcends the limits of earthly time and space. Jesus has presented his hearers with paradoxical teachings about himself as child, about himself as a presence within a community of gatherers, and about life on earth as an enactment of the kingdom of heaven. But this moment of sublime teaching does not last, for then (18:21) Peter interjects a question that has nothing to do with these matters. Sublimity turns into bathos as Peter puzzles over a number (How many times shall I forgive my brother—seven?), which is similar to the disciples' earlier concern about degree (Who is the greatest?).

Peter's non sequitur is a delayed reaction to the discourse about the sinning brother, as his repetition ("If my brother") indicates. In Jesus's discourse, the brother sinned, and the listener is enjoined to provide repeated opportunities for brotherhood. Peter's response reveals the beauty of and the trouble with the specific in anecdote and narrative: whatever is concrete and solid can impress itself upon the imagination, but it also can become a stumbling block. Since Jesus's method for attempting to regain the brother had three steps, Peter tries to get a clear rule about number—one that can be understood easily and thus make clearer the way to the kingdom of heaven. Furthermore, he wants to clear up what happens if the brother keeps sinning: "Lord, if my brother sins against me, how often should I forgive? As many as seven times?"

Peter, in his obsession with number, has blundered into a sublime discourse whose mystery is expressed in numbers (two or three is really, with Jesus, three or four). The numbers—telling the brother three times, and the gathering of two or three—are not in themselves traps at all, but Peter makes them into traps. His proposal of forgiving seven times may seem to him to be generous indeed, but Jesus, who might be provoked legitimately by such numerical obtuseness, rejects Peter's number of seven and offers him an alternative idol: seventy-seven, or seventy times seven. It matters little which, since either is likely to be scandalous to a man who thought of seven as many. Peter has created his own trap or stumbling block, and Jesus, in response, has offered a scandalously large number, which might encourage his obsession or destroy it. But, as if this numerical excess were not enough for Peter or the reader, what follows offers a comparable excess—but in the opposite direction.

The Unforgiving Slave

Jesus's next phrase, "for this reason," suggests that he is about to develop the theme of unlimited forgiveness (or forgiving seventy-seven times), and his entire sentence—"For this reason the kingdom of heaven may be compared to a king who wished to settle accounts

with his slaves"—seems to promise a continuation of his inter-
rupted, sublime theme, the kingdom of heaven on earth, as part of a
narrative about someone (like Peter) who wants to "settle accounts."
In fact, the parable is about a king who forgives someone not three
times, or seven times, or seventy-seven times, but *once*. When the
slave sins (once) after having been forgiven his debt, the king throws
him in jail, apparently forever—until he pays back the equivalent of
millions of dollars.

The parable of the unforgiving slave and the once-forgiving king
is an integral part of the larger narrative not because it relates logically (as the phrase "for this reason" might suggest) to what precedes
it, or because it is a necessary step in the narrative, or because it
fulfills Peter's—or the reader's—expectations, but because it comments on what has gone before and modifies it drastically, even
undermines it. The parable of the unforgiving slave is an integral
part of an unfolding drama of enactment that involves Jesus, the
disciples, and the reader.

We readers are placed in a position similar to Peter, trying to
grasp Jesus's teachings about the kingdom of heaven, and, like Peter,
we may be trying too hard, not hard enough, or in the wrong way.
But whether or not we are like Peter in wanting to nail down the
exact number of times for forgiveness, we are like him in that we
cannot expect to understand Jesus's words without enactment. This
parable offers an enactment of changing and becoming in one relatively laconic sentence: "And out of pity for him, the lord of that
slave released him and forgave him the debt" (18:27). The debt, it is
important to note, is the equivalent of roughly ten million dollars.
The king's first impulse, when the slave was brought to him, is to
sell the slave, his wife, his children, and his possessions, since the
slave could not repay the money. The slave's plea for patience and
his promise to repay all the money lead to a startling, unexpected
turn of events: the king does not accede to the request that he be
patient but instead cancels the debt of ten million dollars. He does
this "out of pity" and for no other reason. He apparently does not
consider what has happened to the money, whether the slave has
used it for good or ill, whether the slave regrets the loss of the
king's money, and so on. It is an extreme, unworldly, unexpected,
un-asked-for, nearly unthinkable, and certainly irrational act of forgiveness. And undeserved, as the slave proves when he cruelly ("seizing him by the throat") refuses to forgive a fellow slave a much
smaller amount (tens rather than millions of dollars) and has him
put into prison until the debt is paid.

The king enacts extraordinary forgiveness toward the slave, but when the servant refuses to enact the same forgiveness toward his fellow servant, the king enacts the servant's actions: he puts him in jail until he pays the debt.[9] The king is capable of anger as well as pity, of punishment as well as forgiveness. He acts not on one principle but successively on radically different principles: first, the principle of expedient recovery, by proposing to sell the slave, his family, and his possessions; second, the principle of following his heart ("pity") without restraint; and, third, the principle of reciprocity, of punishment in kind, in exact imitation of the offense. He begins as the hardened businessman, settling accounts and recouping what losses he can, is suddenly and unexpectedly transformed into an unworldly giver of mercy, and just as suddenly is transformed into the dispenser of justice and punishment. And we are told, in a coda to the parable, that in his final transformation the king is God-like. "So," Jesus says to the disciples after the parable has ended, "my heavenly Father will also do to every one of you, if you do not forgive your brother or sister from your heart" (18:35).

If the parable is read as a response to Peter's question about how many times he should forgive his brother, it does not provide an answer, since the question itself is a stumbling block. Forgiving one time seems to have no more or less authority than forgiving three, or seventy-seven, times. Peter might, however, learn that forgiveness must be "from your heart," as Jesus says and as the king demonstrates. If the parable is read as a comment on the sinning brother discourse, as the final phrase suggests (literally, "forgive *your brother* from your heart"), it raises questions rather than provides answers. The king does not follow the three-step procedure. Is this because the sinner is not his brother but his slave? Perhaps, but the "fellow slaves" do not follow the procedure, either; they go to the king, in distress, and tell him what happened. The procedure, as procedure, it would seem, is no more important than establishing the exact number of times to forgive. What is crucial to forgiveness, but not even mentioned in the sinning brother discourse, would seem to be the heart, the changing and becoming of the whole being, as dramatized by the king. But even this—following the heart—is not enough to save the other: it would not have been enough for recovering the lost sheep, or the sinning brother, and it was not enough to recover the unforgiving slave, who responded to pity with greed and viciousness.

The other essential principle is reciprocity. When the slave does not reciprocate by forgiving *his* debtor, the king imitates the slave by inflicting the slave's punishment of his fellow slave upon the slave himself. And in this, the heavenly Father is like the king; he will imitate "every one of you." The disciples will not continue to receive mercy if they do not themselves give mercy. If the forgiven slave had forgiven his fellow slave, there would have been no distress and no punishment. What the disciples enact on earth *is* life or death, whatever else the kingdom of heaven or Gehenna also may be. If they forgive from the heart, they are binding in heaven and on earth; if they receive a child like the one in their midst, they receive the son of the heavenly Father; if they scandalize little ones, they are worse than if they had been drowned with a millstone around the neck. They may choose to enter life, as the king did, or not. Degrees, methods, and numbers are irrelevant; an action, changing and becoming, is required.

Through the king, the parable offers an enactment of a changing and becoming, but the parable does not function as an exemplary tale. We are not likely to be moved by reading the story to cancel the ten-million-dollar loans (or the ten-dollar loans) we have made; the extravagance of the terms does not invite identification by the disciples or most readers. The parable, however, does offer the reader an opportunity to respond. In fact, the scandalous qualities of the parable insist on a response. Should we be scandalized by the king's extraordinary loan in the first place—ten million dollars to a slave? Is this not astonishingly bad business? Should we be scandalized by the king's initial impulse to sell the servant and his family in order to get back at least part of his money? Should we be scandalized by the king's canceling the entire ten-million-dollar debt? Normal, human forgiveness would seem adequately, perhaps more than adequately, satisfied by patience, allowing the servant to try to pay back as much as he can of what rightfully belongs to the king. Surely there is a legitimate scandal here, no matter how well intentioned the king might be. And does not the fact that the slave is undeserving (because he is vicious and unmerciful himself) confirm that the extravagant forgiveness of debt is scandalous?

And, on the basis of Jesus's earlier teaching, should we be scandalized that the king did not offer to forgive the servant repeatedly? And is there not a theological scandal in Jesus's assertion that the heavenly Father will throw the disciples (and possibly the readers) to the torturers—or somewhere analogous (such as the Gehenna of fire)—if they do not forgive their brothers?

These are all serious stumbling blocks that readers are forced to encounter. Readers may refuse to think about them; they may not want to consider the question, how does it seem to you? They may be indifferent to the king, slave, and heavenly Father; they may invent a parallel text, perhaps an allegory, as a way of avoiding the text that is given; they may be genuinely offended. All of these are encounters, engaging the reader in the act of stumbling or not stumbling.

What Norman Perrin has called "the process of domestication" of parables (199) has led to a habitual form of reading in which readers do not even notice scandals. Naturally, if one does not notice a scandal, one cannot be scandalized or resist being scandalized by it. For Kierkegaard, this domestication is a comfortable way of avoiding the offensive God-man—the phenomenon he found embodied in Bishop Mynster and in institutional Christendom.

This entire passage in Matthew teaches disciples and readers about scandals at the same time as it sets forth scandals. It enacts its own message by forcing the reader into choices of engagement or avoidance, of being scandalized or not. It dramatizes changing and becoming and going astray. In doing this, it presents the reader with the possibility of offense: the possibility of being scandalized by a Jesus of violence (the Jesus of torn-out eye, chopped hand and foot, death by millstone, threat of torture), a Jesus of contradictions (forgive your brother three times? seventy-seven times? once?), or a Jesus of enactments rather than doctrines. Or, on the other hand, it presents the possibility of *not* being scandalized after encountering the scandals ("And blessed is anyone who takes no offense at me"). Matthew, a scribe who has faith in writing, proclaims in his Gospel the provocative good news of Jesus—a character in a narrative, an offense who does not want to offend.

8

Life in the Between: Nathan and the Good Samaritan

Utterance and Response

In chapter 4, I presented Kierkegaard's account of offense, which constitutes the ground of my argument, by examining his narratives of offense and the voices of his speakers. His narratives include such oddities as a judge wrestling with the contradiction of offensive corns on the feet of a beautiful woman, as well as the more weighty attempt by Quidam to extricate himself from an engagement without offending his fiancée. Kierkegaard's various voices belong to a wide range of characters: the aesthetic Johannes the Seducer, the ethical Judge William, and the differently religious Johannes Climacus and Anti-Climacus, among others. The narrative, voice-oriented approach offers a way of presenting Kierkegaard's views without falsifying them as something abstract, mechanical, or systematic. But although Kierkegaard presents the idea of offense through narratives, he does not explore the narrative manifestations of offense in the Gospels, nor does he examine parables as occasions for offense. He makes it clear that Jesus *is* an offense, but apart from his powerful and subtle presentations of the offense and of Jesus as offense, he does not provide us with much in the way of models or tools for the study of Gospel narratives.[1]

A fruitful way of attending to the dynamics of narrative offenses—and one that complements Kierkegaard's narrative unfolding of the offense—may be found in Bakhtin's concept of dialogism or, more accurately (since Bakhtin is as unsympathetic to systems and -isms as Kierkegaard), in what Bakhtin calls the event of the dialogic. The dialogic differs from the dialectical in that it dwells in voices and responses.[2] The dialogic is "the *active reception of other speakers' speech*" (Vološinov, *Marxism*, 117; Bakhtin, *Art and Answerability*, xlii); it exists in the activity *between* subjects, which is where, in Bakhtin's view, life occurs.

Bakhtin had studied both Kierkegaard and Buber before formulating his ideas about the dialogic. In Kierkegaard, he found useful formulations of the single individual, the eternal moment, the collision or crisis, and the historical offense. And in Buber, he found a congenial way of conceiving the dialogic relationships between humans (see Buber's *Between Man and Man*) and between the individual and God (see *I and Thou*).[3] But for our purposes, perhaps the most important source for Bakhtin's ideas on the dialogic and on scandal is Dostoyevski, in whose writings he finds the flowering of the genre of menippean satire.[4] Bakhtin traces Dostoyevski's scandal scenes back to "the basic narrative genres of ancient Christian literature," including the Gospels (*Problems*, 135). The famous scene in *Crime and Punishment* where Raskolnikov first visits Sonya and they read the Gospel is, he says, "an almost perfect Christianized menippea: short dialogic syncrises (faith vs. lack of faith . . .), sharp anacrisis [or provocation, such as Jesus's insults to the Pharisees or the Canaanite woman], oxymoronic combinations ([such as] the thinker-criminal [and] the prostitute-righteous woman), a naked statement of ultimate questions and a reading of the Gospels in a slum setting" (*Problems*, 155). Reading the Gospels in the context of the Bakhtinian dialogic offers a view of them as narratives of crisis, taking place on the threshold, dealing with ultimate questions of life and death, and challenging the listener scandalously.

Such a view begins with an open-ended concept of active utterances, utterances that are responsible and responsive to voices in the past and that anticipate responding voices. As Vološinov, a member of Bakhtin's circle, puts it, "any locution actually said aloud or written down for intelligible communication . . . is the expression and product of the social interaction of three participants: the speaker . . . , the listener . . . , and the topic . . . of speech [or the author, reader, and hero]. . . . The concrete utterance . . . is born, lives, and dies in the process of social interaction between the participants of the utterance" ("Discourse," 105). In Bakhtin's developments of this idea, an utterance includes not just its words but also the dialogic overtones of previous words, to which they are a response, and of later words, those anticipated to come in response. An utterance seeks to generate a response and does not come to life, or to meaning, without a response. "Understanding comes to fruition only in the response," Bakhtin says (*Dialogic Imagination*, 282).

Thus, true understanding is never static or monological; it does not reduce voices to doctrines or ideas to "pellets of intellection," in Lionel Trilling's phrase, or living qualities to things. "The idea is not a subjective individual-psychological formation with 'permanent resident rights' in a person's head," Bakhtin writes; "no, the idea is inter-individual and inter-subjective—the realm of its existence is not individual consciousness but dialogic communion *between* consciousnesses. . . . In this sense the idea is similar to the word. . . . [It] wants to be heard, understood, and 'answered' by other voices from other positions" (*Problems*, 88). Dialogic communication occurs in what Heidegger called *"das Zwischen"* (the between), or Buber *"das Zwischenmensch"* (the inter-human), or Winnicott "potential space." Bakhtin calls it "the boundary" or "threshold"; it is not so much a place as a dialogic event, "a live event, playing itself out between consciousness-voices," as he says of Dostoyevski's representation (*Problems*, 88).

When Jesus provocatively asserts to the disciples that he tells parables to the crowd "in order that 'they may indeed look, but not perceive, and may indeed listen, but not understand,'" we need, as I have argued, to make a Kierkegaardian distinction between the crowd (which is untruth) and the individual (who can be given, though not compelled to receive, secrets or mysteries of the kingdom). And we also need to grapple with the implied distinctions between looking and perceiving, listening and understanding. Perceiving and understanding the kingdom must be done by an individual, but it can never be done by an individual who seeks the kingdom as an object or thing or who believes that truth is a collection of objective facts or doctrines to be grasped. Perceiving and understanding may be seen as something like Bakhtin's "live event," a response that takes place between the individual and the offensive God-man, an answer of faith to a divine other.

This event-response-answer is seen by Matthew as a changing and becoming, and for Matthew the alternative is a terrible "weeping and gnashing of teeth." For the more irenic but not softer Luke, the event is a radical form of *living*; to him, the normal, worldly thing that we call living is often a form of death, an absence of life, since true life is in God. For both Matthew and Luke, the responsive events, or answers to God, involve encounters with a special form of offense or, as Bakhtin prefers to call it in the Dostoyevski book, scandal. Bakhtin argues that the scandal of Christian menippea is not to be found in Hebrew narratives. I have tried to show in chapter 2 that the Gospel offense grows directly out of the Hebrew trap, snare, and stumbling block of Yahweh. Yet I want to argue that Bakhtin's distinction is a valid one. In the Hebrew story of David, Bathsheba, and Nathan and in the Christian parable of the Good Samaritan, we can see how narratives work dialogically and why the menippean and (to use another characteristically Bakhtinian term) carnivalized scandal is a special form of scandal associated with Christian narratives.[5]

David and Nathan: Between I and Thou

The plot of the David and Bathsheba story seems made of the stuff of a tabloid scandal. A high government official, who ought to be away leading his troops, spies on a beautiful naked woman, sends his underlings to fetch her, sleeps with her, attempts to cover up a pregnancy by arranging a visit from the husband, Uriah, who has been valiantly serving his king and people on the battlefield, and plots to have the husband killed when the intended cover-up does not work. Bathsheba is the unwitting femme fatale, a stumbling block to David and, in a different way, to Uriah as well. When David recalls Uriah from the battlefield, asks him some questions to disguise his real motive, and says, "Go down to your house, and wash your feet," Uriah does not go, thereby disobeying something close to a regal command.[6] When David questions him the next day—"Why did you not go down to your house?"—Uriah answers, "The ark and Israel and Judah remain in booths; and my lord Joab and the servants of my lord are camping in the open field; shall I then go to my house, to eat and to drink, and to lie with my wife? As you live, and as your soul lives, I will not do such a thing" (2 Sam. 11:8–11).

It is possible that Uriah has heard of this scandal (the narrator neither encourages nor discourages us from entertaining this idea), but whether he has or not, his speech and action are in striking contrast to David's. There is talk not of washing one's feet but of eating, drinking, and lying with his wife (and the last of these is, of course, precisely what David had in mind). More important, what David has done out of wedlock is to Uriah a scandal even in wedlock. He will not be in a house with his beautiful wife, Bathsheba, when the ark, Israel, and Judah are in booths and his companions are camping in the open fields. As David lives, and as David's soul lives, "I [Uriah] will not do such a thing." In the blunt manner of the forthright soldier, swearing by his fundamental beliefs, Uriah points to the central issue of this entire episode: David's life and David's soul.

Uriah's principled abstinence, however, is no match for a king. Uriah loses his life, and David gains another wife, Uriah's, but, the narrator tells us succinctly, "the thing that David had done displeased the LORD" (2 Sam. 11:27), who sends Nathan to David. What follows is a stumbling block in the form of a trap. Nathan's parable of the little ewe lamb appropriated from a poor man by a rich man to feed his guest is a recounting of David's action in disguise, and it prompts, as it is intended to, David's judgment: "As the LORD lives, the man who has done this deserves to die; he shall restore the lamb fourfold, because he did this thing, and because he had no pity" (12:5–6). David condemns himself to death before he hears Nathan's proverbial words: "You are the man!" (12:7). David's punishment is reciprocal: what he did to Uriah's wife will be done to him, only it will be done openly, not secretly. But still not clear at this point in the story is David's fate, his self-condemned death or life.

David has stumbled into the trap planted by Nathan and God, but a much more critical stumbling block awaits him at the conclusion of Nathan's and God's speech. David's voice in the scandalous events has been deceitful, literally murderous; his voice in response to the parable of the ewe lamb, on the other hand, is full of righteous indignation, worthy of a just king. God's voice brings David to the threshold. He might respond with the voice of the indolent, deceitful king, as he is at the beginning of the story, taking a stroll on the roof after a late-afternoon nap and spying on a naked woman. He might look for excuses, arguing that he did not intend things to turn out the way they did, blaming Uriah's unnatural stubbornness and his bad luck, perhaps something like Saul's weasling response to God when confronted with his disobedient sparing of Agag and the best sheep and oxen. Or, on the other hand, he might respond in the voice of the king who can recognize injustice, even in himself.

In this crisis, David says to Nathan, "I have sinned against the LORD" (12:13). David encounters the stumbling block without stumbling. The rest of the punishment has been withheld until

David's response, defining precisely who is being punished—not a David lost in indolence, deceit, and violence but a kingly David who can recognize injustice in its most difficult guise: in oneself. The double trap has brought him to the threshold of what Uriah called his soul's life, and David has chosen life. His own life is then spared, but his son, Bathsheba's child, the scandalous growth of this affair, must die.

The juxtaposition of David's actions with the rich man and the ewe lamb in the parable, followed by God's speech, is a provocation leading to David's crisis. God's authoritative voice speaks truth, but truth does not live until it is heard and responded to. David hears the voice of God and lives. These dialogic interactions, the activities of the *between*, are where truth in this narrative is found. One might say that David's failure was the result of his transforming his world into objects. Bathsheba becomes to David the objective embodiment of beauty and sexual pleasure; Uriah becomes (if he will get into bed with his wife) the escape from scandal or (when he does not) the incriminating evidence that must be exterminated; and Joab becomes the surrogate military leader and hatchet man. All become reified, objects to serve a self cut off from the responding other, and a self-created means for the soul's death.

At the ultimate crisis, however, David hears and accepts the word of God through Nathan. The remainder of this story is a series of surprising responses. When the child becomes sick, "David therefore pleaded with God for the child; David fasted, and went in and lay all night on the ground" (12:16). He does this for seven days, not eating, not listening or speaking with anyone, except God, who remains silent. When the child dies, the servants are afraid to tell him, but he asks them, "Is the child dead?" (12:19). And when they answer that he is, David's behavior changes drastically, but not as the servants feared: he washes himself, anoints himself, changes his clothes, and eats. His fasting and crying have been a dialogue with a silent God, and his sudden recovery on the child's death reflects his acceptance of God's response: God will not rescind the punishment of the child's death. David then comforts Bathsheba—a new action in this narrative, the result, one might say, of a transformed David, one who had acted scandalously and without "pity" (12:6) but who, at the moment of crisis, does not stumble.

In spite of the fact that this episode raises ultimate questions, juxtaposes the high and the low, and constitutes for David a threshold experience—all characteristic of menippea—it is clearly not what Bakhtin would call a carnivalized narrative; the scandal here is of a different order, which will become clear by looking at a Gospel narrative.

The Dialogic Samaritan

If we read the parable of the Good Samaritan outside its narrative frame in Luke, we lose all sense of the parable as an utterance. It is preceded by the crucial exchange between Jesus and a lawyer:

> Just then a lawyer stood up to test Jesus. "Teacher," he said, "what must I do to inherit eternal life?" [Jesus] said to him, "What is written in the law? What do you read there?" [The lawyer] answered, "You shall love the Lord your God with all your heart, and with all your soul, and with all your strength, and with all your mind; and your neighbor as yourself." And [Jesus] said to him, "You have given the right answer; do this, and you will live." (Luke 10:25–28)

We know more about the lawyer's utterance than his words themselves indicate; we know that he asks the question not in search of truth, or life, but to test Jesus. If Jesus hears this part of the utterance, he does not acknowledge it. He responds ostensibly only to the words themselves, but he responds with more questions rather than with an answer. His questions are themselves a test—what is written? and how do you read? (as the RSV puts it)—questions, incidentally, that bear on us as readers of Luke, but that is another matter.

The lawyer's response to Jesus's questions is impressive, and Jesus acknowledges that he is "right" but then adds, "Do this, and you will live." He here restates as an assertion the question just answered, but with a twist: the original question was not "What must I do to live?" but "What must I do to inherit eternal life?"—not a present process but a future object of desire. Jesus has inoffensively, without hearing or without acknowledging the motive behind the question, elicited a right answer to the wrong question and then supplied the right question. The lawyer does not initially ask the right question because his object is to test Jesus (rather than to find truth) and also no doubt because he assumes that he *is* living. Luke, however, through his hero, Jesus, is throughout his book engaged in the enterprise of bringing the reader or hearer to a reconsideration of what living really is.

The lawyer, who should now know both the right answer and the right question, may if he wishes act upon it, but it will involve a present doing, not only a future inheriting. The narrative makes it clear that he chooses not to act immediately to love God and neighbor, but rather he tries to elevate himself: "But wanting to justify himself, he asked Jesus, 'And who is my neighbor?' Jesus replied, 'A man was going down from Jerusalem to Jericho . . .'" (10:29–30). The parable, however, does not exactly answer the lawyer's self-justifying question. As many critics have noted, Jesus seems to have changed the terms of the question, since the parable does not lead to an answer of the sort the question presupposes—your neighbor is so-and-so—but rather leads to a question (rather than an answer) about *being* a neighbor. Some have supposed that Luke has botched the job of integrating the parable into his narrative, but Jesus's new question brings the lawyer to the unwanted crisis typical of encounters with Jesus: "Which of these three [the priest, Levite, or Samaritan], do you think, was a neighbor to the man who fell into the hands of the robbers?" (10:36). In this entire passage, the questions and responses (including, but not limited to, the parable) are part of a drama, generating meaning in the process of encounter and interaction between speaker and listener in which the lawyer is himself unwittingly brought to the test, forced to a decision on a matter of ultimate importance: life.

Although I have said that Jesus is at first inoffensive in his treatment of this lawyer, the parable Jesus tells as part of this exchange is a different matter; it is inescapably offensive to a Jewish lawyer. Samaritans were untouchables, hated by the Jews, specifically excluded in a midrash on Exodus from being neighbors. A *good* Samaritan would be an oxymoron. Or, as Crossan has said, "Good + Samaritan" is "a contradiction in terms; . . . when good (clerics) and bad (Samaritan) become, respectively, bad and good, a world is being challenged and we are faced with polar reversal" (*In Parables*, 64). This parable is for this lawyer a *skandalon*.

After Jesus reformulates the original question into a new question about neighboring—which of the three was a neighbor?—the lawyer responds, "'The one who showed him mercy.' Jesus said to him, 'Go and do likewise'" (10:37). Does the lawyer say "the one who showed him mercy" (or, literally, the one who did mercy) because he cannot bear to say the hated word *Samaritan*? Or because he has suddenly seen beyond the objectified category of Samaritan and has a new, expanded vision of the compassionate human? His response is unpredeterminable and, here, unknown; this scandal could be the occasion for what Bakhtin calls "the turning point for [the] soul" (*Problems*, 61). Does the lawyer go and do likewise? The narrative is silent. It leaves us suspended in the between, where the live event is. At this eternal moment, on the boundary, the lawyer, who set out to test Jesus and then to justify himself, encounters a *skandalon*, provoked by Jesus into an artistic time and space that Bakhtin would call a "chronotope of the threshold, a chronotope of *crisis* and *break* in life" (*Dialogic Imagination*, 248).

In this passage, there are three distinct potential scandals that bring people to the threshold or boundary. The first is entirely within the parable: it involves the wounded man, who proves to be a scandal to the priest and the Levite but not to the Samaritan. The second exists between the hero of the parable and the listener within the narrative, the lawyer, who hears about a despised Samaritan surpassing the priest and the Levite in neighboring, in compassion, in life. The lawyer is challenged to look and perceive, to listen and understand. If he does so (which we will never know, since the narrative is eternally suspended), his world truly will be turned upside down. Instead of testing or tempting itinerant teachers, instead of justifying himself, instead of providing correct answers that he does not enact, he will have to "do" in the manner of the formerly hated Samaritan; he will have to live by loving God and loving neighbor, and this will mean living in something other than the established and respectable world of priests and Levites. Until this encounter, the lawyer is able to make statements about the world Jesus challenges him to live in—since it is written in the law, and he can read—but he is not able to perceive or understand it.

The third scandal involves Luke's listener or reader, who may or may not have the same attitude toward the Samaritan as the lawyer but who is forced into the boundary by the truncated narrative. The reader witnesses the question-and-response exchanges of Jesus and the lawyer and the interactions of the half-dead man and three travelers not as finalized, completed performances but as dialogic events. Luke does not openly ask his audience, "How do you read?" but he does not have to; the answer will be manifest in the reader's response to this threshold event. The reader, too, encounters doing, loving, and living embodied in the drama of the lawyer, Jesus, and the parable and is personally confronted with the moral imperative—"Go and do likewise"—through the open-endedness of the scene. The reader has little alternative but to agree with the lawyer that the Samaritan proved neighbor to the man, but the reader is not allowed the luxury of approving or condemning the lawyer's response to Jesus's imperative. If there is to be any response, the reader must provide it.

Thus, characters within the parable, the lawyer in the frame narrative, and the reader being addressed by the author are all forced to a threshold and confronted with an obstacle, a possibility of offense. All are called upon to hear, but the possibility of not hearing remains. No one is called upon to interpret a story allegorically, metaphorically, or symbolically; all are called to the threshold to be scandalized or not. The question "How do you read?" is an appeal not to the expertise of lawyers or literary critics but to the single individual who, as Kierkegaard says, exists "before God."

For Bakhtin in his book on Dostoyevski, the utterance, the scandal, and the event in the boundary reveal and create the life of the person. "In dialogue," he says, "a person not only shows himself outwardly, but he becomes for the first time that which he is . . . not only for others but for himself as well. To be means to communicate dialogically" (*Problems*, 252). Jesus's Samaritan *is* a dialogic response to the lawyer, and specifically in the way the lawyer's doctrine, which he knows from the law, has prescribed—a point I will return to. The lawyer, who has begun as a strict monologist with his question traps, his solid answers, and his stratagems to justify himself, has been offered a *skandalon* through Jesus's narrative. The scandal provides an occasion for the lawyer to become like the hated Samaritan, to live in a radically new, and formerly unthinkable, sense. The reader has been presented with a parallel scandal and occasion, through Luke's narration of Jesus's narrative. For the lawyer and the reader, the narrative offers no closure. Both lawyer and reader are left suspended in the moment, the lawyer facing the challenge of a world turned upside down, and the reader facing an imperative of doing mercy that is not performed by the established leaders.

The Official World and the Unseemly

In Bakhtin's view, being means encountering, answering, responding to an other, all of which is done in the boundary between two, which is the dialogic minimum. So it is between David and Nathan, who speaks for God, and between the Samaritan and the half-dead man. When David encounters his own actions disguised in the parable trap, he can judge them correctly. When the lawyer encounters an act of neighboring, he can recognize it. But these similarities mask a more fundamental difference between the two narratives, a difference that hinges on what the narrative *skandalon* disrupts and what, if it is heeded, the *skandalon* leads to.

David's scandal involves a failure in his official role as king and leader of his people, as well as a moral failure. Kings are supposed to lead their armies (as the beginning reminds us, "In the spring of the year, the time when kings go out to battle, David sent Joab"; 2 Sam. 11:1); kings are not supposed to use their power unjustly; kings are not supposed to murder their valiant warriors. Everyone knows this—the people (hence the secrecy with which David veils his deeds), himself (hence his clear understanding of the parable of the ewe lamb), and God (hence God's displeasure and judgment). David's scandal is a violation of the normal, stable world, and Nathan's parable trap is an attempt to recall him to the normal, stable world that it is his official duty to maintain. The parable succeeds in this: David recognizes his guilt and becomes a true king again. Prodded by Joab, he even goes forth to battle. The "freedom" David enjoyed (indolently staying home from battle, engaging in adultery, and covering up his misdeeds by murder) was an ungodly aberration from the norm, after which a reestablished order ensues, although there is an ominous price to be paid in the future.

The *skandalon* encountered by the lawyer who poses questions to Jesus, however, opens up a different kind of breach and leads to different consequences. In referring to scandals in menippea and in Dostoyevski, Bakhtin writes that "they make a breach in the stable, normal ('seemly') course of human affairs and events, they free human behavior from the norms and motivations that predetermine it" (*Problems*, 117). The stable, normal course of human affairs in the parable of the Good Samaritan is represented by the priest and the Levite, those representatives of the established order. The outcast from that order, the Samaritan, encounters a naked man—the representative of no established order but purely of the other. The Samaritan lives in a world that includes robbers, victims, uncompassionate priests and Levites, and untrustworthy innkeepers, and he negotiates his world successfully, but not because he is part of the normal, established world. Instead, he lives because he radically enacts the love of God and the love of neighbor.

The word of God in Jesus's parable is not part of the established order, as it is in the David-Nathan story. The priest, the Levite, and the lawyer might want to claim that it is, but the narrative insists on a gaping difference between the word and kingdom of God on the one hand and the normal, established world on the other. The worldly lawyer, however, can cite Scripture on the issue of eternal life. When Jesus asks him, "What do you read there?" he shows that he knows the Torah: "You shall love [1] the Lord your God with all your [a] heart, and with all your [b] soul, and with all your [c] strength, and with all your [d] mind; and [2] your neighbor as yourself." (Luke 10:27) He is quoting Deuteronomy and Leviticus, not exactly, but certainly close enough to capture the spirit: "You shall love the LORD your God with all your heart, and with all your soul, and with all your might" (Deut. 6:5), and "you shall love your neighbor as yourself" (Lev. 19:18). Indeed, by adding a fourth faculty—mind—the lawyer seems to be overreading in an admirable way. He knows and is zealous about the law. Jesus, however, asks for enactment ("Do this"), and, not succeeding, he tells a story and posits an offense.

Since the narrator tells us, we know that the lawyer wants to justify himself; hence his question, "And who is my neighbor?" If, let us suppose, the lawyer had wanted truth, had wanted life rather than self-justification, what might he have asked instead? "Who is my neighbor?" is a good, lawyerly question that the scribes did ponder (some of them specifically excluding Samaritans from the genus "neighbor"), but a much harder question is "How shall I love God with all my heart, soul, and might?" or, more zealously, "with all my heart, soul, strength, and mind?" Jesus usually does not answer questions directly, and he sometimes answers questions that have not been asked but should have been. So it is in this case.

Jesus tells the lawyer what he does not want to know, and Luke tells the reader what he or she ought to want to know: how to love God and how to love neighbor. The answer, as it happens, fuses the questions and shuns the propositional. The Samaritan's actions are vividly specific not simply to make the narrative believable (Crossan, *In Parables*, 63) or to give the audience time to absorb the unexpected appearance of the Samaritan (Scott, 199) but to respond to the lawyer's scriptural response. The Samaritan sees his neighbor—naked, unknown man:

> and when he saw him, [a] he was moved with pity. [b] He went to him and bandaged his wounds, having poured oil and wine on them. Then [c] he put him on his own animal, brought him to an inn, and took care of him. The next day [d] he took out two denarii, gave them to the innkeeper, and said, "Take care of him; and when I come back, I will repay you whatever more you spend." (Luke 10:33–35)

Jesus's response takes the form of narrative actions that exactly parallel the faculties with which, according to the lawyer, God should be loved. The Samaritan loves God with all his heart (*kardia*, the source and center of the whole inner life [Bauer et al.]) by having pity (*splagchnizomai*), the word repeatedly used for Jesus's response, as, for example, to the leper and to the widow at Nain whose son had died. He loves God with all his soul (*psychē*), meaning in Hellenistic Greek the physical life, the vital principle involving the activity of the whole person (see Turner, 418–19), by enacting his pity—going to the half-dead man, pouring oil and wine on his wounds, and bandaging them. He loves God with all his strength, by physically setting the man on his own animal and taking him to an inn. And he loves God with all his mind (*dianoia*, which Bauer defines as "understanding, intelligence, mind," and also "purpose, plan") by cleverly disarming the notorious greed and untrustworthiness of innkeepers: he will provide some money to the innkeeper right away to care for the man, though he makes it clear that he will return to see that proper care has been given, holding out the carrot of more money. The Samaritan is shrewd as well as compassionate.[7]

This series of actions involving heart, soul, strength, and mind parallels the lawyer's scriptural injunction, but with a surprising twist: the Samaritan is not apparently loving God but loving an unknown neighbor, which is itself an apparent contradiction. Jesus has fused the two questions, one unasked (How do I love God?) and the other asked (Who is my neighbor?), and he has changed the focus from a lawyerly object (the naked man as neighbor) to a human acting (the Samaritan being neighbor). In doing so, he has posed the possibility of offense. That a Samaritan should surpass a priest and a Levite in love, or that he should enact the love of God through the love for this naked man—either of these shocking and surprising activities is sufficient to provoke the lawyer. If the lawyer should be able to accept the scandal of a good Samaritan, he might nonetheless be as surprised that the Samaritan has loved God in this way as the "sheep" or "goats" in Matthew's story are surprised that they have, or have not, loved the son of God, who appeared before them as "one of the least of these who are members of my family"—hungry, thirsty, a stranger, naked, sick, or imprisoned (Matt. 25:34–40).

How to love God and how to recognize a neighbor may be easy enough to cite Scripture about or to ask self-justifying questions about, but they are scandalously difficult to perceive and understand, because perceiving and understanding, in Jesus's parabolic terms, here require a response, action, doing—such as the Samaritan's, who *did* mercy. "Go and do likewise" is a call to scandalous action, scandalous because it requires a turning away from the established, worldly order exemplified by the priest, the Levite, and (at least until the moment of the parable) the lawyer. The Samaritan belongs to Bakhtin's category of "the eccentric"; he is outside the normal, seemly world. To participate in his world of loving God and neighbor, the lawyer, or reader, must turn away from the official order of the priest and the Levite and become eccentric ("out of the center"). David, by contrast, when he responds to Nathan and God, returns *from* being an offense to the established order *to* being a seemly part of that order, a true king.

What Bakhtin calls carnivalized scandal overturns the official, established world, but the scandals of the David-Bathsheba-Nathan story constitute a deviation from established norms only to bring the offender back to those norms. Luke's Good Samaritan story is a carnivalized scandal, as are Jesus's low birth, his motley followers (the mésalliance of high and low characters: the son of God consorting with fishermen, lepers, prostitutes, and tax collectors), his hard sayings ("Whoever comes to me and does not hate father and mother, wife and children, brothers and sisters, yes, and even life itself, cannot be my disciple"; Luke 14:26), his mock crowning as "King of the Jews," and his ignominious death with thieves. The atmosphere of scandal is *essential* to the story of Jesus because he is "eccentric," outside the center of the normal and established order.

This is not to say that the Hebrew narratives do not attack normalcy or the social order or conventional practices. In many narratives, idolatry is normal in the sense of usual for the Israelites, but the normal as standard of judgment in the Israelite world is embodied in the social and religious code of the Ten Commandments. The leaders, such as David and Moses, are expected to uphold this code, and the people are expected to live by it. But such is the gap, at times, between expectations or norms and practice that the great eccentrics of the Hebrew Bible, such as Jeremiah and Ezekiel, are only eccentrics in practice, trying to recall the people to the established norms (seldom realized for long, to be sure) of the Mosaic and Davidic order, which reflect Yahweh's rule. Hosea marries a prostitute not to embrace the lowly or to undermine the social order but as a living metaphor of the harlotry the Israelites have committed by forsaking Yahweh. The established social norms of the narrative world of the Hebrew Bible—whether the Israelites are being a stiff-necked people or not—are from Yahweh. The established social and political norms of Jesus's narrative world in the Gospels are from the priests or Caesar; in this sense, Jesus is a true eccentric, the hero of a what Bakhtin calls "new artistic categories of the scandalous and the eccentric" (*Problems*, 117).

Between Stories

The scandals of both David and the Good Samaritan, however, are dialogic, and they bring David, the Samaritan, and the lawyer to the threshold where they encounter a question of ultimate importance. In the between of the encounter, they must enact a response. From my reading of the Good Samaritan narrative, one might be tempted to arrive at some kind of doctrinal closure, affirming Jesus's message of doing, of good works, of active love. It appears to be, as many critics have called it, an example story.

But such is the non-didactic character of this narrative that we are not allowed to settle even for this propositional truth, as valuable, worthwhile, or above reproach as it may seem. For the Gospels are dialogic not simply within narratives but between and among narratives. Consider the interaction between the story of the Good Samaritan and the one immediately following it, the story of Mary and Martha.[8] After "Go and do likewise," the text continues:

> Now as they [Jesus and the disciples] went on their way, he [Jesus] entered a certain village, where a woman named Martha welcomed him into her home. She had a sister named Mary, who sat at the Lord's feet and listened to what he was saying. But Martha was distracted by her many tasks; so she came to him and asked, "Lord, do you not care that my sister has left me to do all the work by myself? Tell her then to help me." But the Lord answered her, "Martha, Martha, you are worried and distracted by many things; there is need of only one thing. Mary has chosen the better part, which will not be taken away from her." (Luke 10:38–42)

If we have abstracted from the Good Samaritan parable and frame the principle of loving God and neighbor actively, we are immediately forced to call it into question as a propositional, rather than a dialogic, truth. Even if we respond to Jesus's injunction, "Go and do likewise," with agreement and acceptance, we are forced by the following story to reconsider the "likewise" and the "doing." Martha is a doer; further, she is doing time-honored service: providing hospitality to others. It is good manners; it is a biblical virtue, honored in

Scripture; it is essential, since travelers—even divine travelers, as Abraham and Sarah discovered—want food. But here, doing traditional, hospitable service is wrong; not doing is the better part.

Martha plays a role analogous to the lawyer here: she is part of an established order, she knows the rules, and she intends to justify herself. Like the lawyer, she is presented with a scandal: serving her guests is not the better part. Jesus does not insult Martha, but he is severe: he says that she is "worried and distracted by many things" and that she is wrong; he will not tell Mary to help her. His reading of her character and his refusal to uphold the established order of domestic hospitality pose the possibility of offense. For Martha, *not* serving her guests in the prescribed, established ways is not normal or conventional; it is unseemly. But the outcome of this possible offense is not revealed. Like the lawyer, Mary is left in a narrative limbo. Whether she is offended or abandons her misguided service for the "one thing" there is need of we will never know. The conclusion does not exist; once again, the reader is left in the moment of narrative crisis with no resolution.

The narrative withholds not only a conclusion but also an identification of the one thing there is need of. In my experience, most readers feel that they can identify the one thing with certainty, but when pressed to say what the one thing is, they produce a surprising variety of answers. When confronted with the variety, many of them still believe they have come up with the right thing and that the other answers are wrong. But the identity of one thing is made even more questionable by the fact that one Greek text, to which some scholars accord authority, has Jesus say, "One thing is needful, *or a few things*." Here, Mary knows one needful thing, but there may be others as well. In either reading, Martha—and the reader—are not put in the position of trying to puzzle out what, as objective fact, the one needful thing is. David Patterson has said, echoing Bakhtin, "Nothing is more deadly to the spirit than a ready-made answer" (58). Instead, Martha is put in the position of responding to the person of Jesus, even though the response might take the opposite form of the Samaritan's active doing. Supplying a solid thing for Jesus's one thing runs the risk of substituting monological knowing, of the sort the lawyer has of the Scripture, for the dialogic response Jesus seeks and Mary and the Good Samaritan enact.

The story of Mary and Martha, interacting dialogically with the Good Samaritan story and frame, brings the reader to a boundary where ready-made answers are of no use. It, too, is a *skandalon*,

leaving the reader on a threshold beyond the established order, neither in the position of Mary at the Lord's feet nor in the position
of Martha, whose would-be justifying Lord has rebuked her, but
suspended between doing and not doing, confronted by the person
of Jesus. When we examine a parable in isolation, we may want to
conclude that Luke uses parables as examples for his preestablished
meanings or messages (Scott, 28), but, as a writer of the Gospel,
Luke undermines propositional messages and promotes scandalous
encounters.

9

Plot and Story in John

Mythic Plots and Scandalous Stories

According to John Drury, the Gospel of John marks an early but
radical change in Christianity that is still with us: "With John an
era of Christian historiography, of Christianity as popular narrative,
ceases. A great age of Christian doctrine begins. Stories will yield to
creeds" (*Parables*, 164). Stories did indeed yield to creeds, and it
is even tempting to accuse John of promoting this shift, with his
philosophical interest in the Logos and in Jesus as the Word, which
may seem inimical to story. But John's Gospel is the end of an era,
not the beginning of the new era. It is story, not creed. True, John's
Gospel strikes the reader instantly as a different sort of story from
Matthew's, Mark's, or Luke's. For one thing, it contains notably few
parables, and I have in the second part of this book focused primarily, though not exclusively, on parables as scandalous encounters.
But John's Gospel, like the others, is nonetheless a narrative of offense. For John, like the synoptic writers, Jesus is an offense, and
his offensiveness can be seen only in actions. For John, like the
others, scandal lives in story—the story of the disciples, of the Jews
and Gentiles who encounter Jesus, and of the reader who encounters
Jesus's story and life itself, which is John's hero: "I am the life." The
turning away from story to creed, which is a crucial part of the

history of Christianity, is a massive turning away from the offense in narrative that is at the heart of the Gospels.

We cannot imagine a good scandal of the sex-and-politics variety (whether about King David or the local congressman) without a story. But the converse also may be true: in all but the most primitive plots, it is hard to imagine story without scandal, if we take *scandal* in a very broad sense to mean something new, anecdotal, and deviant from a general norm. Scandal is the substance, story the form. But now I am using *scandal* in a much broader sense than the specialized biblical sense I have used earlier. Although I do not intend to abandon my specialized sense, this broad meaning of *scandal* requires an explanation that will in turn be crucial to my argument about the importance of plot and story in John, and about the ascendancy in John of scandalous story over creed or doctrine.

In "The Origin of Plot," Jurij M. Lotman describes two contradictory types of plot. The plot of myth deals with wholeness, with integrated structures, with norms and systems; it has no interest in beginnings and endings because it is essentially timeless or cyclical. It is law forming; it regulates; it provides order. Some (though not Lotman himself) associate it with the Logos. The plot of excess or scandal, on the other hand, which is the peripheral sphere around the central, myth-making sphere, deals with time — linear time — that is composed of discrete events, and it deals with the elements of chance, chaos, the improbable, and the anomalous. It is concerned with "the archive of excesses" in contrast to the "integrated, structural whole" of the mythic plot (173). "Myth," Lotman says, "always speaks about me. 'News,' an anecdote [the plot of excess], speaks about *somebody else*. The first organizes the hearer's world, the second adds interesting details to his knowledge of this world" (163).

Frank Kermode expands and mystifies Lotman on the plot of myth to include the occult — the deeper, darker, and more mysterious; the true, hidden design of the world. His myth, or world-plot, in textual form is "a spiritual encyclopedia," as Homer's *Odyssey* was for James Joyce or as the Hebrew Bible was for the evangelists ("The Bible," 211). Kermode's "scandal," which he links with "story" in contrast to mythic plot, exists in realistic events in time. In scandalous story, things happen in causal but unpredictable ways.

As both Lotman and Kermode make clear, these two antithetical plots are significant because of their relationships with each other. For Lotman (following Bakhtin), this relationship is specifically dialogic. The "wide variety of life" — the archive of excess —

penetrates into "the regulating sphere of theory" at the same time as "mythologism penetrates into the sphere of the excess" (179). By means of this interaction of scandal and myth, "plot represents a powerful means of making sense of life" (182). Kermode sees the Bible as "a book with a plot . . . recurring amid the scandals and excesses of time." It is a book that conceals "behind its stories an occult plot which is a master version of the plot of our world" (223).

John begins his Gospel with mythic plot reduced to the fundamental: "the Word." This is no semiotic structure, as it would be understood by Lotman, but the transcendent Logos. This Logos is, has been, and will be, but it is also beyond time, and it is also the Word made flesh in Jesus and in time. It is John's mythic plot. But Jesus, who is the Word, is manifest in John's text in the form of story, specifically in scandalous story, both in the broad, narrative sense of Lotman's "news" (the Gospels as "good news") and in the Kierkegaardian sense of offense, divine and otherwise.

"In the beginning was the Word, and the Word was with God, and the Word was God. . . . And the Word became flesh and lived among us, and we have seen his glory, the glory as of a father's only son, full of grace and truth" (John 1:1, 14). John's beginning has no birth of the child Jesus but rather goes back before beginnings to the preexistent life, light, glory, and truth that regulate and give meaning to the stories of ordinary human life. John's Logos or Word is identical to Jesus who becomes flesh in time; without him there is no order, regulation, design, or truth. The Logos-Jesus constitutes John's mythic world-plot which, like light, illuminates events in time. John is the antithesis of the postmodern deconstructionist: his text, since it begins with and centers on the Logos, is "logocentric," the bête noir of deconstructionists, and, worse yet, John is willing to name the Logos in the form of flesh.[1]

But even in the midst of John's opening hymn to the Word, there is an intrusion of anecdote and darkness. "He was in the world, and the world came into being through him; yet the world did not know him. He came to what was his own, and his own people did not accept him" (1:10–11). Not knowing is ignorance. Not accepting one in "his own" is something more than ignorance, closer to rejection. When that one is the creator and the Word, this not accepting is the state of being offended, which intrudes upon John's hymn to the Word as it must intrude upon his narrative, since it is in the nature of this fleshly Word to pose the possibility of offense, which may result in not knowing or not accepting.

More specifically, however, the odd intrusion into the opening hymn is the appearance of John the Baptist: "He himself was not the light, but he came to testify to the light" (1:8). He testifies through the paradox of time and hierarchy: "John testified to him and cried out, 'This was he of whom I said, "He who comes after me ranks ahead of me because he was before me"'" (1:15). John the Baptist, who is not light, testifies to the light and truth, because he, unlike the world, comes to know and accept. He, living in time, is not offended by this timeless good news. The hymn to the Word, with its odd interruptive gestures toward the Baptist, is John's way of beginning a story that is peripheral to the ordering Logos or myth at the center. It establishes immediately, however, that whenever the Logos impinges on the world of time, we have the possibility of offense. The dynamics of John's narrative are constituted by the dialogic interaction of the Logos-Jesus on the one hand and, on the other, the good and bad news, the anecdote, the excess, the scandalous story.

The Beloved Disciple and the End of Interpretation

Kermode's assertion that biblical stories conceal an "occult" plot, requiring interpretation, may be placed in radical juxtaposition to Drury's remark that John's parable of the vine is "a quintessentially Johannine allegorical parable": "it presents no problems and needs no interpretation"; "it is not at all enigmatic" (*Parables*, 159, 164). The two assertions suggest two very different approaches to John: positing a virtual requirement for enigma versus positing an essentially lucid text. For interpreters such as Kermode, enigmas are the stuff of interpretive life. In *The Genesis of Secrecy*, Kermode contemplates the enigmatic Man in the Mackintosh who wanders through *Ulysses* and the equally enigmatic Boy in the Shirt, the young man in Matthew and Mark who runs away naked when Jesus is arrested. But Drury, in spite of an allegorical reading based on Hosea, Isaiah, and Jeremiah, sees John as an essentially lucid text. Oddly enough, both are correct about John. John actively wants to bring an end to interpretation, and he has created the Gospel enigma par excellence: the Beloved Disciple. The end of interpretation and interpretive enigmas are crucial to how the reader responds to the scandalous narratives of John's Gospel.

Drury is by no means alone in commenting on the lucidity and non-enigmatic quality of John, leaving aside, perhaps, the opening hymn; one of the first things most readers notice is that John's Jesus is far more open and non-secretive than Jesus in the synoptic

Gospels. But there is nonetheless something patently enigmatic about the Beloved Disciple. Who is this unidentified but preferred disciple? And why is he unidentified? Some have said the Beloved Disciple is the traditional author of the Gospel, John, son of Zebedee, who does not identify himself as the Beloved Disciple out of modesty. Others have argued for John Mark, the supposed author of the Gospel of Mark; others for Lazarus, the only male in John whom Jesus is explicitly said to have loved; others (provocatively) for Judas; and others for no one, the Beloved Disciple as a purely symbolic, ideal Christian disciple. Raymond Brown gives a good account of the pros and cons of most of these candidates in the *Anchor Bible* (xcii–xcviii) and himself favors the candidacy of John, son of Zebedee, though he acknowledges that this is an "ad hoc theory," not subject to proof (cii).

The inescapable literary fact—and one that no reader can afford to ignore—is that the Beloved Disciple is not named, though he is clearly an important part of the narrative action. As the unidentified disciple, he may be the same as the unnamed disciple who, with Andrew, leaves John the Baptist to follow Jesus (1:37–42) and possibly the same as the unnamed disciple who, with Peter, follows Jesus into the courtyard of the high priest (18:15–16). But he is explicitly identified as the Beloved Disciple in six places: at the Last Supper (13:23–26), where he reclines next to Jesus and asks who will betray him; at the cross (19:25–27), where Jesus proclaims that his own mother and the Beloved Disciple are mother and son to each other; after the resurrection (20:2–10), when Mary Magdalene tells Peter and the Beloved Disciple that Jesus is not in the tomb and the two disciples run to look; in the boat, after the resurrection (21:7), when the Beloved Disciple recognizes Jesus; soon after (21:20–23), when Peter, walking with Jesus, sees the Beloved Disciple following and asks about him; and in the penultimate sentence of the Gospel, where he is identified as the witness and author of "these things," though he is referred to by the literal author in the third person ("we know that *his* [the Beloved Disciple's] testimony is true"). This witness is presumably the same person as the one in 19:35, who saw blood and water come from Jesus's body on the cross: "He who saw this has testified so that you also may believe. His testimony is true, and he knows that he tells the truth."

Although it is reasonable to ask the historical question "Who is he?" as readers we must wonder at the odd namelessness of this important disciple. The Beloved Disciple is John's enigma: the one "beloved" by the teacher who told his disciples that he loved them and that they must abide in his love (15:10); the one closest to Jesus, who could ask questions the others dared not; the new son to Jesus's mother; the first disciple to reach the empty tomb and, though second to enter, the first who "saw and believed" in the risen Jesus. And all of these roles are assigned to a nameless character in a Gospel that names the high priest's (Caiaphas's) slave ("The slave's name was Malchus"; 18:10), whose right ear a disciple (Simon Peter) cuts off.

By way of contrast, consider the character of Judas. He is a character difficult to grasp, and also the source of endless historical and theological speculation. But in John he is no enigma. When Jesus tells the disciples that "one of you is a devil," John as omniscient narrator clarifies the reference: "He was speaking of Judas son of Simon Iscariot, for he, though one of the twelve, was going to betray him" (6:70-71). Later, when Judas protests that Mary has wasted expensive ointment by bathing Jesus's feet with it instead of selling it and giving the money to the poor, John clarifies by explaining what Judas's motives were not ("not that he cared about the poor"), identifies his ethos ("he was a thief"), and tells of his stealing from the money box (12:5-6). At the Last Supper, John tells us that the devil put betrayal into Judas's heart (13:2) and that after Judas ate the morsel "Satan entered into him" (13:27). There are plenty of interpretive problems here, but Judas is not, properly speaking, an enigma: he is one of the twelve, he has a named, unambiguous identity—clearly distinguished from another "Judas (not Iscariot)" (14:22)—and he acts from clearly defined motives. He is an objectification of Satan, and no matter what difficult, arguable historical and theological issues this may raise, he, unlike the Beloved Disciple, is not presented by the narrator as an enigma.

John's omniscient, revealing portrayal of Judas is typical, and the enigmatic portrayal of the Beloved Disciple is atypical. When Jesus says something enigmatic, as when he tells the Jews to destroy the temple and he will raise it up in three days, John knows, and tells the reader, what Jesus means: "he was speaking of the temple of his body" (2:21). John knows, and tells the reader, that Jesus is the Word, the true light, the truth, and the glory. Indeed, John's Jesus is more clearly omniscient and certainly less secretive than Mark's Jesus; his words to the high priest in John 18:20 ("I have spoken openly to the world; . . . I have said nothing in secret") would be out of place in any other Gospel. John's omniscience and lucidity seem designed to prevent misunderstanding, misinterpretation, and even interpretation.

But John does not simply assume or assert his right to a lucid omniscience that suppresses interpretation. He argues that his text is based on an eyewitness account and warns that any interpretation of it will corrupt the text. The source of the witness, and the vehicle for the warning, is the Beloved Disciple. At the end, when Peter is told by Jesus, "Follow me," another also follows—the Beloved Disciple. Peter says to Jesus, "Lord, what about him?" and receives a potentially offensive answer (not unlike his response to his mother at the wedding in Cana): "Jesus said to him, 'If it is my will that he remain until I come, what is that to you? Follow me!'" Then the narrator, instead of offering his typical interpretive assistance, adds, "So the rumor spread in the community that this disciple [the Beloved Disciple] would not die. Yet Jesus did not say to him [Peter] that he would not die, but [repeating the exact words], 'If it is my will that he remain until I come, what is that to you?'" (21:21–23). Jesus's words, when "spread in the community" orally, are interpreted by hearers, not unreasonably, to mean that the Beloved Disciple would remain alive until Jesus returned. But John insists, with literal accuracy, that Jesus did not say that; what he actually said can be represented only by repeating the spoken, but now firmly written, words, which constitute a strong warning against interpreting what Jesus has said and what John has written.

The written word is itself sufficient, because it returns directly to the Word, but the written word is not itself complete: "But there are also many other things that Jesus did; if every one of them were written down, I suppose that the world itself could not contain the books that would be written" (21:25). The "many other things that Jesus did" constitute the unmanageable archive of excess. John's Gospel is, he readily admits, only a part, not the whole, but Jesus, the Word, is the whole and is uncontainable. Yet the admittedly partial Gospel is the truth, because its subject is Truth. And as, in the beginning, the Baptist is not light but testifies to the light and the truth, so in the end the Beloved Disciple, the source of words but not the Word, testifies to the Word and to the things that the Word-Jesus has done: "This [the Beloved Disciple] is the disciple who is testifying to these things and has written them, and we know that his testimony is true" (21:24).[2]

Thus, John's narrative omniscience derives from the true testimony of the Beloved Disciple and from knowledge of the Word. His narrative words turn away from charismatic speech to narrative Gospel (Kelber, "Authority," 109–19) and from the oral tradition, which interprets and thus corrupts, to written words as containers of the uncontainable Word. We may nonetheless ask why John should want to use the enigma of the Beloved Disciple to assert the truth of his words and the uninterpretability of them.

The enigmatic Beloved Disciple is John's narrative means for effecting the interaction between anecdote, news, information about others on the one hand, and myth, Logos, truth-for-me, on the other. In 20:30, John tells the reader why he writes: "Now Jesus did many other signs in the presence of his disciples, which are not written in this book. But these are written so that you may come to believe that Jesus is the Messiah, the Son of God, and that through believing you may have life in his name." The good news of John's Gospel is written so that "you may come to believe" and "have life," but one cannot have belief and have life without encountering the possibility of offense, which Jesus warns his disciples of in his farewell discourse: "I have said these things to you to keep you from stumbling [*skandalisthēte*]" (16:1). The alternatives, when confronted with the Word, are belief or offense. The signs are written in John that the reader may believe, but signs also may scandalize. And signs that are seen are, for John, less powerful than what is not seen. When the unbelieving Thomas, on seeing the pierced hands and sides, recognizes Jesus as "My Lord and my God!" Jesus says, "Have you believed because you have seen me? Blessed are those who have not seen and yet have come to believe" (20:28–29).

The disciple who epitomizes this blessedness of not seeing and yet believing is the Beloved Disciple. He arrived at the tomb first, but Peter entered first and "saw" linen wrappings and the cloth. "Then the other disciple, who reached the tomb first, also went in, and he saw and believed; for as yet they did not understand the scripture, that he must rise from the dead" (20:8–9). He saw and believed, but what he saw was not simply linen wrappings and the cloth, not a physical sign, but rather an absence that leads to faith. By not seeing, he sees, and he sees more blessedly than Thomas. John's signs, like the synoptic evangelists' parables, are not intended to be riddles to be interpreted or solved; they are intended to lead one to belief through the possibility of offense.[3] The empty tomb is no sign, but it is a *skandalon*, and through it the Beloved Disciple is the first to see through the eyes of faith the resurrected Jesus in his absence. The enigmatic Beloved Disciple sees what for most could be at best an enigma, but he believes. For him, scandalous story becomes mythic plot, with the Logos-Jesus at the center.

The act of seeing, through the possibility of offense, is the way from news to Logos. The historically nameless disciple may be John

Mark or John, son of Zebedee, or someone else, or no one, but in John's Gospel he will always be the nameless, enigmatic follower who lives both in the narrative time of the anecdote and in the moment of the Logos. He might even be, as Bultmann and, more recently, Kurz have argued, the ideal Christian disciple, a model for the reader. But models have a way of becoming obstacles, and the Beloved Disciple, insofar as he is the object of a historical obsession to identify him, becomes an obstacle, a *skandalon* in his own right.

Through the Beloved Disciple, John affirms that his written words are not to be interpreted; that they are to lead to the one Word, or to offense; that "life in his [Jesus's] name" is accessible to the nameless; that news is lifeless unless it interacts with truth; and that the enigma of life in time as it merges with life in the eternal Word lies not in named identity but in not seeing and seeing.

The Narrative Progress of Offense

John's narrative unfolds as the interaction of the scandalous news with the Logos, culminating with the divine offenses of the cross and the open tomb. Raymond Brown calls chapters 2 through 4 "From Cana to Cana," which usefully calls attention to the physical return and repetition. Jesus turns water into wine at the wedding in Cana, then he travels to Capernaum for two days, then to Jerusalem, where he drives the money changers from the temple and speaks to Nicodemus, then to Aenon ("Springs"), where the Baptist testifies, then back to Galilee, where he speaks to the woman at the well in Samaria, and finally back to Cana, where he cures the official's son, who is ill in Capernaum. These are all events, news, anecdotes, but at the center of them all is Jesus, the Word. They are John's selections ("many other signs . . . are not written in this book"; 20:30) from the archive of excess about other people, and their responses to Jesus are variations on the fundamental alternative: belief or offense. The alternative brings each of the narrative characters into an encounter with the Logos, which must be a personal encounter ("about me," as Lotman says) for those characters. And this personal encounter leads to the reader's encounter that is John's narrative goal: "these are written so that you may come to believe" (20:31).

When Jesus's mother tells him there is no wine left at the wedding in Cana, his response—"Woman, what have I to do with thee?" (2:4, KJV)—was one of Blake's favorite New Testament offenses (see "To Tirzah" in *Songs of Experience*). Others, however, prefer to avoid this offense. The *Interpreter's Bible* (Buttrick) admits that

Jesus's answer "seems harsh" and "may" even "deprecate fussy interference" (although fussy interference is hardly a serious offense), but
the recommended reading is: "Never mind; don't be worried." J. N.
Sanders reassures us that the English translation "gives quite a
wrong impression," that it "is not as harsh as it sounds in English,"
and that "its precise force"—not harsh, certainly—"depends entirely
on the tone of voice with which it is uttered" (110). Raymond Brown
argues that the form of address is "polite," though "peculiar," since a
son is addressing a mother, and that the response "seemingly" implies "simple disengagement," though he points out that there are
other places in the New Testament where the same words clearly
imply hostility. Brown acknowledges that both the hostile and the
disengaged meanings in the Bible involve "some refusal of an inop-
portune involvement" (99). A serious problem with this inoffensive
reading is that Jesus's mother's response to his rejection of her
involvement is to remain involved; she tells the servants to do whatever Jesus tells them to do. John as narrator does not provide a
reassuring interpretation to the seemingly harsh saying because one
is not needed: Jesus is offensive because he is an offense to his
earthly mother and to all the world. The important thing to note
about this passage is not how it can be interpreted as inoffensive
but that Jesus's mother is not offended. Her response is to believe
("Do whatever he tells you"; 2:5) and to follow ("After this he went
down to Capernaum with his mother"; 2:12). After the miracle, only
the response of the disciples is recorded: "his disciples believed in
him" (2:11). And they, too, follow him to Capernaum. They have
read the sign well—not because they have interpreted it accurately
or been appropriately astonished but because they have believed.

   The next anecdote deals with the sellers of oxen, sheep, and
pigeons and the money changers in the temple. The anecdote of the
wedding party is an anecdote about the miraculous transformation
of the contents of ritual purification vessels, but this is an anecdote
about an altogether human event, a cleansing (and thus a transforming) of a desecrated, impure temple. The sellers and money changers
constitute a *skandalon* to Jesus by making "my Father's house" into
"a marketplace" (2:16). His actions in turn scandalize the Jewish
authorities (whom John refers to as "the Jews"), who demand a sign
and receive instead Jesus's cryptic comment about the temple ("Destroy this temple, and in three days I will raise it up"), which offers
the possibility of offense to the Jews ("This temple has been under
construction for forty-six years, and will you raise it up in three
days?"; 2:19–20). Here it might appear that John plays the role of

later commentators by explaining away the offense ("But he was speaking of the temple of his body"). In truth, however, raising the body from the empty tomb will prove to be far more offensive than a spectacular sign like raising the temple.

The effect of the cleansing of the temple is memory: "His disciples remembered that it was written, 'Zeal for your house will consume me'" (2:17). The effect of the exchange with the Jews about the temple/body is *future* memory and belief. "After he was raised from the dead, his disciples remembered that he had said this; and they believed the scripture and the word that Jesus had spoken" (2:22). Jesus's words, which are the Word, lead to offense and faith.

With regard to the disciples (though not "the Jews" and the sellers and money changers), this story has a happy ending. But the story of Nicodemus, like many synoptic stories and parables, is a truncated story, abandoned in suspension, with no conclusion. Nicodemus is unlike the scandalized Jews in that he is a ruler of the Jews who knows, from the signs, that Jesus is "from God"; thus, he appears as one likely to believe and unlikely to be offended. But Nicodemus comes to Jesus not as an individual who lives in the light but as a representative of a group ("we know that you are a teacher who has come from God"; 3:2), hazarding a visit only "by night." Jesus's response is not exactly encouraging and certainly baffling: "Very truly, I tell you, no one can see the kingdom of God without being born from above" (3:3). The issue is not group knowing but individual seeing. But Nicodemus cannot see, as one inevitably cannot in the Johannine night, and Jesus's responses become challenging (the offense as insult): "Are you a [literally, the] teacher of Israel, and yet you do not understand these things? . . . you do not receive our testimony . . . you do not believe" (3:10–12). In the story, we do not know the effect of this speech. Nicodemus simply disappears from the narrative, whether in a state of offense, faith, or bafflement we do not know. His visit by night, however, no matter how well intentioned or how understandable given the risks, is ominous. "Those who walk during the day," John writes, "do not stumble" (11:9), and "those who walk at night stumble" (11:10). Nicodemus does reappear on two brief occasions, first as a modest and hesitant defender of Jesus, questioning the Jewish legal procedures (7:51) and finally as one who helps to bury Jesus, when he comes with an extravagant amount of spices. Like Joseph of Arimathea's faith, Nicodemus's, however hesitant it may be, appears to be qualified and secret, out of fear of the Jews whom he rules.

John the Baptist's faith knows no such hesitations, and he, too, though no ruler, has much to lose, as John reminds us by adding, "John, of course, had not yet been thrown into prison" (3:24). Matthew's and Luke's Baptist has some doubts about whether Jesus is the Messiah, and so he sends his disciples to Jesus to ask if he is the one who is to come. Jesus tells these disciples to report to the Baptist the signs, healings, and good news they have seen and heard and adds, "And blessed is anyone who takes no offense at me" (Matt. 11:6, Luke 7:23). But John's Baptist has no doubts, no need to question Jesus. He does, however, receive reports from his disciples, and the reports are, in their eyes, bad news: "Rabbi [John the Baptist], the one who was with you across the Jordan [Jesus], to whom you testified, here he is baptizing, and all are going to him" (3:26). But their bad news is his good news: the Baptist affirms that he rejoices, that his joy is full. His blessedness is manifest in his refusal to be offended at what seems to his disciples to be an offense.

The Baptist is not offended, but the report of this competition—who is making and baptizing more disciples than whom—is what leads Jesus to begin the journey back to Galilee (4:1–3). Once he has posed the possibility of offense, he has done what he must do, and it is up to the disciples, the Baptist, and the Pharisees to respond as they will. The evangelist's narrative task is to tell the news, so to speak, about the offenses and how they relate to the Word.

The immediately following encounter with the Samaritan woman at the well constitutes the narrative climax of this section, as the most humanly and the most essentially offensive. The offensiveness of Jesus's simple request, "Give me a drink" (4:7), is not immediately apparent. To grasp it, we may turn to historical scholarship, but the first recourse must be to John's lucid narration: "The Samaritan woman said to him, 'How is it that you, a Jew, ask a drink of me, a woman of Samaria?' (Jews do not share things in common with Samaritans.)" (4:9; parentheses in NRSV). John makes a point of telling the reader this because he wants his readers (who may not be contemporary Jews) to understand the possibility of offense. The historical glosses about the source and nature of the powerful antagonisms between Jews and Samaritans are no more than useful elaborations of John's gloss, of his dramatization of the disciples' reaction to the conversation ("They were astonished that he was speaking with a woman"; 4:27), and of his report of what they did not (but presumably wanted to) say to Jesus.

But if the act of conversing itself is potentially offensive, as John insists, the content of the brief conversation contains three more offenses. First, Jesus, the man "tired out by his journey" (4:6), with no means of drawing water from the well and therefore asking her for drink, has the audacity (from the human point of view) to suggest that if she "knew the gift of God, and who it is that is saying to you, 'Give me a drink,' you would have asked him, and he would have given you living water" (4:10), which she may take to mean "spring water." This is hardly a case of good manners, or good rhetoric, from a tired, thirsty man. That the woman finds it potentially offensive is clear from her response: "Are you greater than our ancestor Jacob, who gave us the well?" She correctly perceives that he, supposedly the one in need, is making great claims for himself, and he confirms it by elaborating on his offer of extraordinary water, which he now calls "a spring of water gushing up to eternal life." She is not offended by this claim and offer, though only because she misunderstands: she wants his proffered water so that she will not have to engage in the hard work of drawing more water from Jacob's well.

Jesus then responds with his second offense, "Go, call your husband," knowing supernaturally that she has had five husbands and that she is living now with a man who is not her husband, which he proceeds to tell her about. This could potentially excite the woman's antagonism, but again she is not offended. "Sir, I see that you are a prophet," she says, whereupon she raises the issue of the proper place of worship. Jesus's response, which denigrates the places of both the Samaritans (the mountain) and the Jews (Jerusalem), replacing them with the true worship in a new region of "spirit and truth," elicits her statement of faith—"I know that Messiah is coming"— which in turn leads to Jesus's third offense: his utterance of the divine name, *ego eimi*, I AM, "I am he" (4:26). A tired man, asking for water, announces himself to be a divine being, the Christ; this is what Kierkegaard calls the essential offense.

But, of course, the story is not over. Positing the offense is the beginning, not the end, of spiritual life. The response is all. The woman's response is to leave her water jar (because it cannot contain the living water?) and say to her people, "Come and see a man who told me everything I have ever done! He cannot be the Messiah, can he?" This is the end of our knowledge of the Samaritan woman. Her narrative fate is to pose the question—"He cannot be the Messiah, can he?"—and never come to the answer. Does she eventually believe? Is she eventually offended? We shall never know. She, like Nicodemus, is suspended in narrative darkness, but, unlike Nicodemus, she makes no narrative return.

Perhaps through this narrative ellipsis John suggests that it is easier to believe in the Christ when one hears about him than when

one sees him. Is the Samaritan woman to be envied for what she
sees—a tired Jew who speaks cryptically about mysterious water,
tells her about her sordid past, and says he is divine?

The other Samaritans have it easier: some of them believe because of the woman's testimony—supernatural knowledge of past
scandals at second hand—but after Jesus stays for two days, many
more believe because of his word, and they are able to say, firsthand,
"We know that this is truly the Savior of the world" (4:42). It is no
small matter that the Samaritans of Sychar should accept a traveling
Jew as savior of "the world"—Jews, Samaritans, and the rest—and if
we think about this event, filling in the missing actions, midrash-
style, we might imagine that all the Samaritans must have encountered some offense in this Jewish traveler before believing in him as
savior. But John narrates no dramatic offense to the Samaritan people, who believe. We may recall that in Jerusalem "many believed
in his name because they saw the signs that he was doing. But Jesus
on his part would not entrust himself to them" (2:23–24). Are these
believing Samaritans to be trusted any more than the believing
Jews? Easier is not necessarily better. One who arrives at belief
without having passed through the offense may not be a trusted
believer. The difference between the Samaritan people and the Samaritan woman is at the end a difference between belief and a question, but it is also a difference between belief without dramatized
offense and possible belief based on the possibility of multiple offense. Her challenge, dramatically, is the harder one.

The issue of "the world" is pushed further in the next scene,
when Jesus is approached by the official in Capernaum, whose son
is dying in Cana, some twenty miles away. The savior of the Jews,
then the Samaritans, now becomes the savior of the Gentiles. But
Jesus does not spare this begging Gentile official the possibility of
offense. Jesus says, "Unless you see signs and wonders you will not
believe" (4:48). The official responds, "Sir, come down before my
little boy dies." His petition expresses not disbelief but belief dependent on Jesus's coming down to Cana, which Jesus then indicates is
unnecessary: "Go; your son will live." The official is offended neither
by Jesus's accusation about needing signs and wonders nor by his
refusal to "come down": "The man believed the word that Jesus
spoke to him and started on his way." For the official, the word has
become the Word; his potentially tragic news has encountered the
timeless Logos.

The Gentile official believes without signs (as the Samaritans
do), but in the comic, and happy, ending he is nonetheless hungry

for a sign. When he meets his servants, who are coming to tell him of his child's recovery, he asks when the child began to mend and determines that it was the very hour Jesus had promised he would live—a sign that Jesus was the cause of the child's recovery. And this leads to a doubly happy ending: "he himself believed, along with his whole household." Although the Gentile is not offended when confronted with his need for signs and wonders, he wants them anyway, if they are to be had. This Gentile, like most of the rest of us, prefers a world of time and news, but he is also capable of encountering the Logos in belief.

The Divine Skandalon *Enacted: God as Flesh*

In John's narrative, many Jews believe, a Samaritan village believes, a Gentile household believes. Belief spreads. And the possibility of offense spreads—from a Jewish mother (Jesus's own), to a Jewish ruler (Nicodemus), to a Samaritan woman, to a Gentile official— and with this possibility comes the actual offense, which reaches its narrative climax in the trial and crucifixion of Jesus. But long before this climax, in John's story, the divine offense is manifested in nearly unreadable, or unhearable, starkness. Literally, it is nearly unhearable to the disciples: "This is a hard saying," they say; "who can listen to it?" (6:60, RSV). It becomes readable for us because of the news that surrounds it and the fact that, dramatically, it is news about somebody else, and also because we engage in a kind of automatic interpretation that makes it not only readable but all too readable—almost unremarkable and certainly inoffensive.

The divine offense appears in the context of news about a miraculous and a repulsive feeding. In John 6, the miraculous feeding takes place on a mountain when Jesus feeds the five thousand with the lad's five barley loaves and two fish and has twelve baskets of fragments left over. The crowd responds in a way similar to the Samaritan woman: "This is indeed the prophet who is to come into the world!" (6:14), but the response is not a sign of Johannine belief or faith. In fact, Jesus must escape from them after the miracle because they were "about to come and take him by force to make him king," which is not the kind of glory he has in mind. When evening comes, the disciples leave by boat without Jesus, a strong wind comes up, and, when they are three or four miles out to sea, Jesus appears, walking on the sea, and they are frightened. Jesus's word is the divine word, *egō eimi*, "It is I; do not be afraid" (6:20). The divine appears to them, supernaturally but also physically.

Jesus is taken into the boat, and they are all immediately, and miraculously, at shore.

The next news is that the crowd follows Jesus to the other side, seeking him, but they find him only to have their motives insulted. "Very truly, I tell you, you are looking for me, not because you saw signs, but because you ate your fill of the loaves" (6:26). They seek not because of prophetic signs or the desire to make him their political leader against Rome but because of their bellies—the offense, again, as insult. Furthermore, he instructs them, offensively from their point of view, about the Scripture. In answer to their request for a sign like Moses' manna in the wilderness, Jesus says, "Very truly, I tell you, it was not Moses who gave you the bread from heaven, but it is my Father who gives you the true bread from heaven," and proceeds to offer them another version of the divine offense, the *egō eimi* from a human: "I am the bread of life" (6:32–35). The crowd had wanted to know what they must do to be doing the works of God, and Jesus's answer was to believe in him, Jesus (6:28–29). Their task is to see and believe: "This is indeed the will of my Father, that all who see the Son and believe in him may have eternal life" (6:40). But this they have not done: "you have seen me and yet do not believe" (6:36).

The crowd is offended by the essential offense, murmuring at him as the Israelites had murmured at Moses in the wilderness: "Then the Jews began to complain about him because he said, 'I am the bread that came down from heaven,'" and in their state of offense they affirm that he is mere man, "Jesus, the son of Joseph, whose father and mother we know," and not divine. Jesus, however, does not curse them for disbelief, nor does he soften his offensive message. He repeats his divine connection with God, the necessity of belief in him for eternal life, and the identity of himself, his flesh, and "the living bread" (6:41–51), adding that this bread must be eaten.

Far from being mollified by this, the Jews (as the crowd is now called) respond with violent disputes, saying, "How can this man give us his flesh to eat?" They are offended and angry, and Jesus in the synagogue gives them more to be angry and offended about: "Very truly, I tell you, unless you eat the flesh of the Son of Man *and drink his blood*, you have no life in you. Those who *gnaw on* my flesh and drink my blood have eternal life" (6:53–54). What I have translated as "gnaw on" is usually translated as "eat," the same verb Jesus uses several times in the preceding sentences. But in the Greek this verb is not the same; it means not simply eat, but gnaw, chew, munch, eat audibly, as when animals eat. Jesus continues, "for my flesh is true food and my blood is true drink. Those who *gnaw on* my flesh and drink my blood abide in me, and I in them. . . . Whoever *gnaws on* me will live because of me. . . . The one who *gnaws on* this bread will live forever" (6:55–58).

I am insisting that this is first and foremost an offensive passage, but John himself is sufficiently lucid about the offense not only in Jesus's enactment of it but in the response as well: "When many of his disciples heard it, they said, 'This teaching is difficult; who can accept it?' But Jesus, being aware that his disciples were complaining about it, said to them, 'Does this offend you? [This *skandalizei* you?] . . . But among you there are some who do not believe.' . . . Because of this many of his disciples turned back and no longer went about with him" (6:60–66). The disciples have encountered the essential offense. Jesus has offended them by asserting that he, a human, is the *egō eimi*, the divine I AM, and he has done it in a way that maximizes the offensiveness of his claim. In the Hebrew Bible, to eat one's flesh is to engage in a hostile action. In Psalm 27:2, the speaker laments, "When evildoers assail me *to devour my flesh—* my adversaries and foes—they shall stumble and fall." There, the evildoers who eat his flesh stumble and fall; in Jesus's version, those who do *not* eat his flesh will stumble and fall. The eating or drinking of blood is specifically prohibited by the Torah (e.g., Deut. 12:23–25). In an apocalyptic vision, Ezekiel is instructed by God to call the birds and the beasts together in a sacrificial feast in which they "shall eat flesh and drink blood" of God's enemies (Ezek. 39:17).

Why is it, then, that many commentaries on this passage do not even hint that there is anything offensive about it, in spite of the disciples' own offense, which is specifically remarked on by Jesus? One answer might be that the disciples are simply wrong, misguided; they have misinterpreted the saying, and the commentaries rush to interpret more satisfactorily by eliminating the offense. But we jump altogether too quickly to a "right" interpretation of gnawing on the flesh and drinking the blood. And it is understandable that we do, since who wants to abide in these shocking images? It is only human to want to avoid the inhuman, but it is also only human to want to avoid the divine, as Moses discovered when the Israelites appointed him to speak to God face to face and report back, sparing them the fear and trembling.[4]

It seems evident that John wants his readers as well as his characters—the "Jews" and disciples—to experience the possibility of offense in this passage. That we readers are not the characters in the narrative, that we are not the immediate addressees, makes our response different, of course, but the real reason most modern readers find nothing offensive here is because it is preinterpreted. As Raymond Brown says, "If Jesus's words in 6:53 are to have a favorable meaning, they must refer to the Eucharist. They simply reproduce the words we hear in the Synoptic account of the institution of the Eucharist (Matt. 26:26-28): 'Take, *eat;* this is *my body;* . . . *drink* . . . this is *my blood*'" (284-85). Some who reject this interpretation argue that the passage has a favorable meaning because it speaks of receiving Christ spiritually through faith. But are Jesus's words necessarily to have a favorable meaning? Perhaps they are to be as offensive as they patently are.

It may be that the eucharistic overtones of this passage are "universally recognized" (Culpepper, 197), but if so we should be careful that universal truths do not stand in the way of reading particular words accurately. It would be more accurate to say, with Colin Brown, that the eucharist is about what is described in John 6, but John 6 is not about the eucharist (2: 535)—at least, there is no hard evidence actually within John's text that he is writing about the eucharist. Historically speaking, some form of the eucharist existed when John wrote, but, dramatically speaking, the eucharist does not exist when Jesus speaks in John 6 (because, chronologically, there has been no Last Supper yet), and John does not include any talk about eating flesh or drinking blood in his version of the Last Supper, thereby missing an excellent opportunity to invite a eucharistic interpretation of the earlier passage. John 6 is, whatever else one may say of it, offensive drama. John's warning against interpreting Jesus's words about the Beloved Disciple (21:23) is appropriate here: Jesus "did not say" that this referred to the eucharist or to spiritual faith; he said what he said. And what he said is an offense.

When I discussed in chapter 7 the notoriously scandalous passage in Matthew about plucking out one's eye and cutting off one's hand or foot, I argued that the passage could, and should, be read literally but hypothetically and that when read in this way, Jesus is certainly offensive but is not actually advocating the idolatry of plucking out one's own eye. But to read John 6 literally is, well, a greater challenge. Jesus says straightforwardly that they must gnaw on his flesh and drink his blood, without the *if* clauses of the eye, hand, and foot passage. It sounds distressingly like cannibalism, which is not much better, if that, than plucking out one's eye. We are stuck with two choices: interpretation (of the he-really-means variety) or responding as the disciples do and acknowledging it as a hard, offensive saying. We do not know the name of the Beloved Disciple, and I am inclined to acknowledge that we do not know the meaning of this hard passage. But we nonetheless do, emphatically, have the character and actions of the Beloved Disciple in the text, and we can and ought to have the offense of John 6.

My emphasis on drama in this passage has led me to what may seem like know-nothing-ism. One might object that even if John opposes interpretation at the end of his book (in a passage that may not have been written by John), he is a highly symbolic writer, himself given to interpretation. When Jesus says "temple," John tells us that he means "body." When John says "night" and "darkness," we sense a metaphorical meaning that contrasts with Jesus's proclamation, "I am the light of the world." When he says "gnaw on my flesh" and "drink my blood," why may he not have meant "take the eucharist"? I am not inclined to interpret it so because John—metaphysician, symbolist, and self-conscious narrator that he is—does not incorporate in his text any evidence that he, or Jesus, is suggesting an explicit meaning, as he does somewhat crudely with "temple" and more subtly with "night" and "darkness." The evidence about the eucharist is external, and if one wishes to accept it (as many people certainly will), I would still want to call attention to the primacy of offensive drama. My literalism does have its limits: there is no actual cannibalism in this passage, of the sort that anthropologists study in the field, and "I am the bread of life" is metaphor. But Jesus's extension of the basic metaphor to gnawing flesh and drinking blood is, if still metaphor, certainly scandalous metaphor. And, I am inclined to add, uninterpretable, scandalous metaphor.

The other common interpretation—that Jesus is referring to receiving him spiritually through faith—does have some textual basis. Shortly after saying that he who gnaws on his flesh and drinks his blood has eternal life and "abides in me," he says, "It is the spirit that gives life; the flesh is useless. The words that I have spoken to you are spirit and life" (6:63). This, it might be argued, suggests that eating flesh is a metaphor for abiding in the spirit, or the Logos, who is Jesus. If this is true, does it allow us to interpret "gnawing on flesh" as "abiding in spirit"? Certainly not, since such interpretation removes the offense, and the dramatic offense is the heart of the hard saying. Of the words referred to in Jesus's statement, "The words that I have spoken to you are spirit and life," Bultmann's comment is apt: "But the words are precisely the *skandalon!*" (*Gospel*, 446). The words are an offense, as the Word made flesh must be. There can be no abiding in the spirit without passing through the offense. Interpretation, which domesticates the offense, robs John's words of their "spirit and life."

Bultmann asserts that the offense of the Gospel "is brought out as strongly as possible" by the phrase "the Word became flesh" (1: 14), because it is in Jesus's "sheer humanity that he is the Revealer." This, he says, is "the paradox which runs through the whole gospel: the *doxa* [glory] is not to be seen *alongside* the *sarx* [flesh], nor through the [flesh] as through a window; it is to be seen in the [flesh] and nowhere else. If man wishes to see the [glory], then it is on the [flesh] that he must concentrate his attention." Revelation is present in the person of Jesus only in "a peculiar *hiddenness*." Thus, "the event of revelation is a question, is an offence" (*Gospel*, 62–63). O'Day raises a legitimate objection when she argues that "Bultmann's focus is . . . on the *person* of Jesus, not on the Gospel text" (658). I want to alter, and double, Bultmann's focus: the Gospel narratives themselves are like the (represented) person of Jesus in that they bring the audience to an encounter and a crisis. They are occasions for offense.

The words in John 6 are not to be interpreted in the sense of finding some hidden spiritual content that in any way serves as a substitute for them; they are to bring the dramatic characters and the readers to the moment of crisis, the moment of offense or belief. That they do this to the characters in the text is evident by John's report that many disciples no longer go with Jesus—they have been scandalized—as well as by the contrary response of Peter when Jesus asks if the twelve disciples also wish to go away: "Lord, to whom can we go? You have the words of eternal life. We have come to believe and know that you are the Holy One of God" (6:68–69). This is a moment of triumph, of faith over offense. But it is a short-lived moment, for Jesus's response to Peter carries in it a new possibility of offense: "Did I not choose you, the twelve? Yet one of you is a devil" (6:70).

Provocations and Passion

We have followed John's Jesus through a series of confrontations and provocations, culminating with his assertion of the divine I AM in a repugnant encounter. Of course, the series does not end with this. At the Feast of Tabernacles, Jesus confronts his enemies with the question, "Why are you looking for an opportunity to kill me?" (7:19) and proclaims that anyone who wants "living water" must come to him (7:38), while the people debate the scandal of his earthly origin (see Nathanael's earlier question, "Can anything good come out of Nazareth?"; 1:46). He confronts the scribes and Pharisees, who are about to stone the adulterous woman, and tells the Pharisees, "I am the light of the world" (8:12). He tells the "Jews who had believed in him"—belief is no protection from offense—that the truth will make them free, which offends them because they assume they are already free ("We are descendants of Abraham and have never been slaves to anyone"; 8:33). And he provokes them further by telling them they are not from Abraham but from "your father the devil" (8:44). As a result of these provocations, the object of the stoning is now no longer an adulteress but Jesus himself (8:59).

The story of Jesus giving sight to the man born blind offers a striking variation on this theme. In curing him, Jesus announces again, "I am the light of the world," but the man born blind, as he comes to see the literal light of the world and later the spiritual light, the glory ("Lord, I believe"; 9:37-38), is dramatized as an earthly parody of Jesus. As Jesus has been sent by the Father (a motif often repeated), the man born blind is sent to "the pool of Siloam (which means Sent)" (9:7). When neighbors try to identify him, the man says, *egō eimi*, "I am the man" (9:9). When the Jews quiz him repeatedly about his sight, he becomes sarcastically offensive, echoing Jesus's charge against the Jews ("you cannot bear to hear my word"; 8:43, RSV) by saying to them, "I have told you already, and you would not listen. Why do you want to hear it again? Do you also want to become his disciples?" (9:27). And the Jews become offended by him, "and they drove him out" (9:34), as they will later turn against Jesus by demanding that he be crucified.

At the Feast of the Dedication, Jesus proclaims, "The Father and I are one" (10:30), and "the Jews" want to stone him for what is clearly Kierkegaard's essential offense: "It is not for a good work that we are going to stone you, but for blasphemy, because you, though only a human being, are making yourself God" (10:33). At the Passion, they say he must die by crucifixion "because he has claimed to be the Son of God" (19:7). Thus, the Passion becomes, for John, the work of offended people against the one in their midst who has committed the essential offense.

John's story of the Passion is the story of varying forms of blindness and hardness of the heart. Like Matthew's unbelievers, John's unbelievers hear but do not understand and see but do not perceive. The lack of hearing is dramatized: God speaks in a voice from heaven—"I have glorified it, and I will glorify it again" (12:28)—and the crowd that heard it thinks it is thunder, while others think an angel has spoken. The lack of seeing is spoken of figuratively by Jesus, who is himself the light: "The light is with you for a little longer. Walk while you have the light, so that the darkness may not overtake you. If you walk in the darkness, you do not know where you are going" (12:35). John quotes Isaiah to explain their blindness and hardness, using the same passage Matthew and Mark had used to explain the obstructive power of parables: "He has blinded their eyes and hardened their heart, so that they might not look with their eyes, and understand with their heart and turn—and I would heal them" (John 12:40; cf. Matt. 13:13–15, Mark 4:12). He who reveals also may obstruct. He who is the light also brings darkness, as John has already made clear in the episode of the man born blind: "Jesus said, 'I came into this world for judgment so that those who do not see may see, and those who do see may become blind'" (9:39). The new seeing Jesus brings is glory (*doxa*); Isaiah spoke prophetically "because he saw his [Jesus's] glory" (12:41).

Some do not see the glory, as they do not hear the Father, and some see, darkly, but cannot act on their seeing. Many authorities, such as Nicodemus, seem to hang between belief and offense in a kind of narrative limbo. "Nevertheless many, even of the authorities, believed in him [Jesus]. But because of the Pharisees they did not confess it, for fear that they would be put out of the synagogue; for they loved human glory more than the glory that comes from God" (12:42–43). But the narrative impetus for the Passion story is what Kierkegaard calls active offense. During the Last Supper, the offensive diction of John 6 returns when Jesus, speaking of Judas Iscariot, quotes Psalm 41:9: "The one who *gnawed on* my bread has lifted his heel against me" (13:18).[5] Judas has done the offensive gnawing that Jesus requires of believers, and yet he is now about to betray Jesus. Even one who has passed through the offense may not be a trusted believer. Judas, who has been scandalized by Mary's using costly ointment to anoint Jesus's feet (12:3–6), now literally and figuratively enters the darkness of offense: "He immediately went out. And it was night" (13:30).

What follows this exit is Jesus's "farewell discourse" (13:31–17:26) to the remaining disciples, with its message of love, promise of the Holy Spirit, and assertion of the *egō eimi* ("I am the way, and the truth, and the life"; "I am the true vine") and eternal life. But it also contains a promise of denial, hatred, persecution, and tribulation, which are both the cause and the effect of offense. In this discourse, Jesus speaks of them as a warning to the disciples, to prevent them from being offended.

> I have said these things to you to keep you from stumbling [literally, these things I have said to you so that you will not be offended (*skandalisthēte*)]. They will put you out of the synagogues. Indeed, an hour is coming when those who kill you will think that by doing so they are offering worship to God. And they will do this because they have not known the Father or me. But I have said these things to you so that when their hour comes you may remember that I told you about them. (16:1-4)

They will kill you because of their offense, their not knowing and not believing. The double danger is that their offense, manifested in the persecution of Jesus and then of the disciples, may lead to the disciples' offense.

This possibility is immediately dramatized by Peter. Peter is a believer. He speaks the truth ("We have come to believe and know," he tells Jesus, "that you are the Holy One of God"; 6:69). He thinks he is willing to give his life for Jesus ("I will lay down my life for you"; 13:37). But when confronted with questions about being a disciple or about being seen with Jesus, he denies Jesus three times. In the empty tomb, he sees physical objects, the linen wrappings and cloth, while the "other disciple" sees and believes. But finally, he sees the risen Jesus and affirms his love three times, paralleling in faith the three denials of his offense (21:15-17).

Occasions for Offense

My argument in this book has been that the Gospels are occasions for offense. These occasions are offered in order to bring the reader to belief, but true belief can occur only through the possibility of offense; hence it is more appropriate to call them occasions for offense than occasions for belief, even though the latter is the desirable end. "Blessed is anyone who takes no offense at me." Repeatedly in John, some people believe for a while, only to turn against Jesus and become part of the crowd that wants to stone or crucify him. In Matthew's parable of the sower, the seeds sown on rocky ground immediately spring up but are soon scorched and wither; they are said to represent those who hear the word with joy and endure for a while but, when persecution or tribulation arise because of the word, are immediately offended. Belief may be replaced by offense when it exists in time. Matthew's kingdom of God and John's eternal life are outside time, as is the Kierkegaardian moment of encounter and crisis, but our ordinary, mortal lives, our stories, are lived and narrated in time.

Kingdom, life, and the moment are at the center of the Gospels. But when the Word is made flesh, it must exist in time, where plants wither and humans are offended, and where such things become news. The Gospels' occasions for offense must be realized through narrative, since good news (the "gospel") and bad news alike are naturally conveyed through narrative, even when the subject is Truth, the Logos, the Word. The Word makes itself known, if at all, through narrative words, by telling stories about Jesus, who is the Word made flesh—itself an offense, as Kierkegaard and the Gospels themselves amply demonstrate.

The Gospels tell stories of Jesus, but they are kerygmatic stories; that is, they are stories that proclaim good news. They are not essentially kerygmatic creeds or proclamations of doctrines. They proclaim a narrative Jesus, a presence whose identity must be known, if it is to be known at all, through the medium of news, anecdote, story, by means of which the hearer or reader may encounter the possibility of offense that Jesus *is*. This encounter inevitably involves a crisis, a moment in which Jesus's identity may be seen through the eyes of offense or, having passed through the offense, through the eyes of a believing faith.

Hans Frei's phrase "the eclipse of Biblical narrative" refers to the loss to criticism and theology of the form the evangelists chose to write in: narrative. The form is obvious to any reader and is essential to the Gospel writers' Jesus, but it undeniably has a way of being supplanted by Deism, historicism, hermeneutical systems, creeds, or doctrines. Now that the eclipse is waning (one hopes) and the Bible is once again being approached as narrative, we are in a position to recover the Gospels' narrative sense of Jesus as *skandalon*. By domesticating it, ignoring it, or translating it away, we remove the means of seeing and encountering the hero of their narratives. It is not the only quality of Jesus that the Gospels offer, to be sure; John's counterpart is *doxa*, Jesus's glory, manifested narratively in the signs, the person of Jesus, and the responses of those, like the man born blind, who see with belief. But this glory cannot exist without narrative offense.

G. K. Chesterton observed that a stereoscopic view has much to recommend it when encountering Christian orthodoxy: we see two different pictures at once, and yet we see all the better for that. We need this stereoscopic view, but we need more than it for encountering the Gospels as narratives. A view of a single, static thing with depth—an image in a stereoscope—will not do; the view should be rather of an action, specifically an action that involves news interacting with the Word. Even this extension to action, however, is not adequate, for it suggests an observer apart from the observed. The Gospel writers require something more radical. As the news encounters the Word, so the reader is invited to encounter both myth and story in a dialogic interaction that leads to an either/or: either offense or faith.

Notes

Chapter 1

1. For theological expositions of the *skandalon* in English (translated from German), see Gustav Stählin's article *"Skandalon, skandalizō"* in Kittel and Friedrich's *Theological Dictionary of the New Testament* and Joachim Guhrt's article "Offence, Scandal, Stumbling Block" in Colin Brown's *New International Dictionary of New Testament Theology*. Both articles survey the few references to the term in classical literature, its origins in the Hebrew Bible and appearances in the Septuagint, and its uses in the New Testament, and both contain bibliographic references to the limited scholarship on the idea. Neither article, however, makes any reference to the two most significant thinkers who deal with offense: Kierkegaard (1813–55) and Calvin, who wrote a treatise on the subject in 1550.

2. David Lawton chooses *skandalon* as his illustration of the difficulty of finding English equivalents for Greek words (73).

3. See the appendix for translations from the NRSV. The King James Version translates the Greek more uniformly than any modern English translation. It almost always translates the noun or verb with some form of "offense"; when it does not, it uses "stumblingblock" (three times) and "occasion of stumbling" and "occasion to fall" (once each). Nonetheless, because of the modern idiom and improved accuracy of the NRSV, I have quoted from it, unless otherwise noted. When italicized words appear in my quotations from the NRSV, the italics are mine.

4. There are two major exceptions to my generalization. The first is Gustav Stählin, whose article in the *New Testament Dictionary of Theol-*

171

ogy is a summary of his 1930 book entitled *Skandalon*, a thorough philological treatise, in German. (Earlier philological notes on the *skandalon* had
been written by Carr, Moulton, and Moffatt.) The second is Helmut Bintz,
whose book (1969) is a response to Karl Barth. Bintz recognizes the importance of Kierkegaard and asserts that the *skandalon* is the fundamental
problem of religious doctrines. It and the gospel message must be subjected
to constant reinterpretation, in the light of contemporary situations. Barth
himself mentions the concept occasionally, e.g., in *Dogmatics*, where he
refers to Jesus as "a truth which, looked at from the standpoint of all historical results, is completely novel and offensive! To the Greeks foolishness, to
the Jews a stumbling-block" (67). Rudolf Bultmann also refers occasionally
to the offense or stumbling block, e.g., in *Jesus Christ and Mythology* (36,
39). (For additional references, see Zahrnt, 213n; Neill and Wright, 242n;
and below, in chapter 9.) In France, a series of articles appeared in *Foi et Vie*
(1947) by Bosc, Daniélou, Maury, Parain, Vischer, and Westphal discussing
aspects of the New Testament *scandale*. Francois Mauriac, in *The Stumbling Block* (1952), attacks cults within Catholicism and Protestant error,
but he speaks as one scandalized rather than as one interested in the subject
of stumbling blocks. A French Catholic theologian, Alphonse Humbert
(1954), analyzes the religious aspects of the idea; his distinctions are appropriated by T. C. O'Brien in the entry "Scandal" in *Encylopedic Dictionary
of Religion*. A good, short dictionary entry under "Offense" will be found in
Nigel Turner's *Christian Words* (294–98). Geoffrey Clive's "Seven Types of
Offense" (1958) is a more expansive discussion of offense, not much concerned with the New Testament but rather with modern culture and literature from Dostoyevski to Mann. And Ronald Knox (1949) has written engag-
ingly on the problems of translating the term in a chapter entitled "Justice
and Scandal in the Gospels" (59–73).

5. Girard, in a 1964 essay on Camus's *The Stranger*, quotes one of
Kierkegaard's many explorations of offense as a way of explaining Mersault's
defiance and despair. In the passage Girard quotes, Kierkegaard says that
the despairing man "is offended by [his despair], or rather from it he takes
occasion to be offended at the whole of existence" (*To Double Business
Bound*, 26; Girard is quoting from *The Sickness unto Death*, 71). The discussions of the *skandalon* in the journal *Foi et Vie*, published before Girard
moved from France to the United States, also may have called his attention
to the idea.

6. Here is Derrida in another mode, as the bringer of scandals: "We
must decide to scandalize those . . . obscurantist advocates of poetics — impotent censors above all — shocked by what can be done with a dictionary. . . . We have to scandalize them, make them cry out still louder — in
the first place because it is fun to do so, and why deny ourselves the pleasure" (*Signéponge*, 120).

7. For example, Naomi Schor, in an article called "The Scandal of Real-

offence." But
being signifi-
oman offers a
nding his mis-

words" to the
g." They were
us, chauvinis-
h to deny the
deflected the

man in Mark's
sus. Thus, the
"the apostolic

mikhshol is
el 25:31, when
ehold, thereby
cience"). Else-
olasin, and *as-*

God's name for
aya, to be, but
is that we will
as we will find
eneid, but that
nd understand-

nue to call the
er."

lheinz Müller,
offenses I have
ent of the idea,
Paul's positive
age, we would
he oldest place
apostle makes
feiture of salva-
at also . . . ulti-

ating is clear in

iterature, argues that at the time of
representational mode wedded to the
nale energy." Therefore, realism, the
is now scandalous. But Sand's novel
of its sexual nature and, to the critic
listic novel. Now, "*Lélia*, undoubtedly
writing in France, continues to be a
critical establishment. . . . *Lélia* will
e repressed until the aesthetic values
nte-Beuve begin to be questioned and
Bernstein's *The Celebration of Scan-*
n Urban Fiction, which starts from
to be scandalous, a challenge to the
ntions of representation in fiction as

Girard's use of the *skandalon*, refers
of the Secondary. By this he means
ed to being among the principal or
but it nonetheless affects the princi-
history—in both "scandalous and ben-
"scandalized" at literature (205), since
response to history. "Any society and
ss and secure in their sense of the
ativity an irritant, even a *skandalon*.
man order: they partake of irrational-
ction, and dispersion are part of their
t deconstruct the principal but rather
principal to progress. "Unlike Jacques
g, perhaps, too much reforming zeal
this relationship" of the principal (or
arginal; xi) but rather to promote "a
nt sectors of what exists" (xii). Clear-
fferent from the biblical *skandalon*,
promotes, accommodation. The bibli-
Kierkegaard might say, not both/and.

ter 2

he insult) altogether in his *Anchor*
W. F. Albright), but he addresses the
mmentary on Mark (1986, p. 321).
ommentary on Matthew, Davies and
modern interpreters have focused on
h probably, they say, means "house

dog" as opposed to stray or wild dog) as an attempt "to lesse
Davies and Allison do not go on to understand the offense
cant in the story. In their reading, much like Burkill's, the
"riposte," a "spirited exchange" that "argues her case" of ext
sion to her, a Gentile (2: 554–56).

F. W. Beares, like Klausner, refers to Jesus's "offensiv
woman as "the worst kind of chauvinism," an "atrocious say
coined, Beares theorizes, after the time of Jesus by some zea
tic prophet, but neither Mark nor Matthew was "bold enou
authenticity of the saying," as they should have, though the
emphasis from the saying to the act of healing (342–44).

Elisabeth Schüssler Fiorenza sees the Syrophoenician w
version (7:24–30) as winning a theological argument with J
woman is "a sign of the historical leadership" of women an
'foremother' of all gentile Christians" (138).

3. In Leviticus 19:14 and Psalms 119:165, the Hebre
translated by the Greek *skandalon* in LXX, as it is in 1 Sam
Abigail pleads with David to spare the males of her hou
avoiding "offense of heart" (KJV; NRSV has "pangs of co
where, the LXX translators used *ptōma, skōla, basanon,*
thenountes for the Hebrew *mikhshol* (Carr, 62).

4. Gabriel Josipovici comments on the implications of
us as readers: "YHWH . . . identifies himself with the verb
as an *activity* rather than as an *essence.* . . . For us this me
not find stories *about* him in this book [the Hebrew Bible]
stories about Marduk in *Enuma Elish* or about Juno in the
the stories in this book will be our only way of discovering
ing him" (74).

5. The authorship of this letter is disputed, but I cont
author Peter, meaning "whoever wrote the First Letter of Pe

Chapter 3

1. Paul's use of the *skandalon* has been studied by K.
who offers another formulation of the negative and positiv
been discussing. Müller points out that the Hebrew equiva
though entirely negative, is necessary for the existence o
meaning: "Without the negative meaning of the Jewish u
not be able to transpose the word to a positive meaning. At
in the Pauline corpus, which the noun *skandalon* marks, th
the cross known as an offense, able to effect . . . not only fo
tion and physical hardship [as in the Hebrew Scriptures], b
mate salvation" (122).

2. The identity of the *skandalon* with eating and form
the Greek text, even if slightly ambiguous in the translatio

Chapter 4

1. Most Kierkegaard scholars discuss or at least mention the offense, since it is central to Kierkegaard's religious thought, but no one has dealt with it extensively. The only article on the subject is an anonymous essay in *Times Literary Supplement* ("The 'Offence' of the God-Man," March 27, 1937). Good introductions to Kierkegaard's thought may be found in books by Malantschuk, Collins, and Gardiner and essays by Auden, Webb, and LeFevre. Especially helpful are two books by Malantschuk—the short introduction, *Kierkegaard's Way to the Truth*, and the longer, more complete *Kierkegaard's Thought*—as well as his brief essays in the notes of Kierkegaard's *Journals*, vols. 1-4. Excellent studies of the pseudonymous writings have been written by Mark C. Taylor, Evans, and, most recently, Hartshorne.

2. *Dialectic* is a methodological term Kierkegaard uses frequently. By it, he means "a consistent thinking through of the central Christian concepts," as Malantschuk says (*Journals*, 1: 525). The thinking through often takes the form of posing choices among opposites or contradictions, as is evident in Anti-Climacus's formulations here and in the recurrent either/or throughout Kierkegaard's writings. Adorno puts it this way: "According to Kierkegaard's philosophy, dialectic is to be conceived as the movement of individual human consciousness through contradictions" (32).

3. It is characteristic of Climacus's religious detachment (as an observer but certainly not a Christian believer) that he should avoid the religious title, "Christ," and refer to "the god" (*Guden*) rather than "God" (*Gud*).

Chapter 5

1. Some influential scholars argue that these lines do not refer specifically to Jesus's parables but rather to his teachings in general and that they do not imply obstruction but simply obscurity to outsiders. Joachim Jeremias argues that Mark 4:11-12 was a later insertion—"Mark 4:10 was originally followed by v. 13" (18, 13-14)—and that Mark, when he later inserted v. 11-12, "erroneously understood" *parabolē* as parable, whereas in fact, according to Jeremias, Mark 4:11-12 "has no reference whatever to the parables of Jesus" and "affords no criterion for the interpretation of parables" (18). Ian T. Ramsey cites Jeremias's reading with full approval, noting that "the notorious verse, when set within the correct context and rightly interpreted along these lines, . . . loses its scandal and difficulty" (11). Just so. But should we want, or be willing, to lose scandal and difficulty through interpretation that requires a reconstruction of the existing text? Even Jeremias, as he reinterprets this offensive passage, affirms "the perpetual twofold issue of all preaching of the gospel: . . . deliverance and offence" (18). Jeremias himself is not trying to eliminate the offense but rather to eliminate the notion that parables are necessarily obscure and therefore require

allegorical interpretation. For a critique of Jeremias, see Bernard Brandon Scott (22–25). Robert Fowler takes a different line for avoiding Mark's notorious verse. Although he attends admirably to some of the offenses in Mark, such as the fig tree (96–97), he rejects the direct meaning of 4:12 on the grounds that it "is exactly opposite to what we would expect Jesus to say." Therefore, he argues, we should read it as irony—"maybe" Jesus's irony but "at least" the narrator's (102).

2. For a fine study of idolatry, see Owen Barfield's *Saving the Appearances*.

3. I pursue the notion of parables as revealers of desire further in the third section of chapter 6.

4. It may be argued that the phrase "God-man," found so frequently in Kierkegaard's works and elsewhere, is, strictly speaking, applicable only to Jesus in the Gospel of John, where Jesus is explicitly the incarnation of God and the preexistent Son of God, who has become man in the flesh. Most biblical scholars maintain that the synoptic Gospels do not present Jesus as the incarnation, though some suggest that the Johannine incarnation is implicit in the synoptic Gospels (e.g., recently, Williams, 205). Mark announces that Jesus is Christ, the Son of God, at the outset (1:1); and before the high priest Mark's Jesus responds with the divine "I am" to the priest's question, "Are you the Messiah, the Son of the Blessed One?" (14:61–62). In Matthew, when Jesus is baptized, the Spirit of God descends on him and a heavenly voice says, "This is my Son, the Beloved" (3:17). In Luke, Jesus is announced as the Son of God, born to a virgin by means of the Holy Spirit and "the power of the Most High" (1:35). But only in John, among the four Gospels, is Jesus the preexistent Son of God who "became flesh" (1:14) in the world. In using "God-man," I am not trying to impose a Johannine incarnation on the other Gospels but to capture the offensive duality of Jesus as, on the one hand, the Son of God, the Messiah, or the incarnate divine *and*, on the other hand, man.

5. An excellent discussion of medieval interpretations of all Gospel parables may be found in Stephen L. Wailes, *Medieval Allegories of Jesus' Parables*.

6. For discussions of parable criticism in this century, see Norman Perrin, *Jesus and the Language of the Kingdom*, 91–181; Warren S. Kissinger, *The Parables of Jesus*; and William A. Beardslee, "Recent Literary Criticism," 177–83.

7. Both Funk and Crossan reflect the emphases of an earlier scholar, Amos Wilder, who brought an extraordinary literary sensibility to the study of parables. In an early essay, later reprinted in *Jesus' Parables*, Wilder wrote that "a true metaphor or symbol is more than a sign, it is a bearer of the reality to which it refers. The hearer not only learns about that reality, he participates in it. He is invaded by it. . . . Jesus' speech had the character, not of instruction and ideas, but of compelling imagination, of spell, of mythical shock and transformation" (83).

8. The antecedent of "its" is "qualifier," which Ricoeur identifies as the kingdom of God. The qualifier, kingdom of God, confers on parables and related literary genre their specific "religious" usage, through its "odd," "extravagant," "paradoxical," "scandalous" meaning (*Biblical Hermeneutics*, 32–33, 119–21).

Chapter 6

1. One diverse group of scholars, calling themselves the Jesus Seminar, has published the results of its pollings on "what Jesus really said" (ix) in Funk et al., *The Parables of Jesus*. The parable of the sower, in Matthew 13, for example, is judged to be authentic (although not resoundingly so), but all of the allegorical interpretations attributed by Matthew to Jesus are judged inauthentic. Not all critics are persuaded by this dismissive attitude toward the allegorical interpretations. John Drury, for example, has argued strongly that Mark should be read in the context of a tradition of allegorical parables ("Origins," 187). I agree that the allegorical tradition, along with other traditions, is significant, but those traditions need to be viewed within the context of Jesus as *skandalon* and bringer of offense. Quite apart from this historical debate, however, my reading of Matthew must take the allegorical interpretations into account because they are in the text. My way of doing this is to take them seriously as part of *Matthew's* narrative. This begs the historical question of whether Jesus actually spoke the allegorical interpretations, but it does attend to the important issue of "the realistic or history-like quality of biblical narratives" (Frei, 16).

2. Kingsbury and Drury (*The Parables*, 82–88) are among the few critics who read Matthew 13 itself as a narrative. Kingsbury sees it as a dramatic "turning point" in the narrative, when Jesus turns away from the Jews and toward his disciples (130), and Drury widens the perspective to a historical turning point between creation (when things are hidden) and doomsday (when things are revealed). In parables, and in Jesus in Matthew 13, things are both hidden and revealed, Drury believes. But, contrary to my argument in this chapter, in spite of their differing emphases, both critics assume that the disciples positively succeed in learning how to "see" and "hear" through Jesus's training.

3. I refer to Matthew 13:52 as a parable, following Drury (*The Parables*, 114), Patte (196), Green (137), C. Brown (2: 750), and others, for several reasons: it is grammatically similar to most other parables in Matthew 13 ("kingdom of heaven" in the subject, linked by "is like" to a metaphorical predicate); it is immediately followed by a reference to "these parables" (13: 53), which appears to me to refer to the master of the household as well as to the other seven parables; and it contains verbal links with the earlier parables. But Donahue refers to it as a "saying" (65), Scott as an "evaluation" (25n), and Hendriksen as a "description" (55); and others, such as Jeremias and the authors of the Anchor Matthew, clearly do not want to call it a

parable. C. Brown indulges in understatement when he says, "There is a measure of scholarly disagreement as to what properly constitutes a parable or parabolic saying" (2: 749). This is likely to remain the case, since the fifty appearances of *parabolē* in the New Testament refer to quite different things, from symbol or ritual (Heb. 9:9) to proverb (Luke 4:23), riddle (Mark 7:17), and short narrative (Matt. 13:3).

4. This issue has attracted a number of commentators. Derrett, in *Law in the New Testament*, argues that the finder was "perfectly entitled in morals and in law to do what he did" (6), but given the complexities of his argument, Derrett remains puzzled about why "Matthew gave no clue to help us to see the point of our parable" (3).

Chapter 7

1. For an excellent discussion of the oral nature of the historical gospel and its contrast to the literary nature of the Gospels in the New Testament, see Werner Kelber's *The Oral and Written Gospel*.

2. Literally, the Greek *gehenna* (usually translated as "hell") refers to a ravine near Jerusalem where refuse was burned and where infant sacrifice had taken place in much earlier times. The term takes on symbolic meaning in Matthew, but the idea of hell as an actual place ruled by Satan, characterized by tortures and punishments, originated well after the Gospels. See C. Brown, 1: 208-9.

3. In the Sermon on the Mount, Jesus makes clear the falsity of this idolatrous *if* by commenting on the interconnectedness of eye and body: "The eye is the lamp of the body. So, if your eye is healthy, your whole body will be full of light; but if your eye is unhealthy, your whole body will be full of darkness" (Matt. 6:22-23).

4. The hand, foot, or eye is for Origen the allegorical equivalent of the *skandalon*, which he defines as "those who pervert the simple folk who are easily led astray from sound teaching" (*Contra Celsum*, 314).

5. David Daube comments that paying by the coin from the fish is "a course which formally, in semblance, amounts to perfect compliance, so will avoid any discord, while, in reality, they part with nothing that is genuinely their own, so are not subjecting themselves to the impost" (in Sanders, 127).

6. It should be noted that Jesus's inoffensive response also harbors a potential offense: telling an adult to be a child is an assault on the normal assumption that the good resides in adulthood, experience, maturity, and accumulated wisdom.

7. The NRSV translates *adelphos* as "member of the church," but I will use the more literal "brother" to emphasize the link between this passage and Matthew 18:35, where Jesus talks again about forgiving your brother (*adelphos*, translated in NRSV here as "brother or sister").

8. Jesus's saying about binding and loosing applies most immediately

to the sinning brother, but it also applies to what follows, the parable of the unforgiving slave, which turns on actions of binding and loosing. The king out of pity looses the slave from his debt (18:27, using the same Greek verb stem as in 18:18) and later, out of anger, asks the slave if he was not bound to have mercy on his fellow slave (18:33, using the same verb stem as in 18:18). Likewise, though without the verbal repetitions, the temple tax episode turns on the question of whether Jesus is bound to pay, or loosed from paying, the temple tax. Thus, the binding/loosing theme begins in the temple tax episode with a tension between obscure theory and practice, moves in the sinning brother episode to clarity in theory but no outcome in practice, and ends in the parable with a clear dramatic application, the binding and loosing being applied to the slave and finally to "my heavenly Father" and "every one of you."

9. The forgiveness is extraordinary in part because it does not require prior repentance. Raymund Schwager makes the important temporal distinction: "The master's willingness to forgive is unconditional in the sense that it has no antecedent conditions; it does have a consequent condition: the favored servant is expected to behave in a new way" (112).

Chapter 8

1. The obvious exception to this—though Kierkegaard himself does not apply it to the Gospels—is irony. His thesis, *The Concept of Irony*, is a classic exposition of irony, and some of its ideas have been applied to the Gospel of John by Paul Duke.

2. "Take a dialogue and remove the voices (the partitioning of voices), remove the intonations (emotional and individualizing ones), carve out abstract concepts and judgments from living words and responses, cram everything into one abstract consciousness—and that's how you get dialectics" (Bakhtin, *Speech Genres*, 146).

3. Nina Perlina has illuminated Bakhtin's thought, especially on authoritative discourse, by reference to Buber's works. She argues, "One can find Bakhtin in Buber and Buber in Bakhtin in every philosophic premise of their writings" (26).

4. Menippean satire, or menippea, is one of the literary forms (along with the Socratic dialogue, symposia, and others) between the serious genres (tragedy and epic) and comedy; they are serious-smiling, or serio-comic forms. The menippea gets its name from Menippus of Gadara, who lived in the third century B.C.E. The menippea by Lucian, Apuleius, Petronius, and Juvenal are characterized as a genre by a mockery of serious forms, exaggeration, digression, extraordinary situations, slum naturalism, and, Bakhtin says, "naked 'ultimate questions'": "In [menippea] ultimate philosophical positions are put to the test" (*Problems*, 115).

5. The menippea is a literary form that, like other serio-comic genres, manifests a carnival sense of the world. "Carnival is a pageant without

footlights and without a division into performers and spectators. In carnival everyone is an active participant, everyone communes in the carnival act. Carnival is not contemplated and, strictly speaking, not even performed; its participants *live* in it, they live by its laws as long as those laws are in effect; that is they live a *carnivalistic life*. Because carnivalistic life is life drawn out of its *usual* rut, it is to some extent 'life turned inside out,' 'the reverse side of the world' (*'monde à l'envers'*)" (Bakhtin, *Problems*, 122).

6. I am indebted here and elsewhere to Meir Sternberg's fine analysis of this story in *The Poetics of Biblical Narrative* (190–222).

7. If, as is usually assumed, Luke is following Mark 12:30, he has altered Mark's ordering of the faculties in such a way that they fit his own narrative of the Samaritan, which is found only in Luke. Mark's ordering is: "and you shall love the Lord your God with all your heart, and with all your soul, and with all your mind, and with all your strength." Matthew (22:37) omits "strength" altogether.

8. Lawton notes the narrative relationship between the two stories by calling the Mary-Martha episode a "corrective" of the injunction to *do* (150). Talbert also reads the Good Samaritan story together with the Mary and Martha story, arguing that "To love one's neighbor means to act like the Samaritan. To love God means to act like Mary" (126). He takes as his interpretive principle the statement of Rabbi Akiva: "Every section in scripture is explained by the one that stands next to it" (125). A Bakhtinian emendation would create a related, but different, principle: Every section of scripture is *answered* (but not corrected) by the one that stands next to it, and also answered by the addressee. Behind such a principle lies a sense of the text as "utterance" (Bakhtin, *Speech Genres*, 104) and of "contextual meaning," which refers to interaction not only among parts of the text but also between the text and the addressee. Contextual meaning "always includes two (as a dialogic minimum)" (170).

Chapter 9

1. This is not to say that one cannot undertake a deconstruction of John's Logos. For example, Kelber, in his discussion of John's prologue, asserts that "at best . . . there exists a plurality of original *logoi* [words]" rather than "the johannine concept of the single *Logos* [Word]." The Word in the beginning "reveals itself as being dependent on a prior otherness which was always already there. . . . The fourth gospel, no less than Nietzsche, Freud, Heidegger or Derrida, affirms a decentering" ("Birth," 130–31). My reading of John does not follow this line of argument but rather assumes "the johannine concept of the single Logos" as the founding myth, or the spiritual encyclopedia, antecedent to the scandalous news.

2. For a discussion of the odd shift from "we" to "his," see Raymond Brown, xcii–cii, 1124–25, who argues that John, son of Zebedee, is the Beloved Disciple and the author (as "authority") of the Gospel of John, though not its

literal writer. The writer ("we"), Brown argues, was probably a follower of John ("he"). Many scholars believe that chapter 21 was written by a different hand from that of the earlier chapters. If so, this bold addendum preserves and uses the enigma of the Beloved Disciple in a way consistent with his earlier appearances.

3. "Blessed are those who have not seen and yet have come to believe" points, within the text, to the Beloved Disciple. But it also points, outside the text, to the reader (Warner, "Art of Rational Persuasion," 162).

4. Reynolds Price, in his admirable essay on John in *Incarnation*, tries to bring the reader to see afresh "the hair-raising newness" of John. This passage, for Price, is one of the more hair-raising. "To say that one can give 'living water' may be no more than the poetic claim of a spiritual teacher. To call oneself the 'bread of life' approaches the megalomanic. But for one man to thrust through the Hebrew dread of eating blood and of human sacrifice and apparently to demand the actual consumption of his physical body is a deed that cries out for drastic response—exile, confinement for lunacy, immediate stoning. Or obedience" (49–50).

5. My translation. John has not quoted the Psalm exactly. The Septuagint has "ate" (*esthiein*); John has substituted the animalistic "gnawed on" (*trogein*) to echo the offense of his chapter 6.

Works Cited

Adorno, Theodor W. *Kierkegaard: Construction of the Aesthetic*. Trans. Robert Hullot-Kentor. Minneapolis: University of Minnesota Press, 1989. Orig. pub. 1962.

Albright, W. F., and C. S. Mann, eds. *Matthew. The Anchor Bible*. Garden City: Doubleday, 1971.

Alter, Robert, and Frank Kermode, eds. *The Literary Guide to the Bible*. Cambridge: Harvard University Press, 1987.

Anonymous. "The 'Offence' of the God-Man: Kierkegaard's Way of Faith." *Times Literary Supplement*, 27 March 1937: 229–30. Response by Laura Riding, "Letters," *Times Literary Supplement*, 10 April 1937: 275.

Aristophanes. *The Acharnians*. Vol. 1 of *Aristophanes*. 3 vols. Trans. Benjamin B. Rogers. Cambridge: Harvard University Press, 1960. 1–117.

Auden, W. H. "Søren Kierkegaard." *Forewords and Afterwords*. New York: Vintage, 1989. 168–81. Orig. pub. in *The Living Thoughts of Kierkegaard*, 1952.

Bakhtin, Mikhail. *Art and Answerability: Early Philosophical Essays*. Ed. and trans. Michael Holquist and Vadim Liapunov. Austin: University of Texas Press, 1990.

———. *The Dialogic Imagination*. Ed. and trans. Michael Holquist and Caryl Emerson. Austin: University of Texas Press, 1981.

———. *Problems of Dostoevsky's Poetics*. Ed. and trans. Caryl Emerson. Minneapolis: University of Minnesota Press, 1984.

———. *Speech Genres and Other Late Essays*. Trans. Vern W. McGee. Austin: University of Texas Press, 1986.

Barfield, Owen. *History in English Words*, 2nd ed. London: Faber, 1953.

_____. *Saving the Appearances: A Study in Idolatry*. New York: Harcourt, 1965. Orig. pub. 1957.

Barth, Karl. *Dogmatics in Outline*. New York: Harper, 1959. Orig. pub. 1949.

Bauer, Walter, William F. Arndt, F. Wilbur Gingrich, and Frederick W. Danker. *A Greek-English Lexicon of the New Testament and Other Early Christian Literature*, 2nd ed. Chicago: University of Chicago Press, 1979.

Beardslee, William A. "Recent Literary Criticism." In Epp and MacRae, 175–98.

Beares, Francis Wright. *The Gospel according to Matthew: A Commentary*. Oxford: Blackwell, 1981.

Behler, Ernst. *Irony and the Discourse of Modernity*. Seattle: University of Washington Press, 1990.

Bernstein, Carol L. *The Celebration of Scandal: Toward the Sublime in Victorian Urban Fiction*. University Park: Pennsylvania State University Press, 1991.

Bintz, Helmut. *Das Skandalon als Grundlagenproblem der Dogmatik*. Berlin: De Gruyter, 1969.

Bion, W. R. *Attention and Interpretation*. New York: Basic Books, 1970.

Blake, William. *The Marriage of Heaven and Hell*. Ed. Sir Geoffrey Keynes. Oxford: Oxford University Press, 1975.

_____. *The Poetry and Prose of William Blake*. Ed. David V. Erdman. Garden City: Doubleday, 1965.

_____. *Songs of Innocence and of Experience*. Ed. Sir Geoffrey Keynes. Oxford: Oxford University Press, 1970.

Bloom, Harold. *The Book of J*. Trans. David Rosenberg. New York: Grove Weidenfeld, 1990.

Booth, Wayne. *The Rhetoric of Fiction*, 2nd ed. Chicago: University of Chicago Press, 1983.

Bosc, Jean. "L'Eglise et le scandale." *Foi et Vie* 45 (1947): 671–76.

Brown, Colin, ed. *The New International Dictionary of New Testament Theology*. 4 vols. Grand Rapids: Zondervan, 1975–78.

Brown, Raymond E., S.S. *The Gospel According to John*. 2 vols. *The Anchor Bible*. Garden City: Doubleday, 1966, 1970.

Bruns, Gerald L. "Midrash and Allegory." In Alter and Kermode, 625–46.

Buber, Martin. *Between Man and Man*. Trans. Roger Gregor Smith. New York: Macmillan, 1965.

_____. *I and Thou*. Trans. Walter Kaufman. New York: Scribner, 1970.

_____. *Werke*. 3 vols. Munich: Kösel, 1962.

Buechner, Frederick. *Lion Country*. New York: Atheneum, 1971.

Bultmann, Rudolf. "*Aischunō*." In Kittel and Friedrich, 1: 189–90.

_____. *The Gospel of John: A Commentary*. Trans. G. R. Beasley-Murray, R. W. N. Hoare, and J. K. Riches. Philadelphia: Westminster, 1971.

_____. *Jesus and the Word*. Trans. L. P. Smith and E. H. Lantero. New York: Scribner, 1958. Orig. pub. 1926.

_____. *Jesus Christ and Mythology*. New York: Scribner, 1958.

Bundy, W. E. *Jesus and the First Three Gospels*. Cambridge: Harvard University Press, 1955.

Burkill, T. A. *New Light on the Earliest Gospel*. Ithaca: Cornell University Press, 1972.

Buttrick, George Arthur, gen. ed. *The Interpreter's Bible*. 12 vols. New York: Abingdon, 1951–57.

Calvin, John. *Concerning Scandals*. Trans. John W. Fraser. Grand Rapids: Eerdmans, 1978. Orig. pub. 1550.

Calvino, Italo. *If on a winter's night a traveler*. Trans. William Weaver. New York: Harcourt, 1981.

Carr, Arthur. *Horae Biblicae*. London: Hodder, 1903.

Charles, R. H. *The Apocrypha and Pseudepigrapha of the Old Testament*. 2 vols. Oxford: Clarendon, 1913.

Charlesworth, James H. *The Old Testament Pseudepigrapha*. 2 vols. Garden City: Doubleday, 1983–85.

Chesterton, Gilbert K. *Orthodoxy*. New York: Dodd, 1949. Orig. pub. 1908.

Clark, Katerina, and Michael Holquist. *Mikhail Bakhtin*. Cambridge: Harvard University Press, 1984.

Clive, Geoffrey. "Seven Types of Offense." *Lutheran Quarterly* 10 (1958): 11–25.

Collins, James. *The Mind of Kierkegaard*. Princeton: Princeton University Press, 1983. Orig. pub. 1953.

Conzelmann, Hans. *1 Corinthians: A Commentary on the First Epistle to the Corinthians*. Trans. James W. Leitch. Philadephia: Fortress, 1975. Orig. pub. 1969.

Corn, Alfred, ed. *Incarnation: Contemporary Writers on the New Testament*. New York: Viking, 1990.

Crossan, John Dominic. *Cliffs of Fall: Paradox and Polyvalence in the Parables of Jesus*. New York: Seabury, 1980.

_____. *In Parables: The Challenge of the Historical Jesus*. San Francisco: Harper, 1973.

Culpepper, R. Alan. *Anatomy of the Fourth Gospel: A Study in Literary Design*. Philadelphia: Fortress, 1983.

Daniélou, Jean. "Le Scandale de la division entre les chrétiens." *Foi et Vie* 45 (1947): 677–80.

Daube, David. "Temple Tax." In E. P. Sanders, 124–34.

Davies, W. D., and Dale C. Allison, Jr. *A Critical and Exegetical Commentary on the Gospel according to Saint Matthew*. 3 vols. Edinburgh: Clark, 1988, 1991.

Derrett, J. Duncan M. *Law in the New Testament*. London: Darton, 1970.

Derrida, Jacques. *Signéponge/Signsponge*. Trans. Richard Rand. New York: Columbia University Press, 1984.

_____. *Writing and Difference*. Trans. Alan Bass. London: Routledge, 1978.

Dillard, Annie. *An American Childhood*. New York: Harper, 1987.

Dodd, C. H. *The Parables of the Kingdom*, rev. ed. New York: Scribner, 1961.

Donahue, John R. *The Gospel in Parable: Metaphor, Narrative, and Theology in the Synoptic Gospels*. Philadelphia: Fortress, 1988.

Drury, John. "Origins of Mark's Parables." In Wadsworth, 171–89.

_____. *The Parables in the Gospels: History and Allegory*. New York: Crossroad, 1985.

Duke, Paul D. *Irony in the Fourth Gospel*. Atlanta: John Knox Press, 1985.

Eco, Umberto. "The Scandal of Metaphor: Metaphorology and Semiotics." *Poetics Today* 4 (1983): 217–57.

Epp, Eldon Jay, and George W. MacRae, eds. *The New Testament and Its Modern Interpreters*. Philadelphia: Fortress, 1989.

Evans, C. Stephen. *Kierkegaard's "Fragments" and "Postscript": The Religious Philosophy of Johannes Climacus*. Atlantic Highlands: Humanities, 1983.

Filson, Floyd V. *A Commentary on the Gospel according to St. Matthew*. New York: Harper, 1960.

Fiorenza, Elisabeth Schüssler. *In Memory of Her: A Feminist Theological Reconstruction of Christian Origins*. New York: Crossroad, 1983.

Fitzmyer, Joseph A. *The Gospel According to Luke (I–IX). The Anchor Bible*. Garden City: Doubleday, 1981.

Fowler, Robert M. *Let the Reader Understand: Reader-Response Criticism and the Gospel of Mark*. Minneapolis: Fortress, 1991.

Frei, Hans. *The Eclipse of Biblical Narrative: A Study in Eighteenth and Nineteenth Century Hermeneutics*. New Haven: Yale University Press, 1974.

Fuchs, Ernst. *Studies of the Historical Jesus*. London: SCM, 1964.

Funk, Robert W. *Language, Hermeneutic, and Word of God: The Problem of Language in the New Testament and Contemporary Theology*. New York: Harper, 1966.

Funk, Robert W., Bernard Brandon Scott, and James R. Butts. *The Parables of Jesus: A Report of the Jesus Seminar*. Sonoma: Polebridge, 1988.

Gardiner, Patrick. *Kierkegaard*. Oxford: Oxford University Press, 1988.

Gingrich, F. Wilbur. *Shorter Lexicon of the Greek New Testament*, 2nd ed. Rev. Frederick W. Danker. Chicago: University of Chicago Press, 1983.

Girard, René. *Job: The Victim of His People*. Trans. Yvonne Freccero. Stanford: Stanford University Press, 1987.

_____. *The Scapegoat*. Trans. Yvonne Freccero. Baltimore: Johns Hopkins University Press, 1986.

_____. *Things Hidden since the Foundation of the World*. Trans. Stephen Bann and Michael Metteer. Stanford: Stanford University Press, 1987.

_____. *To Double Business Bound: Essays on Literature, Mimesis, and Anthropology*. Baltimore: Johns Hopkins University Press, 1978.

_____. *Violence and the Sacred.* Trans. Patrick Gregory. Baltimore: Johns Hopkins University Press, 1977.

Greek New Testament, 3rd ed. Ed. Kurt Aland et al. Stuttgart: United Bible Society, 1983.

Green, H. Benedict. *The Gospel According to Matthew. The New Clarendon Bible.* London: Oxford University Press, 1975.

Guhrt, Joachim. "Offence, Scandal, Stumbling Block." In Colin Brown, 2: 705–10.

Hartshorne, M. Holmes. *Kierkegaard, Godly Deceiver: The Nature and Meaning of His Pseudonymous Writings.* New York: Columbia University Press, 1990.

Hendriksen, William. *New Testament Commentary: Exposition of the Gospel according to Matthew.* Grand Rapids: Baker, 1973.

Humbert, Alphonse. "Essai d'une théologie du scandale dans les Synoptiques." *Biblica* 35 (1954): 1–28.

Jeremias, Joachim. *The Parables of Jesus,* rev. ed. New York: Scribner, 1972.

Jerusalem Bible. Ed. Alexander Jones. Garden City: Doubleday, 1966.

Josipovici, Gabriel. *The Book of God: A Response to the Bible.* New Haven: Yale University Press, 1988.

Jülicher, Adolf. *Die Gleichnisreden Jesu.* Darmstadt: Wissenschaftliche Buchgesellschaft, 1976. Orig. pub. 1888–99.

Kelber, Werner H. "The Authority of the Word in St. John's Gospel: Charismatic Speech, Narrative Text, Logocentric Metaphysics." *Oral Tradition* 2 (1987): 108–31.

_____. "The Birth of a Beginning: John 1:1–18." *Semeia* 52 (1940): 121–44.

_____. *The Oral and the Written Gospel: The Hermeneutics of Speaking and Writing in the Synoptic Tradition, Mark, Paul, and Q.* Philadelphia: Fortress, 1983.

Kermode, Frank. "The Bible: Story and Plot." In *An Appetite for Poetry.* Cambridge: Harvard University Press, 1989.

_____. *The Genesis of Secrecy: On the Interpretation of Narrative.* Cambridge: Harvard University Press, 1979.

Kierkegaard, Søren. *Attack upon "Christendom."* Trans. Walter Lowrie. Princeton: Princeton University Press, 1968.

_____. *The Concept of Anxiety.* Trans. Reidar Thomte and Albert B. Anderson. Princeton: Princeton University Press, 1980.

_____. *The Concept of Irony.* Trans. Howard V. Hong and Edna H. Hong. Princeton: Princeton University Press, 1989.

_____. *Concluding Unscientific Postscript to Philosophical Fragments.* 2 vols. Trans. Howard V. Hong and Edna H. Hong. Princeton: Princeton University Press, 1992.

_____. *Eighteen Upbuilding Discourses.* Trans. Howard V. Hong and Edna H. Hong. Princeton: Princeton University Press, 1990.

_____. *Either/Or: Part I.* Trans. Howard V. Hong and Edna H. Hong. Princeton: Princeton University Press, 1987.

_____. *Either/Or: Part II*. Trans. Howard V. Hong and Edna H. Hong. Princeton: Princeton University Press, 1987.

_____. *Fear and Trembling; Repetition*. Trans. Howard V. Hong and Edna H. Hong. Princeton: Princeton University Press, 1983.

_____. *Philosophical Fragments; Johannes Climacus*. Trans. Howard V. Hong and Edna H. Hong. Princeton: Princeton University Press, 1985.

_____. *The Point of View*. Trans. Walter Lowrie. London: Oxford University Press, 1939.

_____. *Practice in Christianity*. Trans. Howard V. Hong and Edna H. Hong. Princeton: Princeton University Press, 1991.

_____. *The Sickness unto Death*. Trans. Howard V. Hong and Edna H. Hong. Princeton: Princeton University Press, 1980.

_____. *Søren Kierkegaard's Journals and Papers*. 7 vols. Trans. Howard V. Hong and Edna H. Hong, assisted by Gregor Malantschuk. Bloomington: Indiana University Press, 1967–78.

_____. *Stages on Life's Way*. Trans. Howard V. Hong and Edna H. Hong. Princeton: Princeton University Press, 1988.

_____. *Works of Love*. Trans. Howard V. Hong and Edna H. Hong. New York: Harper, 1962.

Kingsbury, J. D. *The Parables of Jesus in Matthew 13: A Study in Redaction-Criticism*. London: SPCK, 1969.

Kissinger, Warren S. *The Parables of Jesus: A History of Interpretation and Bibliography*. Metuchen: Scarecrow, 1979.

Kittel, Gerhard, and Gerhard Friedrich, eds. *Theological Dictionary of the New Testament*. 10 vols. Trans. Geoffrey W. Bromiley. Grand Rapids: Eerdmans, 1964–76.

Klausner, Joseph. *Jesus of Nazareth*. Trans. Herbert Danby. New York: Macmillan, 1959.

Knox, Ronald. *The Trials of a Translator*. New York: Sheed, 1949.

Kurz, William S. "The Beloved Disciple and Implied Readers." *Biblical Theology Bulletin* 19 (1989): 100–107.

Lawton, David. *Faith, Text and History: The Bible in English*. Charlottesville: University Press of Virginia, 1990.

LeFevre, Perry D. *The Prayers of Kierkegaard*. Chicago: University of Chicago Press, 1956.

Lévi-Strauss, Claude. *The Elementary Structures of Kinship*, rev. ed. Trans. James H. Bell et al. Boston: Beacon, 1969.

Lotman, Jurij M. "The Origin of Plot in the Light of Topology." *Poetics Today* 1 (1979): 161–84.

Malantschuk, Gregor. *Kierkegaard's Thought*. Trans. Howard V. Hong and Edna H. Hong. Princeton: Princeton University Press, 1971. Orig. pub. 1968.

_____. *Kierkegaard's Way to the Truth: An Introduction to the Authorship of Søren Kierkegaard*. Trans. Mary Michelsen. N.P.: Reitzels, 1987. Orig. pub. 1963.

Mann, C. S., ed. *Mark. The Anchor Bible.* Garden City: Doubleday, 1986.

Marshall, I. Howard. *Kept by the Power of God: A Study of Perseverance and Falling Away.* London: Epworth, 1969.

Mauriac, Francois. *The Stumbling Block.* New York: Philosophical Library, 1952. Orig. pub. 1948.

Maury, Pierre. "Le scandale et la nécessité du scandale." *Foi et Vie* 45 (1947): 664–70.

Moffatt, James. "Jesus upon 'Stumbling-blocks.'" *Expository Times* 26 (1914–15): 406–9.

Moore, Stephen D. *Literary Criticism and the Gospels: The Theoretical Challenge.* New Haven: Yale University Press, 1989.

Moulton, James H. "Skandalon." *Expository Times* 26 (1914–15): 331–32.

Müller, Karlheinz. *Anstoss und Gericht: Eine Studie zum jüdischen Hintergrund des paulinischen Skandalon-Begriffs. Studien zum Alten und Neuen Testament.* Munich: Kösel, 1969.

Neill, Stephen, and Tom Wright. *The Interpretation of the New Testament, 1861–1986,* new ed. Oxford: Oxford University Press, 1988.

Nemoianu, Virgil. *A Theory of the Secondary: Literature, Progress, and Reaction.* Baltimore: Johns Hopkins University Press, 1989.

O'Brien, T. C. "Scandal." In *Encyclopedic Dictionary of Religion.* Ed. Paul Kevin Meagher. Washington: Corpus, 1979.

O'Day, Gail R. "Narrative Mode and Theological Claim: A Study in the Fourth Gospel." *Journal of Biblical Literature* 105 (1986): 657–68.

Origen. *Contra Celsum.* Trans. Henry Chadwick. Cambridge: Cambridge University Press, 1953.

Parain, Brice. "Le Scandale de la vérité." *Foi et Vie* 45 (1947): 658–63.

Patte, Daniel. *The Gospel according to Matthew: A Structural Commentary on Matthew's Faith.* Philadelphia: Fortress, 1987.

Patterson, David. *Literature and Spirit: Essays on Bakhtin and His Contemporaries.* Lexington: University of Kentucky Press, 1988.

Perlina, Nina. "Mikhail Bakhtin and Martin Buber: Problems of Dialogic Imagination." *Studies in Twentieth Century Literature* 9 (1984): 13–28.

Perrin, Norman. *Jesus and the Language of the Kingdom: Symbol and Metaphor in New Testament Interpretation.* Philadelphia: Fortress, 1976.

Phillips, Gary A. "History and Text: The Reader in Context in Matthew's Parables Discourse." *Semeia* 31 (1985): 111–38.

Price, Reynolds. "The Gospel According to Saint John." In Corn, 38–72.

Ramsey, Ian T. *Christian Discourse: Some Logical Explorations.* London: Oxford University Press, 1965.

Ricoeur, Paul. "Biblical Hermeneutics." *Semeia* 4 (1975): 26–148.

———. "The 'Kingdom' in the Parables of Jesus." *Anglican Theological Review* 623 (1981): 165–69.

———. *A Ricoeur Reader: Reflection and Imagination.* Ed. Mario J. Valdés. Toronto: University of Toronto Press, 1991.

Sanders, E. P., ed. *Jesus, the Gospels, and the Church*. Macon: Mercer University Press, 1987.

Sanders, J. N., and B. A. Mastin. *A Commentary on the Gospel According to St. John*. New York: Harper, 1968.

Schor, Naomi. "The Scandal of Realism." In *A New History of French Literature*. Ed. Denis Hollier. Cambridge: Harvard University Press, 1989. 656–61.

Schwager, Raymund. "Christ's Death and the Prophetic Critique of Sacrifice." *Semeia* 33 (1985): 109–23.

Scott, Bernard Brandon. *Hear Then the Parable: A Commentary on the Parables of Jesus*. Minneapolis: Fortress, 1989.

Stählin, Gustav. "*Skandalon, skandalizō*." In Kittel and Friedrich, 7: 339–58.

———. *Skandalon: Untersuchungen zur Geschichte eines biblischen Begriffs*. Gütersloh: Bertelsmann, 1930.

Starobinski, Jean. "The Struggle with Legion: A Literary Analysis of Mark 5:1–20." *New Literary History* 4 (1973): 331–56.

Sternberg, Meir. *The Poetics of Biblical Narrative: Ideological Literature and the Drama of Reading*. Bloomington: Indiana University Press, 1985.

Swift, Jonathan. "An Argument against Abolishing Christianity." Vol. 3 of *Prose Works*. Ed. Temple Scott. London: Bell, 1909. 5–19.

Talbert, Charles H. *Reading Luke: A Literary and Theological Commentary on the Third Gospel*. New York: Crossroad, 1982.

Taylor, Mark C. *Kierkegaard's Pseudonymous Authorship: A Study of Time and the Self*. Princeton: Princeton University Press, 1975.

Taylor, Mark Lloyd. "Ordeal and Repetition in Kierkegaard's Treatment of Abraham and Job." In *Foundations of Kierkegaard's Vision of Community*. Ed. George B. Connell and C. Stephen Evans. New Jersey: Humanities Press, 1992.

Trilling, Lionel. *The Opposing Self*. New York: Viking, 1955.

Turner, Nigel. *Christian Words*. Edinburgh: Clark, 1980.

Via, Dan Otto, Jr. *The Parables: Their Literary and Existential Dimension*. Philadelphia: Fortress, 1967.

Vischer, Wilhelm. "Jésus, le scandale et les scandales dans l'évangile selon Matthieu." *Foi et Vie* 45 (1947): 652–57.

Vološinov, V. N. "Discourse in Life and Discourse in Art." In *Freudianism*. Appendix I, 93–116.

———. *Freudianism: A Critical Sketch*. Trans. I. R. Titunik. Bloomington: Indiana University Press, 1987.

———. *Marxism and the Philosophy of Language*. Trans. Ladislav Matejka and I. R. Titunik. Cambridge: Harvard University Press, 1986.

Wadsworth, Michael, ed. *Ways of Reading the Bible*. Sussex: Harvester, 1981.

Wailes, Stephen L. *Medieval Allegories of Jesus' Parables*. Berkeley: University of California Press, 1987.

Warner, Martin. "The Art of Rational Persuasion." In Warner, *The Bible*, 153–77.

Warner, Martin, ed. *The Bible as Rhetoric: Studies in Biblical Persuasion and Credibility*. London: Routledge, 1990.

Webb, Eugene. *The Philosophers of Consciousness*. Seattle: University of Washington Press, 1988.

Westphal, Charles. "Brève réponse au Père Daniélou." *Foi et Vie* 45 (1947): 681–86.

Wilder, Amos. *Jesus' Parables and the War of Myths: Essays on Imagination in the Scripture*. Ed. James Breech. Philadelphia: Fortress, 1982.

Williams, James G. *The Bible, Violence, and the Sacred: Liberation from the Myths of Sanctioned Violence*. San Francisco: Harper, 1991.

Winnicott, D. W. *Playing and Reality*. New York: Basic Books, 1971.

Zahrnt, Heinz. *The Question of God: Protestant Theology in the Twentieth Century*. Trans. R. A. Wilson. New York: Harcourt, 1966.

Appendix: Selected Greek Words Relevant to Offense and Their Appearances in the New Testament

The selected Greek words listed in I, below, are the most important words that relate to the idea of the offense, though not the only ones. The brief definitions given here reflect the problems all modern translators and lexicographers face when trying to translate these words. This is evident from the list of all the words' appearances in the New Testament (in II, below), where the translations from the New Revised Standard Version (NRSV) are often different from the definitions in the first list. For fuller definitions and references, see Bauer, Arndt, Gingrich, and Danker, *A Greek-English Lexicon*; and for discussions of theological content, see the dictionaries of Kittel and Friedrich and of C. Brown.

In the second list, when the text includes a form of *skandal-*, the reference is in italics, as in *Matt. 5:29*. The Greek word in parentheses following each New Testament translation is always given in the same basic form as that word in the first list, but occasionally, to call attention to differences or to avoid confusion, the actual word as it appears in *The Greek New Testament* is given in brackets. Where the NRSV provides an alternative translation, it is indicated in this way: [*alt.* stumbles].

I. Selected Greek Words
(definitions from Gingrich, Shorter Lexicon)

skandalizō: cause to be caught or to fall, i.e., cause to sin, be led into sin, fall away; be repelled by someone, take offense at someone; give offense to, anger, shock.

skandalon: trap; temptation to sin, enticement; that which gives offense or causes revulsion, that which arouses opposition, an object of anger or disapproval, a stain, fault, etc.; *petra skandalou* a stone that causes people to fall.

aproskopos: blameless; clear; giving no offense.

proskomma: stumbling, offense; the opportunity to take offense, obstacle, hindrance.

proskopē: an occasion for taking offense.

proskoptō: *transitive* strike; *intransitive* stumble, beat against; take offense at, feel repugnance for, reject.

II. Appearances in the New Testament

Matt. 4:6, so that you will not dash your foot against a stone (*proskoptō*).

Matt. 5:29, If your right eye causes you to sin, tear it out (*skandalizō*).

Matt. 5:30, And if your right hand causes you to sin, cut it off (*skandalizō*).

Matt. 7:27, the winds blew and beat against [*prosekopsan*] that house, and it fell (*proskoptō*).

Matt. 11:6, And blessed is anyone who takes no offense at me (*skandalizō*).

Matt. 13:21, when trouble or persecution arises on account of the word, that person immediately falls away [*alt.* stumbles] (*skandalizō*).

Matt. 13:41, they will collect out of his kingdom all causes of sin (*skandalon*).

Matt. 13:57, And they took offense at him (*skandalizō*).

Matt. 15:12, Do you know that the Pharisees took offense when they heard what you said? (*skandalizō*).

Matt. 16:23, Get behind me, Satan! You are a stumbling block to me (*skandalon*).

Matt. 17:27, However, so that we do not give offense to them, go to the sea (*skandalizō*).

Matt. 18:6, If any of you put a stumbling block before one of these little ones who believe in me (*skandalizō*).

Matt. 18:7, Woe to the world because of stumbling blocks! (*skandalon*). Occasions for stumbling are bound to come (*skandalon*), but woe to the one by whom the stumbling block comes! (*skandalon*).

Matt. 18:8, If your hand or your foot causes you to stumble, cut it off (*skandalizō*).

Matt. 18:9, And if your eye causes you to stumble, tear it out (*skandalizō*).

Matt. 24:10, Then many will fall away [*alt.* stumble] (*skandalizō*).

Matt. 26:31, You will all become deserters because of me this night (*skandalizō*).

Matt. 26:33, Though all become deserters because of you (*skandalizō*), I will never desert you (*skandalizō*).

Mark 4:17, when trouble or persecution arises on account of the word, immediately they fall away [*alt.* stumble] (*skandalizō*).

Mark 6:3, And they took offense [*alt.* stumbled] at him (*skandalizō*).

Mark 9:42, If any of you put a stumbling block before one of these little ones who believe in me (*skandalizō*).

Mark 9:43, If your hand causes you to stumble, cut it off (*skandalizō*).

Mark 9:45, And if your foot causes you to stumble, cut it off (*skandalizō*).

Mark 9:47, And if your eye causes you to stumble, tear it out (*skandalizō*).

Mark 14:27, Jesus said to them, "You will all become deserters" (*skandalizō*).

Mark 14:29, Even though all become deserters, I will not (*skandalizō*).

Luke 4:11, so that you will not dash your foot against a stone (*proskoptō*).

Luke 7:23, And blessed is anyone who takes no offense at me (*skandalizō*).

Luke 17:1, Occasions for stumbling are bound to come, but woe to anyone by whom they come! (*skandalon*).

Luke 17:2, than for you to cause one of these little ones to stumble (*skandalizō*).

John 6:61, Jesus . . . said to them, "Does this offend you?" (*skandalizō*).

John 11:9, Those who walk during the day do not stumble, because they see the light of this world (*proskoptō*).

John 11:10, But those who walk at night stumble, because the light is not in them (*proskoptō*).

John 16.1, I have said these things to you to keep you from stumbling (*skandalizō*).

Acts 24:16, Therefore I do my best always to have a clear [*aproskopon*] conscience toward God and all people (*aproskopos*).

Rom. 9:32, They have stumbled [*prosekopsan*] over the stumbling stone [*lithō tou proskommatos*] (*proskoptō, proskomma*).

Rom. 9:33, See, I am laying in Zion a stone that will make people stumble [*lithon proskommatos*], a rock that will make them fall [*petran skandalou*]. (*proskomma, skandalon*).

Rom. 11:9, And David says, "Let their table become a snare [*pagida*] and a trap [*thēran*], a stumbling block [*skandalon*] and a retribution for them" (*skandalon*).

Rom. 14:13, never to put a stumbling block [*proskomma*] or hindrance [*skandalon*] in the way of another (*proskomma, skandalon*).

Rom. 14:20, but it is wrong for you to make others fall by what you eat (*proskomma*).

Rom. 14:21, it is good not to eat meat or drink wine or do anything that makes your brother or sister stumble (*proskoptō*).

Rom. 16:17, I urge you, brothers and sisters, to keep an eye on those who cause dissensions and offenses (*skandalon*).

1 Cor. 1:23, but we proclaim Christ crucified, a stumbling block [*skandalon*] to Jews and foolishness [*mōrian*] to Gentiles (*skandalon*).

1 Cor. 8:9, But take care that this liberty of yours does not somehow become a stumbling block to the weak (*proskomma*).

1 Cor. 8:13, Therefore, if food is a cause of their falling (*skandalizō*), I will never eat meat, so that I may not cause one of them to fall (*skandalizō*).

1 Cor. 10:32, Give no offense to Jews or to Greeks or to the church of God (*aproskopos*).

2 Cor. 6:3, We are putting no obstacle in anyone's way, so that no fault may be found with our ministry (*proskopē*).

2 Cor. 11:29, Who is made to stumble, and I am not indignant? (*skandalizō*).

Gal. 5:11, In that case the offense of the cross has been removed (*skandalon*).

Phil. 1:10, so that in the day of Christ you may be pure and blameless (*aproskopos*).

1 Pet. 2:8, A stone that makes them stumble [*lithos proskommatos*] (*proskomma*), and a rock that makes them fall [*petra skanda-lou*] (*skandalon*). They stumble because they disobey the word (*proskoptō*).

1 John 2:10, Whoever loves a brother or sister lives in the light, and in such a person there is no cause for stumbling (*skandalon*).

Rev. 2:14, the teaching of Balaam, who taught Balak to put a stumbling block before the people of Israel (*skandalon*).

Index